RELIGION AND YOUTH

For a variety of reasons we need to know more about the religious lives of young people. This book tells us why, in addition to supplying – in abundance – facts, figures, examples and explanations about a complex but fascinating subject. I recommend it very warmly.

Grace Davie, University of Exeter, UK

What is the future of religion given the responses of young people?
What impact do existing religious forms have on youth?
What kind of spirituality and religion are young people creating for themselves?

Written by leading scholars in the field, *Religion and Youth* presents an accessible, yet cutting edge, guide to the key issues in the study of youth and religion, including methodological perspectives. It provides a key teaching text in these areas for undergraduates, and a book of rigorous scholarship for postgraduates, academics and practitioners.

Offering the first comprehensive international perspective on the sociology of youth and religion, this book reveals key geographical and organisational variables as well as the complexities of the engagement between youth and religion. The book is divided into six parts organised around central themes: Generation X and their legacy; The Big Picture – surveys of belief and practice in the USA, UK and Australia; Expression – how young people construct and live out their religion and spirituality; Identity – the role of religion in shaping young people's sense of self and social belonging; Transmission – passing on the faith (or not); Researching Youth Religion – debates, issues and techniques in researching young people's religion and spirituality. James Beckford writes the Foreword and Linda Woodhead the Epilogue.

THEOLOGY AND RELIGION IN INTERDISCIPLINARY PERSPECTIVE
SERIES IN ASSOCIATION WITH THE
BSA SOCIOLOGY OF RELIGION STUDY GROUP

BSA Sociology of Religion Study Group Series editor:
Pink Dandelion and the publications committee

Theology and Religion in Interdisciplinary Perspective Series editors:
Douglas Davies and Richard Fenn

The British Sociological Association Sociology of Religion Study Group began in 1975 and provides the primary forum in Britain for scholarship in the sociology of religion. The nature of religion remains of key academic interest and this series draws on the latest worldwide scholarship in compelling and coherent collections on critical themes. Secularisation and the future of religion; gender; the negotiation and presentation of religious identities, beliefs and values; and the interplay between group and individual in religious settings are some of the areas addressed. Ultimately, these books reflect not just on religious life but on how wider society is affected by the enduring religious framing of human relationships, morality and the nature of society itself.

This series is part of the broader *Theology and Religion in Interdisciplinary Perspective Series* edited by Douglas Davies and Richard Fenn.

Other titles published in the BSA Sociology of Religion Study Group Series

Exploring Religion and the Sacred in a Media Age
Edited by Christopher Deacy and Elisabeth Arweck
ISBN 978-0-7546-6527-4 (HBK)

Religion and the Individual
Belief, Practice, Identity
Edited by Abby Day
ISBN 978-0-7546-6122-1 (HBK)

Women and Religion in the West
Challenging Secularization
Edited by Kristin Aune, Sonya Sharma and Giselle Vincett
ISBN 978-0-7546-5870-2 (HBK)

A Sociology of Spirituality
Edited by Kieran Flanagan and Peter C. Jupp
ISBN 978-0-7546-5458-2 (HBK)

Religion and Youth

Edited by

SYLVIA COLLINS-MAYO
Kingston University, UK

PINK DANDELION
University of Birmingham, UK

ASHGATE

Published by
Ashgate Publishing Limited
Wey Court East
Union Road
Farnham
Surrey, GU9 7PT
England

Ashgate Publishing Company
Suite 420
101 Cherry Street
Burlington
VT 05401-4405
USA

www.ashgate.com

British Library Cataloguing in Publication Data
Religion and youth. – (Theology and religion in interdisciplinary perspective series)
  1. Youth – Religious life.
  I. Series II. Collins-Mayo, Sylvia. III. Dandelion, Pink. IV. British Sociological
  Association. Sociology of Religion Study Group.
  200.8'35'091821—dc22

Library of Congress Cataloging-in-Publication Data
Collins-Mayo, Sylvia.
  Religion and youth / Sylvia Collins-Mayo and Pink Dandelion.
      p. cm.—(Theology and religion in interdisciplinary perspective series in
  association with the BSA Sociology of Religion Study Group)
    Includes bibliographical references and index.
      ISBN 978-0-7546-6764-3 (hardcover : alk. paper)—ISBN 978-0-7546-6768-1 (pbk. :
  alk. paper)
    1. Youth—Religious life. I. Dandelion, Pink. II. Title.

    BL625.47.C65 2010
    200.83509182'1—dc22

                                                                              2009053876

ISBN 9780754667643 (hbk)
ISBN 9780754667681 (pbk)
ISBN 9781409407256 (ebk)

Mixed Sources
Product group from well-managed forests and other controlled sources
www.fsc.org Cert no. SA-COC-1565
© 1996 Forest Stewardship Council
FSC

Printed and bound in Great Britain by
MPG Books Group, UK

Contents

List of Figures

List of Tables

List of Contributors

Sarah J. Abramson received her bachelor's degree in Religious Studies from Wesleyan University in the United States, and her master's degree in Gender and Social Policy from the London School of Economics (LSE). She is currently a PhD candidate in the Sociology Department at LSE, and is also the Senior Policy Researcher for the Board of Deputies of British Jews.

Elisabeth Arweck is Senior Research Fellow in the Warwick Religions and Education Research Unit (WRERU), Institute of Education, University of Warwick and Editor of the *Journal of Contemporary Religion*. Her recent research has focused on the religious socialisation and nurture of young people in mixed-faith families. She is currently exploring young people's views of religious diversity. Recent publications include a number of co-authored articles (with Eleanor Nesbitt), *Researching New Religious Movements in the West* (Routledge 2007), and (co-edited) volumes, such as *Exploring Religion and the Sacred in a Media Age* (with Chris Deacy, Ashgate 2009) and *Reading Religion in Text and Context* (with Peter Collins, Ashgate 2006).

Kristin Aune is Senior Lecturer in Sociology at the University of Derby. Her research focuses on gender, youth, feminism and contemporary Christianity. She is currently engaged in a large AHRC/ESRC-funded project examining Christian identity amongst undergraduate students. In addition to book chapters and journal articles, she has published several books, including most recently *Women and Religion in the West: Challenging Secularization* (with Sonya Sharma and Giselle Vincett, Ashgate 2008). Her new book *Reclaiming the F Word: The New Feminist Movement* (with Catherine Redfern) will be published in 2010 by Zed Books.

Tom Beaudoin is Associate Professor of Theology at Fordham University, in the Graduate School of Religion. He is the author of *Witness to Dispossession: The Vocation of a Postmodern Theologian* (2008), *Consuming Faith: Integrating Who We Are With What We Buy* (2003) and *Virtual Faith: The Irreverent Spiritual Quest of Generation X* (1998).

James A. Beckford, Fellow of the British Academy, is Professor Emeritus of Sociology at the University of Warwick and President-Elect of the Society for the Scientific Study of Religion. His recent books include: *Social Theory and Religion* (2003), *Muslims in Prison: Challenge and Change in Britain and France* (with D. Joly and F. Khosrokhavar, 2005), *Theorising Religion: Classical and Contemporary*

Debates (edited with J. Walliss, 2006) and *The SAGE Handbook of the Sociology of Religion* (edited with N.J. Demerath III, 2007). His current research interests include prison chaplaincy, religion and the state, and Muslims in Europe.

Leise Christensen is a Lecturer at Theological Pedagogical Centre in Loegumkloster, Denmark. She teaches Pedagogy of Religion and Old Testament studies. Christensen's PhD thesis was in Old Testament studies and was titled 'The Necessity of Contradiction. Continuity via Ambiguity in the Book of Ecclesiastes' (University of Aarhus, 2001). Other works include books and articles within the field of practical theology.

Sylvia Collins-Mayo is Principal Lecturer in Sociology at Kingston University. She completed her PhD on young people's faith at the University of Surrey in 1997. Her post-doctoral research interests have continued to focus on youth religion with particular reference to the everyday faith of young people from Christian backgrounds. She is currently researching the role of Christian-based youth work in the religious development of unchurched young people. She is co-author of *Making Sense of Generation Y* (2006).

Elizabeth Cooksey is Associate Professor of Sociology and Associate Director of the Center for Human Resource Research at the Ohio State University where she was responsible for the design of the 1979 National Longitudinal Study of Youth, Child and Young Adult data collections. Her research focuses primarily on social, demographic and behavioural issues during adolescence and young adulthood.

Denise Cush is Professor of Religion and Education at Bath Spa University. Her teaching and research areas include Religious Education in international perspective, Buddhism, Hinduism, Christianity and Contemporary Spiritualities (including teenage witches and young Pagans). She is currently Chair of the Association of University Lecturers in Religion and Education, and on the Editorial Board of the *British Journal of Religious Education*. Recent publications include 'Religious and Cultural Plurality in Education', in S. Ward, ed., *Education Studies: A Student Guide* (2nd edn) (Routledge Falmer 2008). 'Wise Young Women: Beliefs, Values and Influences in the Adoption of Witchcraft by Teenage Girls in England', in Hannah E. Johnston and Peg Aloi, eds, *The New Generation Witches: Teenage Witchcraft in Contemporary Culture* (Ashgate 2007) and (co-edited with C. Robinson, M. York and L. Foulston) *Encyclopedia of Hinduism* (Routledge 2008). However she is probably best known for her A-level textbook *Buddhism* (Hodder and Stoughton 1994).

Pink Dandelion is Professor of Quaker Studies at the University of Birmingham and directs the work of the Centre for Postgraduate Quaker Studies, Woodbrooke and the University of Birmingham. He edits *Quaker Studies* and acts as Series Editor for the Edwin Mellen series in Quaker Studies. His books include

The Quakers: A Very Short Introduction (2008) (with Jackie Leach Scully), *Good and Evil: Quaker Perspectives* (2007), *Introduction to Quakerism* (2007), *The Liturgies of Quakerism* (2005), *The Creation of Quaker Theory* (2004), the co-authored *Towards Tragedy/Reclaiming Hope* (2004) and *The Sociological Analysis of the Theology of Quakers: The Silent Revolution* (1996).

Abby Day is a Research Fellow in the Department of Anthropology, University of Sussex where she is Principal Investigator on an ESRC-funded project: *A Longitudinal Qualitative Study of Belief and Identity.* She is Co-Convenor, with Prof. Gordon Lynch, Birkbeck, University of London, of an AHRC/ESRC Religion and Society network: Young People and the Cultural Performance of Belief. Her books include, *Belief and Social Identity in the Modern World: Believing in Belonging* (Oxford University Press, forthcoming) and an edited volume, *Religion and the Individual* (Ashgate 2008).

Tessa Dooms is a Researcher for the African Religious Health Assets Programme (ARHAP) and a sessional lecturer at the University of the Witwatersrand in South Africa. Her research is primarily positioned in the field of sociology of religion, and in particular the link between religion and sexuality. She is currently a postgraduate student at Wits University. The title of her MA dissertation is: 'Reconstructing discourse, reconstructing power and recognising assets at the intersection of religion and adolescent sexual wellbeing'. Her other interests include youth culture, health and Pentecostalism in South Africa.

Duncan Dormor is the Dean of St John's College in the University of Cambridge where he lectures in sociology of religion and applied Christian ethics. His books include, *An Acceptable Sacrifice: Homosexuality and the Church* (co-edited with Jeremy Morris), *Anglicanism the Answer to Modernity* (2003) (co-edited with Jack McDonald and Jeremy Caddick) and *Just Cohabiting? The Church, Sex and Getting Married* (2004).

Sarah Dunlop is a Research Fellow in the Centre for the Study of Theology, Religion and Culture at King's College London. She uses visual ethnographic research methods to study the spirituality and religious practices of young people and is currently working on a project to discover the worldviews of young Polish migrants in the UK. She has written *Visualising Hope: Exploring the Spirituality of Young People in Eastern and Central Europe* (YTC Press 2005).

Richard Flory is Associate Professor (Research) of Sociology, and Senior Research Associate in the Center for Religion and Civic Culture at the University of Southern California. He is the author/editor of *Growing up in America: The Power of Race in the Lives of Teens* (Stanford University Press 2010), *Finding Faith: The Spiritual Quest of the Post-Boomer Generation* (Rutgers University Press 2008) and *GenX Religion* (Routledge 2000).

Leslie Francis is Professor of Religions and Education within the Warwick Religions and Education Research Unit, University of Warwick, Canon Theologian at Bangor Cathedral, Visiting Professor at York St John University, Visiting Professor at Glyndwr University, and Research Associate in the Centre for the Study of Religion and Psychology in the Danielsen Institute at Boston University USA. His recent books include *The Gospel in the Willows* (2010), *Empirical Theology in Texts and Tables* (2009), *The Mind of the Anglican Clergy* (2009), *Preaching with All Our Soul* (2008), *Gone for Good? Church Leaving and Returning in the 21st Century* (with Philip Richter, 2007), *British Methodism* (2006), *Urban Hope and Spiritual Health* (with Mandy Robbins) (2005), *Fragmented Faith* (2005) and *Faith and Psychology* (2005).

Mathew Guest is Lecturer in Theology and Religion at Durham University. He has published widely in the sociology of religion, specialising in contemporary evangelical Christianity in Western cultures. His books include, *Evangelical Identity and Contemporary Culture: A Congregational Study in Innovation* (2007), *Bishops, Wives and Children: Spiritual Capital across the Generations* (with Douglas Davies) (2007) and *Congregational Studies in the UK: Christianity in a Post-Christian Context* (co-edited with Karin Tusting and Linda Woodhead) (2004).

Alana Harris holds the Darby Fellowship in History at Lincoln College, University of Oxford. Her research interests span nineteenth- and twentieth-century British history, gender history and the sociology of religion. Recent publications include *Redefining Christian Britain: Post-1945 Perspectives* (2007) (with Jane Garnett and others) and she is currently preparing her doctoral thesis, 'Faith in the Family: Transformations in English Catholic Spirituality and Popular Religion, 1945–82', for publication.

Jeannine Heynes is the Coordinator of Religious Education and Membership Development at First Parish in Milton, a Unitarian Universalist church in Massachusetts. In her doctoral thesis, 'An Exploration of Girls' Perceptions of, and Views on, the Representation of Women and Gender in Religious Education' (University of Manchester 2008) she engages with issues of gender and education, feminist theologies, and the voices and experiences of girls. Jeannine has presented papers at a variety of academic conferences and has been a guest lecturer at the University of Manchester, the University of Hull and Eastern University speaking about gender, education and religion.

Ida Marie Høeg is Researcher at the Centre for Church Research (KIFO), Norway. In several journals and books she has published empirical studies in the field of ritual studies and sociology of religion. Her main research interests are religious and secular rites of passage, Church of Norway members' relation to the church, and gender and religion.

Wolfgang Ilg is Project Manager in Practical Theology and Religious Education and Researcher in Psychology at the University of Tübingen, Germany. In several books he has published empirical studies in the field of confirmation work, youth work and international youth exchange.

Gordon Lynch is Professor of Sociology of Religion and Director of the Centre for Religion and Contemporary Society within the Department of Psychosocial Studies at Birkbeck College, London. He has been co-chair of the Religion, Media and Culture Group within the American Academy of Religion and is currently chair of the British Sociological Association's Sociology of Religion study group. He has written on religion and contemporary Western culture, including *Understanding Theology and Popular Culture* (Blackwell 2005) and *The New Spirituality* (IB Tauris 2007). He is currently working on different projects exploring the intersections between religion and contemporary media, theorising religion, and the use of the sacred as a focus for sociological analysis.

Michael Mason is a Senior Research Fellow at Australian Catholic University's Quality of Life and Social Justice Research Centre in Melbourne. He works across the fields of sociology, religion studies and theology, with interests in sociological theories of religion, multidisciplinary, phenomenological and mixed-method approaches, and a research focus on religion in Australia and religious experience. He has been a principal investigator in several national sociological surveys on religion and spirituality. His most recent book is *The Spirit of Generation Y: Young People's Spirituality in a Changing Australia* (2007, with co-authors Andrew Singleton and Ruth Webber).

Donald E. Miller is Firestone Professor of Religion at the University of Southern California and executive director of the Center for Religion and Civic Culture. He is the author, co-author or editor of nine books, his most recent being *Finding Faith: The Spiritual Quest of the Post-Boomer Generation* (2008) and *Global Pentecostalism: The New Face of Christian Social Engagement* (2007). His earlier works include *Armenia: Portraits of Survival and Hope* (2003), *GenX Religion* (2000), *Reinventing American Protestantism* (1997), *Survivors: An Oral History of the Armenian Genocide* (1993), *Homeless Families: The Struggle for Dignity* (1993), *Writing and Research in Religious Studies* (1992) and *The Case for Liberal Christianity* (1981).

Pia Karlsson Minganti is a Researcher at the Department of Ethnology, History of Religions and Gender Studies at Stockholm University and Visiting Research Fellow at the Department of Politics, Institutions, History at University of Bologna. Since the mid-1990s she has been specialising on Muslims in Sweden. Her PhD was on 'Islamic Revival and Young Women's Negotiations on Gender in Contemporary Sweden' (Stockholm University, 2007). Karlsson Minganti is currently leading a research project focused on members in Muslim youth organisations in Sweden and Italy.

Karenza Moore is Lecturer in Crimininology at Lancaster University. Karenza has eight years' experience of research and publication on drug use, particularly in leisure settings. She has also published on social aspects of new technologies and global electronic dance music (EDM) club cultures. Alongside Dr Fiona Measham she conducted the first UK study on ketamine use amongst British EDM clubbers. Karenza is Reviews Editor for *Dancecult: Journal of Electronic Dance Music Culture* and co-founder of http://www.clubbingresearch.com/. She is currently Principal Investigator on a British Academy research project looking at GHB/GBL use in the UK.

Eleanor Nesbitt is a Professor in Religions and Education at the University of Warwick and has recently directed a study of the religious identity formation of young people in 'mixed-faith' families. She is Reviews Editor for the *Journal of Punjab Studies*. Her books include *Sikhism: A Very Short Introduction* (2005), *Intercultural Education: Ethnographic and Religious Approaches* (2004), *Interfaith Pilgrims: Living Truth and Truthful Living* (2003), *The Religious Lives of Sikh Children: A Coventry Based Study* (2000), and (with Gopinder Kaur) *Guru Nanak* (1999) and (with Robert Jackson) *Hindu Children in Britain* (1993).

Kati Niemelä, ThD, MEd, is a Senior Researcher at the Church Research Institute in Finland and an Adjunct Professor of Religious Education at the University of Helsinki. Her main research interests are youth and religion, church confirmation training, church membership and disaffilation, and church personnel and career development. In these areas she has published numerous books and articles.

Phil Rankin was previously Fellow in the Spirituality of Young People at Sarum College. While Fellow he completed a three-year research project, the report of which is entitled *Buried Spirituality* (2005). He is currently a facilitator and trainer based in Northern Ireland.

Philip Richter is Dean of Studies and Director of Education at STETS (the Southern Theological Education & Training Scheme), based in Salisbury. He is Convenor of the BSA Sociology of Religion Study Group and is a Methodist Minister. His books include *Sunday: A Photo Essay* (2007) and *Gone for Good? Church Leaving and Returning in the 21st Century* (with Leslie J. Francis, 2007).

Mandy Robbins is Senior Research Fellow at the Warwick Religions and Education Research Unit, Institute of Education, University of Warwick. She teaches on the distance learning MA in Religious Education. She is managing editor of *Rural Theology: International, Ecumenical and Interdisciplinary Perspectives*. Her books include *Clergywomen in the Church of England: A Psychological Study* (2008), *Urban Hope and Spiritual Health: The Adolescent Voice* (with Leslie J. Francis, 2005).

Nicholas M. Shepherd is the Executive Team Leader for the Centre for Youth Ministry (CYM) with whom he also tutors in practical theology. CYM provides professionally accredited undergraduate and postgraduate training and ongoing professional development in Christian youth work in the UK and Ireland. Nick edits the *Journal of Youth and Theology* and has recently gained his PhD in practical theology through King's College, London.

Jasjit Singh is a doctoral student at the University of Leeds, studying the transmission of religion among young British Sikhs (18–30) as part of the AHRC/ESRC Religion and Society programme. Having completed an MA in Religion and Public Life in 2008 during which he focused on the views of young British Sikhs on hair and the turban, Jasjit is looking to examine how young British Sikhs relate to tradition and authority in the face of modernity and globalisation as part of his PhD. For further details see www.personal.leeds.ac.uk/~trs5j2s.

Christian Smith is currently the William R. Kenan, Jr Professor of Sociology at the University of Notre Dame, Director of the Center for the Sociology of Religion and Principal Investigator of the National Study of Youth and Religion. He recently served as Associate Chair of the Department of Sociology at the University of North Carolina at Chapel Hill, from 2000 to 2005. Smith is the author, co-author, or editor of numerous books, including *Soul Searching: The Religious and Spiritual Lives of American Teenagers* (2005), *Passing the Plate: Why American Christians Don't Give Away More Money* (2008), *Moral, Believing Animals: Human Culture and Personhood* (2003), *The Secular Revolution: Power, Interests, and Conflict in the Secularization of American Public Life* (2003), *American Evangelicalism: Embattled and Thriving* (1998) and *The Emergence of Liberation Theology: Radical Religion and Social Movement Theory* (1991).

David Tacey is Reader in Literature and Psychoanalytic Studies at La Trobe University, Melbourne. His special interest is the search for meaning in the post-modern cultural context. He is the author of nine books, including *ReEnchantment* (2000), *The Spirituality Revolution* (2003) and *Edge of the Sacred* (2009). With Ann Casement, he edited *The Idea of the Numinous: Contemporary Jungian and Psychoanalytic Perspectives* (2006). His books have been translated into several languages. Recently, his *How to Read Jung* (2007) has been translated into Chinese and Korean.

Giselle Vincett is a Postdoctoral Research Fellow at the University of Edinburgh. She is currently researching religion and spirituality amongst young people in socially deprived areas in the UK. Giselle's publications include an edited volume entitled *Women and Religion in the West: Challenging Secularization* (with Kristin Aune and Sonya Sharma) (Ashgate 2008), 'Spirituality' (with Linda Woodhead) in *Religions in the Modern World* (Routledge 2009) and '(Dis)Engagements with Christianity Amongst Young People in England and Scotland' (with Sylvie Collins-Mayo) in *The Annual Review of the Sociology of Religion* (2009).

Pirjo Kristiina Virtanen is a researcher at the University of Helsinki, the Department of World Cultures. Her field of speciality is Amazonian indigenous peoples. Her articles include 'Amazonian Native Youths and Notions of Indigeneity in Urban Areas' (2010), 'New Interethnic Relations and Native Perceptions of Human-to-Human Relations in Brazilian Amazonia' (2009), 'Shamanism and Indigenous Youthhood in the Brazilian Amazonia' (2009), and 'Multidimensional Tradition: Native Young People and Their Construction of Indigenousness in Brazilian Amazonia' (2007). Her doctoral dissertation is entitled 'Changing Lived Worlds of Contemporary Amazonian Native Young People: Manchineri Youths in the Reserve and the City, Brazil-Acre' (2007). She has co-edited *Local and Global Encounters: Norms, Identities, Representations* (2009).

David Voas is Simon Professor of Population Studies in the Institute for Social Change at the University of Manchester. He leads a number of cross-national projects using large social surveys and serves as the British director of the European Values Study. With the support of the UK funding councils he is setting up an online centre for British data on religion (www.brin.ac.uk).

R. Stephen Warner is Professor of Sociology, Emeritus, at the University of Illinois at Chicago. He is author of *New Wine in Old Wineskins: Evangelicals and Liberals in a Small-Town Church* (1988) and *A Church of Our Own: Disestablishment and Diversity in American Religion* (2005) and co-editor of *Gatherings in Diaspora: Religious Communities and the New Immigration* (1998) and *Korean Americans and their Religions: Pilgrims and Missionaries from a Different Shore* (2001). With Rhys H. Williams he is at work on a report from the Youth and Religion Project under the working title *Navigating To Faith: Forming American Youth as Christians, Muslims, and Hindus* (under contract with Rutgers University Press).

Rhys H. Williams is Professor and Chair of Sociology at Loyola University, Chicago. He also directs the McNamara Center for the Social Study of Religion. His publications include *A Bridging of Faiths: Religion and Politics in a New England City* (with N.J. Demerath III, 1992), *Cultural Wars in American Politics: Critical Reviews of a Popular Myth* (1997), and the forthcoming *Navigating to Faith* (with R. Stephen Warner). He also has published articles in journals such as the *American Sociological Review*, *Sociological Theory*, *Social Problems* and *Sociology of Religion*. From 2003 to 2008 he was editor of the *Journal for the Scientific Study of Religion*, and in 2009–10 is president of the Association for the Sociology of Religion.

Linda Woodhead is Professor of Sociology of Religion at Lancaster University, and Visiting Professor at Aarhus University. Her interest is religion and change in contemporary society. She currently directs a £12m UK research programme on 'Religion and Society', consisting of 75 separate projects. Her publications include *The Spiritual Revolution* (with Paul Heelas, 2005), *Christianity: A Very Short Introduction* (2004) and *Religions in the Modern World* (2nd edn) (2009).

Foreword

Questions about youth and religion have been central to discussions about continuity and change in every religious tradition. At the same time, the attitudes of young people towards religion throw light on the social and cultural circumstances in which they live. This is why studies of youth and religion insist on making connections with central features of society such as the family, economy, education, politics, law, friendship, entertainment, gender relations, sexuality, consumerism, the media and sport. The chapters in this book show just how strong these connections are – and what different forms they take – in all the different countries discussed by contributors.

Contributors to this book show not only that studies of youth and religion have changed in various ways since the mid-twentieth century but also that these changes reflect wider shifts in many societies – as well as in social scientific ways of understanding them. Three of these shifts are of special significance because they reflect scholars' changing intellectual reasons for studying religion and young people.

First, there has been a shift away from the tendency to confine studies of youth and religion to formal processes of religious socialisation. This reflects a general decline among mainstream Christian churches in the importance attached to the orthodoxy of beliefs taught to, and supposedly accepted by, young people. But it also signifies a departure from the underlying image of young people as relatively passive recipients of religious knowledge. Admittedly, scholars remain interested in the processes of religious socialisation in families, religious organisations, schools and voluntary associations. Nevertheless, there is a growing recognition that young people can exercise a high degree of critical autonomy in making their own decisions about what to believe and how to translate their beliefs into action. Young people's use of new communications technologies and social networking sites – on a global scale – only enhances their opportunities for creative responses to formal socialisation in religion and to induction into religious ways of life. Most importantly, it can foster *bricolage* and the creation of do-it-yourself types of religion and spirituality that manage to combine intense subjectivity with emergent collective identities.

Second, interest in young people and religion was at a low level in the 1970s and 1980s among social scientists, particularly in Europe, when priority tended to be given to concerns with youth unemployment, youth subcultures, new social movements and cultural resistance to aspects of capitalism. This was also an era in which the declining social significance of religion was widely assumed to be its most interesting feature. As a result, evidence of falling rates of infant baptism, confirmation and religious marriage in Christian churches was taken to imply that young people were in the vanguard of what some French sociologists used to call the 'exit' from religion. Nevertheless, the dawn of the twenty-first century saw questions about young people and religion recapture the interest of social scientists in many parts of the world. This shift began with studies of the controversial capacity of transnational new religious movements to mobilise predominantly young followers; and it continued with the flowering of interest in the notion of spiritualities and, in particular, their expression among mainly young people in such forms as vampirism, Goth culture, Satanism, Wicca and paganism. Interest is currently high in the positive and negative connections between these spiritualities and the participation of young people in social movements and campaigns for peace, human rights, environmentalism and animal liberation.

Third, sociological research on religion in recent decades has underlined the importance of understanding young people in relation to their historical contexts. Instead of regarding the experience of being young as a fixed and uniform stage of the life-cycle which is merely repeated from generation to generation, the tendency now is to look for the distinctive features of particular cohorts of people who were young at particular historical junctures. For, while there are certainly bodily, emotional and social characteristics that are broadly typical of all young people, their lives are nevertheless heavily shaped by events and conditions that pertain uniquely to the years of their youth in particular places. This approach has made it possible to identify the distinctive characteristics – in terms of their religious beliefs and practices – of, for example, 'baby boomers', 'Generation Xers' or 'Muslims born in Britain in the 1980s'. However, this research is less concerned with regular, long-term patterns of religious continuity and change from generation to generation than with the distinctiveness of cohorts at particular times and places.

In short, the engagement of young people with religions and spiritualities is not only interesting in itself but is also a challenge to social scientists who seek to understand broader patterns of continuity and change in the development of societies and cultures. This book is therefore a timely contribution by distinguished scholars from many countries to debates that go to the heart of important questions about the past, present and future of youth and religion.

James A. Beckford
University of Warwick

Introduction

Sylvia Collins-Mayo

If we are to understand religion in contemporary society and glimpse its future, we need to turn our attention to young people. Young people are the generation at the forefront of cultural and social change. It is their engagement with religion, religious ideas and institutions that tell us how resilient beliefs and practices are, and how religions might adapt, transform and innovate in relation to wider social and cultural trends. Yet, it is only in the last decade or so that sociologists have started to devote much attention to age and religion. Before then, most of the discussion on young people's religiosity was left to educationalists, psychologists and practitioners concerned with youth ministry. Equally, religion has attracted only sporadic attention from youth studies scholars, even though religion – and more broadly spirituality – can be a core dimension of personhood, an important source of values, life purpose and communal belonging, and a vehicle for marking the transition from adolescence to adulthood. The sociology of youth religion is therefore 'the new kid on the block', but as an emerging sub-disciplinary field has much to contribute both to our understanding of religion and young people. In this book we bring together leading international scholars to discuss six central themes around religion and youth. In so doing, the collection highlights some of the most important researches that have focused on youth religion over the last ten years as well as introducing significant new studies,[1] which together provide a kaleidoscopic view of contemporary youth religion in Western Europe, the United States and Australia, and open up a new research agenda for years to come.

Perhaps the most salient point that stands out in the sociological analysis of age and religion in recent literature is that young people growing up in late modern Western societies tend to be less religious than older people, at least in terms of institutional religion. Young people are less likely to identify with any one religious tradition than their older contemporaries, less likely to subscribe to the creed of a major world religion and less likely to attend a place of worship on a regular basis (Davie 2000; Voas and Crockett 2005). This observation immediately raises questions. The first is concerned with the extent to which an interest in religion may be dependent on the life cycle. Is it the case that young people are 'naturally' less religious than older people because religion tends to deal with 'ultimate concerns' and experiences that are more likely to arise later in life – in the words of Cyndi Lauper, do 'girls just wanna have fun'? Perhaps with the accumulation

---

[1]   Many of the chapters included in this volume were presented as papers at the British Sociological Association Sociology of Religion Study Group conference in 2008.

of significant life events non-religious young people will become religious older people. Or is it the case that young people generation on generation are 'losing their religion'? A second question follows. If there is a generational trend away from institutional religion, are young people basically succumbing to the forces of secularisation (a perspective that seems to have gone out of fashion), or are there sacralising influences running parallel which are changing the way young people relate to religion thereby keeping the sacred alive and meaningful? If the latter, then what significance does religion in its new forms have both for the individual and for wider society? A third set of questions relates to the transmission of faith. If young people are less religious than older people is it because older people have failed to pass faith on effectively? This is Brown's (2001) conclusion from his historical analysis of religious in change in Britain. For him, loss of piety amongst women in the 1960s due to wider socio-cultural changes undermined the process of religious socialisation. What 'spiritual capital', then, do young people inherit today?

The answers to all these questions are complex and contingent – different pictures emerge depending on where you look. In this respect whilst 'youth' is a helpful category for analysing broad trends and monitoring general patterns of religious change (as in generational analysis), there is a danger of over-generalising and treating young people as if they constitute a distinct homogeneous group. Clearly they do not. Youth is constructed differently in different societies, and the experience of youth within different societies varies according to social class, gender, ethnicity, ability and so on. In discussing youth most of the contributors to this volume have focused on teenagers or young adults up to the age of 25. This in itself encompasses a broad spectrum of positions in terms of personal development and stages in the life course. However, if 'youth' is understood as the period of transition from dependent childhood to independent adulthood rather than simply a chronological period, Western societies can be said to be witnessing an extension of youth, which will make youth as a category even more varied. The traditional markers of adulthood – financial independence, a home outside the family of origin, marriage or cohabitation and a family of one's own – are taking longer to achieve. Commentators on youth sometimes talk of 'yo-yo' transitions (Biggart and Walther 2006) – a young person may make several forays into independence before they finally establish themselves as fully independent. Consequently the period of youth may sometimes exceed 25 years. At the other end of the age-range, the commercialisation of youth has reached into pre-adolescence. 'Tweenagers' (10–13 year-olds) are encouraged to imitate their older peers in patterns of consumption and attitude (Mayo and Nairn 2009). In summary, youth is a diverse category. Our aim in this book is therefore to consider both broad trends in youth religion to get an idea of the 'big picture' but also to consider specific cases of young people's relationship to religion in order to understand something of its local particularities. We cannot, of course, provide an exhaustive account of the latter, but rather we highlight the variety of ways young people engage with religion in late modern society.

Our opening two sections are concerned with the broad picture. In Part I we present some of the insights of generational analysis. Flory and Miller, whose collection of papers *GenX Religion* (2000) has become essential reading for anyone interested in youth religion, begin the discussion by considering how young people in the United States have engaged with religion in the post-boomer era from 1976 onwards. A chief dimension and distinctive feature of youth religion during this period is the embracing (or counter-culture rejection) of digital media. Young people today live in an age of globalisation supported by rapidly advancing media and communications technologies. This has impacted on how young people engage with religion, both in terms of belief and practice. Beaudoin, also reflecting on the United States, made a similar point in his seminal book *Virtual Faith* (1998). He argued that the development of media in relation to popular culture did not just change how young people related to existing religion, rather for many young people popular culture *replaced* institutional religion as basis for making sense of the world. In chapter 2 Collins-Mayo and Beaudoin consider this legacy for young people today. Changing the nature of analysis from qualitative to quantitative, in chapter 3 Voas addresses head-on the question we raise above concerning generational change versus life course and period effects. He leaves us in no doubt of the importance of the former. Lynch concludes Part I with a thoughtful critique of generational analysis as it pertains to religion, identifying some of its weaknesses as well as strengths.

Part II presents the results of three comprehensive surveys of young people's religious attitudes, beliefs and practices in the United States (Smith, chapter 5), England and Wales (Robbins and Francis, chapter 6) and Australia (Mason, chapter 7). Each of these studies allows us to grasp the big picture of young people's religiosity and demonstrate some common features of late modern youth religion in different parts of the world. It seems from these surveys that there are some secularising tendencies in evidence, particularly in relation to traditional Christianity. Christian beliefs still have some currency for the young people, but are embraced in a selective manner with a degree of uncertainty and little personal significance on a day-to-day basis. On the other hand each survey shows signs of religious – or spiritual – adaptation.

Parts III and IV pick up the theme of sacralisation in different ways. Tacey, author of *The Spirituality Revolution* (2003), writes from a multidisciplinary perspective in chapter 8 to bring our attention to spirituality (rather than religiosity) as a core dimension of personhood. Drawing on his experiences of teaching students in Australia, he concludes that young people, often bought up outside of any religious tradition, are searching for a type of spiritually that will nurture an authentic inner self. Traditional religious forms are too restrictive to fulfil this need, but since young people are, in his view, inherently spiritual the decline of institutional religion does not result in secularisation but instead frees up space for spirituality to develop in new ways.

The spiritual revolution thesis in various guises has stimulated some important empirical research (e.g. Heelas and Woodhead 2005) as well as fitting with broader analysis of the nature of late modern society. Giddens (1991), Beck and Beck-Gernsheim (2002) and others have argued that structural individualisation is a characteristic of late modern society. In contrast with previous generations when life choices were fairly limited and biographies assumed standard trajectories, today young people are faced with many different choices concerning the path their life might take and who they want to become; as such they are required to engage in a reflexive process of identity construction whether they like it or not. This is both exciting and unnerving – young people are not constrained by traditional expectations, but neither do they have equal access to resources that will enable them to realise the choices they want to make; nor can they be entirely sure of the consequences of decisions made in an unpredictable global society. Culture provides the raw materials for this reflexive construction of self, most notably through patterns of material consumption and the creation of 'lifestyle' (Miles 2000). Spiritual traditions potentially provide another resource for those who want to use them, whether that be in the form of New Age practices, psycho-therapeutic or drug cultures, neo-traditional paganism, or even traditional institutional religion, or a combination of all of these things. The important point from the perspective of sacralisation in late modernity is that whatever form of spirituality is adopted it is increasingly a matter of individual choice, and that choice is informed by the need to nurture an authentic 'subjective-life' from Heelas and Woodhead (2005). An important additional point is made by Beck and Beck-Gernsheim in their analysis of individualisation – individualisation does not mean ignoring others or following an ethic of pure self-interest. Young people can and do, live for others whilst thinking of themselves (2002, 28).

Parts III and IV therefore continue our exploration of young people's relationship to religion by looking at range of ways in which they draw on spiritual traditions and what significance such beliefs and practices have in terms of how they live their lives and develop their identity. In chapter 9 Virtanen explores the contemporary shamanic practices of young people in the Brazilian Amazon. Cush (chapter 10) examines teenage girls' involvement in witchcraft in England, whilst Moore (chapter 11) takes our attention to spiritual expression in relation to electronic dance music clubbing. Both Cush and Moore indicate the significance of popular culture as an influence on spirituality in these rather different contexts, and so echo the point made in chapter 2. Day's discussion on 'believing in belonging' (chapter 12) highlights the significance of personal relationships as a source of meaning that can supplant religious beliefs altogether. She also provides evidence of moral thinking and confirms the view that young people follow similar moral perspectives to previous generations but that they place the authority for their decisions in their own selves rather than in an external religious authority. Cooksey and Dooms (chapter 13) further consider the relationship between religion, moral thinking and behaviour in terms of sexual practices amongst young people in the United States and South Africa.

Part IV focuses more specifically on identity. It is the case that in Western Europe religion has come back into the public sphere (it never left it in the United States), largely in relation to questions around how to best accommodate increasing religious diversity or to contain the possibility of religiously motivated violence. Both of these policy-related issues disproportionately affect young people, especially Muslim youth. Due to migration and higher birth rates amongst minority religious groups, the youth population has greater degrees of religious pluralism than older generations. This has raised the profile for religion and in some cases has encouraged young people to re-engage with religious tradition. The radicalisation of a religious minority has led to interfaith tensions, Islamaphobia aimed at young Muslims and, to counter, entrenchment of conservative religious identities. Minganti (chapter 14) explores the theme of Muslim identity construction, focusing on Sweden and the confluent narratives of religion, gender and race. The relationship between gender and religion is also of interest to Heynes (chapter 15) in her analysis of teenage girls' reactions to RE material in English schools. Singh (chapter 16) considers identity from the perspective of young British Sikhs and their use of the symbols of hair and turban in embodying identity. Harris (chapter 17) and Shepherd (chapter 18) turn our attention to Christian identity construction in different locations. Harris considers the ways in which the traditional practice of pilgrimage (in her case Lourdes in France) can be a means by which faith identity can be developed, and Shepherd looks at Christian youth groups as a context for negotiating identity.

Part V is concerned with the process of religious transmission. As we identified at the beginning, one of the reasons put forward for young people's lack of religiosity is that late modernity is not conducive to the transmission of faith (Hervieu-Léger 2000). In this section we therefore look at both the process and experience of transmission. Warner and Williams (chapter 19) open the discussion by considering different patterns of religious transmission within families of different faith groups in the United States. Their comment that families have to 'work hard' to socialise their children reinforces the point that in late modernity religious transmission does not come easily. Arweck and Nesbitt (chapter 20) consider the experience of transmission within families too, but this time in England and in relation to the complex case of mixed-faith families. Guest (chapter 21) also identifies a special category of families in terms of religious transmission, Church of England clergy families. His discussion considers the transmission of 'spiritual capital' in this setting. Christensen et al. (chapter 22) take us to the more formal institutional means of establishing young people in their faith, by looking at Christian confirmations classes and the meaning confirmation holds in different European societies.

In Part VI we take a step back from the details of research findings in order to give some attention to methodological issues around researching young people and religion. It is an experientially focused contribution to a growing body of literature which is specifically concerned with how best to research youth both from an ethical as well as practical point of view (Fraser et al. 2004; Heath et al. 2009).

In chapter 23 Collins-Mayo and Rankin consider the values and pitfalls of different approaches to youth religion drawing on their experiences of both quantitative and qualitative methods. Voas (chapter 24) highlights the value of quantitative analysis and survey work. He discusses issues around the measurement of religion and data collection. He also notes the possibilities and benefits of secondary analysis of existing data sets. Dunlop and Richter (chapter 25) take us in a qualitative direction and draw attention to new methodological developments in the use of visual methods and photography. Aune and Vincett (chapter 26) remind us of the importance of considering social diversity in analysing youth religion. In their case gender is the point of reference, others could have been chosen. Abramson (chapter 27) concludes this section by reflecting on the 'insider-outsider' problem that remains an important methodological consideration in contemporary sociology of religion, using her experience as a Jewish researcher studying youth movements within British Judaism.

In the Conclusion, Pink Dandelion reflects on what we can learn from this collection and its importance for future research. Finally, in the Epilogue, Linda Woodhead comments on the emerging sociology of youth religion from her perspective as Director of the AHRC/ESRC[2] Religion and Society Programme in the United Kingdom which in 2008/9 invested £4m in commissioned researches into youth religion. The work is therefore set to continue; this book offers a staging post on way.

---

[2]   Arts and Humanities Research Council/Economic and Social Research Council.

PART I
Generations and their Legacy

The years following the end of World War 2 have been witness to rapid socio-cultural changes in the West. Shifts in patterns of education, employment, communication, consumption, family life and geographical mobility have all been associated with changes in people's attitudes towards, and involvement in, religion. One of the ways researchers have tried to document and analyse these changes has been in terms of generational differences. Three generations are commonly referred to in the literature: baby boomers (those born in the 15 to 20 years immediately after the War), Generation X (those born in the 1960s and 1970s) and Generation Y sometimes called the Millennial Generation (those born in the 1980s and 1990s). The first three chapters of this section focus on how the post-boomers differ from previous generations. Flory and Miller focus on post-boomers in the United States. Collins-Mayo and Beaudoin consider the particular significance of popular culture and digital media for the religiosity of Generation X and Y. Voas considers explanations that underpin generational religious change. Lynch changes our focus a little and offers a critique of the generational approach used by researchers to document and understand young people's religion.

Chapter 1

The Expressive Communalism of Post-Boomer Religion in the USA[1]

Richard Flory and Donald E. Miller

Introduction

The 'post-boomer' generations may constitute an entirely new consciousness in terms of how they relate to religion in the twenty-first century. Individuals who were born after 1975 grew up using computers, finding information on the internet, and, more recently, carrying digital devices that seem to be appendages to their bodies – cell phones, iPods, and Blackberrys. Even pre-teens are snapping pictures with their phones. Coffee shops are filled with people of all ages downloading email messages on their computers, swapping music files, watching the latest webisode of their favourite TV programs, and texting, twittering, and checking Facebook updates on their iPhones.

In many ways, we are on the front end of this revolution. It is only in the last several years that people discarded their film cameras for digital replacements. While thousands of trees are still being chopped down each year to produce books such as this one, there is every reason to think that most future communication will be digital in form. E-books are already available in which text is supplemented by video and audio clips. Increasingly people are replacing their morning ritual of reading the newspaper with their first cup of coffee and instead are clocking a few minutes scanning headlines online before they turn to breakfast. Indeed, it will not be too long until you could be reading this book on some convenient device balanced on your knee that will enable you to listen to the latest worship music, see video clips of church services in Nigeria or Brazil, and interact in real time with religious leaders as if they were sitting in the living room with you. Articles with text will not disappear, but they will be nested within an interactive media framework.

One result of the digital revolution is that people are exposed to multiple worldviews in visually rich formats. The religious implication of this cultural change is that people have to struggle with the issue of pluralism in ways that are historically unique. The old argument about pluralism was that it promoted secularization, because how could one possibly hold to an exclusive religious perspective when one was faced daily with an incredible variety of competing

---

[1] Material used in this chapter has been previously published in Flory and Miller (2004, 2007a, 2007b, 2008).

options? In other words, how could they all be true and why should one worldview be privileged over the others?

More recently – especially when everyone did not become agnostic relativists – the argument about the effect of pluralism changed. Having multiple options from which one could choose produced competition within the religious marketplace and, very possibly, better products. Under religious monopolies lazy members of the priestly class could survive without serving their client population or engaging in innovation. Today this is not possible. Within Christianity, for example, there are multiple niche markets catering to specific consumer needs. One size does not fit all, and some mega-churches are accommodating themselves to this fact by having simultaneous worship services, each with different music, different liturgical styles, and corresponding different clienteles (see, for example, McConnell 2009; Thumma 2007; Surratt et al. 2006).

While religion is not a business, it must be responsive to changes in the marketplace because if it does not, it will be deemed irrelevant. This is precisely what is happening to many of the historic Protestant denominations in the USA. At one time, the so-called 'mainline' churches claimed the majority of Americans. Today these churches are increasingly filled with graying heads. They may expound 'sophisticated' theological arguments by well-educated clergy, but they are culturally out of touch, packaging their religion in ways that does not communicate to a broad range of the American population – and especially to the post-boomer generations.

The dilemma of the moribund mainline denominations raises the question of whether churches that are prospering today, including many megachurches, are prepared to address the needs of the post-boomer generations. From our interviews with post-boomers, as well as consulting a number of reports from surveys of post-boomer religiosity (National Institute on Spirituality in Higher Education 2000–2003) and other studies of the lives of American post-boomers (see, for example, Winograd and Hais 2008; Wuthnow 2007) several distinct patterns emerge that we suspect have a lot to do with the fact that they are children of the digital age.

Here are some characteristics of post-boomers:

- They perceive religion to be a choice and not an obligation.
- Religious labels, including denominational identifications, are relatively unimportant to them.
- They are typically tolerant of other people's beliefs and, in fact, enjoy the variety of different religious practices that they see on campus.
- Religious authority is internal rather than located in some external source, such as the hierarchy of a church.
- They see more value in religious experience than in a codified set of beliefs.
- They affirm the idea of being on a religious journey rather than embracing a static set of beliefs and practices.

- If they join a religious group, they are more interested in the authenticity of the people—their honesty, openness, and humility – than they are in an authoritarian presentation of the truth.
- They have no problem being eclectic in their religious taste, which sometimes includes creating their own hybrid religious identities.
- They want to make a difference in the world and therefore believe that religion should address issues of justice and equality.

Obviously these characteristics do not describe every post-boomer, rather that they are found in unique ways among post-boomers that are related to the experiences they have had while growing up, influencing how they approach relationships, jobs, and even how they understand and participate in religion. That said, we would not expect all post-boomers to act in exactly the same ways, rather that there would be a range of responses to the challenges of a changing culture that are related to their formative experiences and to their time and place in history (see Mannheim 1952, and Schuman and Scott 1989 for this basic framework on generations).

Cultural influences

There are several cultural factors that have shaped the perspectives of post-boomers, many of which are related to the digital revolution.

First, post-boomers take globalization for granted. From the day they were born they have had access to multiple worldviews, simply by clicking the button on their television remote, or now, through their cell phones. They have grown up with the knowledge that their culture, their belief system, their style of life is simply one among many. Furthermore, they realize that the world is interconnected, both economically as well as ecologically. For some post-boomers, this exposure is threatening and they have retreated into a fundamentalist ghetto of racist and ideologically isolated beliefs, where they are right and everyone else is wrong. But this is not the majority viewpoint of post-boomers – especially those who are educated and live in urban areas interacting with a wide variety of persons and cultures. These individuals tend to believe that the world is a richer and more interesting place because of the variety of cultures and belief systems that surround them.

Second, post-boomers have grown up in an incredibly cynical period in the USA. They believe that most politicians are corrupt, that priests molest children, that Evangelical pastors have affairs, that corporations promote faulty products and otherwise exploit their unwitting customers, and that few people can be trusted. Hence, it is not surprising that many post-boomers chant the mantra that 'I am spiritual but not religious' (see Fuller 2001), because they distrust institutions of all sorts, including religious organizations. Philosophically, they imbibe an informal expression of postmodernism that sees any comprehensive belief system as inadequate, because there are no universal truths. Reality depends on where one stands, on one's perspective. At best, truth is partial and perhaps there is no truth at all. Based on what they have seen in their lives, they believe that money, power, and self-interest control the world.

Third, post-boomers live with residual fear – of environmental disaster, the collapse of the American – and global – economy, the decline of the USA as a superpower, and of the next terrorist attack, which may be just around the corner. Many post-boomers think the USA is living on borrowed time given the state of the US economy and its reliance on foreign oil. They are genuinely frightened by the emergence of other countries as economic superpowers and thus competitors to the USA. They notice that most of the smart science students at their university were born someplace other than the USA, and they wonder what is wrong with our educational system. Many post-boomers question if they will be able to sustain the lifestyle that their parents achieved. How could they ever afford to buy a house that is comparable to the one in which they grew up?

Post-Boomer religious responses to culture

Research on spirituality suggests that particularly since the 1960s, spirituality has become decoupled from religion, with many people pursuing their own private, individualistic, and noninstitutionalized spiritual journey, where the individual spiritual quest for fulfillment takes precedence over membership in, or commitment to, the religious community (see, for example, Bellah et al. 1985; Roof 1993, 1999; Wuthnow 1994, 1998, 2001). Among post-boomers however, we have found an understanding and approach to religion that, based on their formative experiences and general outlook, are different than what is described in the literature. For example, although post-boomers tend not to accept social institutions of any sort unquestioningly, we have found that they are willing to participate in religious institutions, although within certain limits. They carefully choose the types of institutions within which they participate, they are more interested in the relationships and community that they find there than in the institution itself, and they can be somewhat fluid in their institutional commitments, often participating in more than one institutional setting at the same time.

Further, post-boomers live in a digitally driven, symbolically saturated culture, one that they can easily access and participate in, and thus many are seeking religious experience in ways that seek to include various combinations of symbols, traditions, rituals, and expressiveness. These range from reinvigorating ancient symbols and rituals within their own religious traditions, to borrowing from other traditions and even creating their own rituals and symbols in order to have an embodied spiritual experience.

The post-boomer spiritual quest that we describe here is quite different than the individual spiritual quest as described in much of the literature, in particular in terms of their commitment to a religious community within which they seek a physical experience of the spiritual, and where they actively live out their spiritual lives as part of their commitment to both the religious community and the surrounding community. We think of this as an embodied spirituality that is both personal and social. post-boomers seek individual spiritual experience and fulfillment in the community of believers, where meaning is both constructed and directed outward in service to others, both within the religious community and the larger community where they are located.

Within the context of the way that post-boomers have experienced the world, and out of which their basic outlook on the world has been formed, we have identified three different religious responses to cultural change among post-boomers. First there are the *Appropriators* who tend to embrace the latest cultural fad in their style of worship and programming. In all of their activities, whether in a worship service, a Christian rock concert, or even a mission trip, Appropriators seek to provide a compelling and 'relevant' religious experience for individual participants. In this, both churches and independent ministries seek to create these experiences through imitating, or *appropriating,* trends found in the larger culture and ultimately popularizing these into a form of pop-Christianity that is primarily oriented toward an individual spiritual experience. For Appropriators, it is the desire for relevance and to produce products mirroring the trends in the larger culture that drives their efforts. In many ways, they have created an almost parallel world to the larger culture in which the individual believer finds refuge from the challenges of suburban life, where they can find a safe community of similar people within which to pursue their spiritual journey.

In contrast to the cultural imitation of the Appropriators, a second response is what we have called the *Reclaimers*, because they seek to resurrect various liturgical forms and practices from the past (e.g., the 'bells and smells' of the Catholic, Orthodox or Anglican traditions), finding the worship in many mega-churches to be shallow. Reclaimers are reacting to the sterile worship locations of most mega-churches and the emphasis on entertaining worship. They happily forego the skits and jokes and Hawaiian shirts of Appropriator clergy in favor of a Gothic cathedral, flowing incense, candles on a well-worn altar, robed priests and dim light streaming in through stained glass. They believe that tradition has value – that the saints of ancient times developed liturgical and meditation practices that have the potential to bring one closer to God. While they are backward looking, they are surprisingly postmodern in their desire to unite mind and body in mystical union with the Holy. Although some Reclaimers seek out Orthodox churches (for example, Greek or Russian) in which to worship, a much larger group of people are turning to the Anglican tradition and especially to those congregations that prize the sensuality of 'high church' liturgy. In terms of the digital revolution, Reclaimers typically see the church as a refuge from the bombardment of the commercial world. Worship is a time to shut out the external buzz of contemporary life and move inward to a place where God's presence can be felt more than proclaimed in words.

Finally, we identify a relatively small group of churches that are true *Innovators* in that they are not simply packaging cultural elements and rebranding them with a

Christian label, but instead they are seeking to embody the essence of Christianity in genuinely authentic ways that relate to the culture. Innovators represent a constantly evolving, or *innovating*, approach to religious and spiritual beliefs and practices. Many of these are newer, less established groups that are affiliated with the 'emerging church' movement, while others are established churches and ministries that are innovating within their own traditions. These groups, whether emerging or more established churches, frame their approach in contrast to what they see as an overly institutionalized and inwardly focused church to one that is focused on building community, both within the religious group and with the surrounding community. These churches are introducing various forms of ritual and symbol into their worship services along with new forms of religious and community life that emphasize community and belonging, as well as service, within the religious community and to the larger community (Flory and Miller 2008).

Expressive communalism

What then do these three different approaches to religion have in common? We have argued that the common experiences of post-boomers have resulted in a similar understanding of the world, yet have presented three different religious responses to the challenges and opportunities that post-boomers perceive in the larger culture. We believe that each of the three responses we have identified represent a larger desire for religious expression, spiritual experience, and a sense of both belonging, and service to, a community.

None of the three responses we have identified fit neatly into the individualistic spirituality identified in previous research. That is, although there are certainly individualistic elements found in each of these responses, each also, and in most cases equally, emphasize elements that relate to community – both in the sense of belonging and in serving. This is not to suggest, however, that they have somehow removed themselves from the individualism that pervades American society, rather that their individual spiritual quest is mediated through the communities in which they are active and in which they seek membership and belonging.

The importance of embodiment and community for post-boomers, whether through using one's body in worship or in living out, or embodying, Christian teachings, suggests that there are many who are seeking a new form of spirituality that goes beyond the individualistic questing that characterizes much of the sociological literature on spirituality. The responses we have identified, whether embracing or resisting these trends, have shown that there is a new, or perhaps renewed, emphasis on an embodied worship and service, and a desire for seeking, creating, and committing to a particular faith community. It is in the context of these faith communities where one can be both personally fulfilled, and where one can serve others, whether in one's own religious community, or the with homeless in Los Angeles, or AIDS victims in Africa.

Thus, whether it is through the stained glass, icons, and incense of the liturgical traditions, or the creation of various art-works intended to express their particular spiritual experience, or service to others, these only have personal meaning within the context of the religious community. These young people are not the spiritual consumers of their parents' generation, rather they are seeking both a deep spiritual experience and a community experience, each of which provides them with meaning in their lives, and each is meaningless without the other. We believe that we are witnessing the emergence of a new form of spirituality, what we are calling *Expressive Communalism*, that although related to the individualistic forms of spirituality as noted above, is also distinct from them. post-boomers have embedded their lives in spiritual communities in which their desire and need for both expressive/experiential activities, whether through art, music, or service-oriented activities, and for a close-knit, physical community and communion with others, are met. These young people are seeking out a different approach to spirituality in response to the shortcomings they see as inherent in what they have previously experienced. In this, post-boomers are seeking to develop a balance for an extreme individualism through the religious experience and spiritual meaning found in an expressive community of fellow believers.

Chapter 2

Religion, Pop Culture and 'Virtual Faith'

Sylvia Collins-Mayo and Tom Beaudoin

In this first section of *Religion and Youth* we are concerned with the religious legacy of generations. Looking at the numbers of young people hanging out in our shopping malls over the course of an average weekend compared to the numbers filling the pews in church at least two points of the legacy seem clear. First, fewer young people are inheriting a habit of churchgoing than in the past. Second, they are, however, inheriting a love of shopping and popular culture. Neither post-materialist values (Ingleheart 1990) nor a worldwide credit crunch seems to be persuading young people that it is better to pray than to purchase. Generation Y are 'consumer kids' (Mayo and Nairn 2009) and they got to be so under the influence of baby boomers and GenXers.

What's in a generational name?

Before we consider the generational legacy further it is as a well to define our terms. Following Mannheim (1952), a generation is a group of people born around the same time who live through a particular set of social, cultural, economic and political circumstances during the formative years of early adulthood. These socio-historic conditions come to shape how they see the world, the values they hold and the characteristic ways in which they approach life that distinguishes them from generations that have gone before or will come after. Theorists differ in the labels they put on generations and the particular birth years they cover. Others critique the value of thinking in terms of generations at all (see Lynch 2002 and chapter 4 herein).

Notwithstanding some of the problems of generational theory, generational descriptions do at least allow us to get a hold on some broad features which can be a useful starting point for thinking about young people's experiences and patterns of social and religious change. Specifying the intra-generational variety can be (as in this book) teased out later.

The times they are a changin'

Generation X is normally taken to include those born during the 1960s and 1970s. They are the inheritors of the post-war generation – the so-called 'baby boomers' (see Voas, chapter 3). Baby boomers are associated with the counter-culture movement of the 1960s which saw a liberalisation of social and political attitudes. They were the first generation, for instance, to benefit from the contraceptive pill and saw the relaxing of laws around divorce and homosexuality. Disillusioned with the old social institutions, boomers sought new freedoms through political activism such as the civil rights movement, second-wave feminism and peace campaigns in both the United States and Britain. In terms of religion, boomers were inclined to move away from church, or at least from the denominations and congregations they had grown up in. In his commentary on post-1950s North America, Wuthnow (1998) describes the 1960s as a time of transition from a 'spirituality of dwelling', where religious life was embedded in family, congregation and community, to a 'spirituality of seeking' whereby individuals took an eclectic approach to their spiritual life, drawing on a range of traditions. A key emphasis in seeker-spirituality was the emancipation of self, authenticity and the enhancement of 'subjective life' (to borrow a recent phrase from Heelas and Woodhead 2005). The spiritual orientation of North American boomers was echoed to some degree across the Atlantic in Britain. It ran alongside, however, an even more widespread phenomenon: namely, a growing apathy and indifference towards spirituality altogether in favour of materialistic, self-oriented, hedonistic consumption. Indeed in both Britain and the United States a youth market had opened up to boomers and was rapidly expanding – its wares were popular culture: pop music, fashion, magazines, pop art, films, cartoons and the like.

The legacy to Generation X

Reaching early adulthood during the 1980s and 1990s, Generation X picked up the social and cultural legacy of the boomers and it was not an easy one. Much of the boomer optimism dissipated in the 1970s as the counter-culture movement failed to realise its aims and Western economies became subject to a recession following the 1973 oil crisis. Youth unemployment, anxieties around nuclear war and a growing awareness of environmental problems troubled GenXers in both the United States and Britain. So too did rising divorce rates and AIDS, a legacy of 1960s sexual liberation. Large numbers of GenXers grew up in families with parents absent by divorce or through long working hours – mums as well as dads. This meant that GenX children to some degree were left to look after themselves (winning them the title 'latch-key' kids) and consequently they spent much of their time growing up watching television, listening to pop music (or watching it on MTV), playing computer games, surfing a nascent internet and generally enjoying the pleasures of popular culture:

> This entry into the world of pop culture at such a young age is one reason our
> generation [GenX] is unique. Whereas baby boomers also had an intimate
> relationship with popular and media culture, GenXers found it at an earlier,

more critical age and without the familial supervision of previous generations. (Beaudoin 1998, 5)

Institutional religion found it hard to compete. boomers disillusioned with the church and prioritising personal authenticity in their own spiritual life were disinclined to socialise their children into (or 'impose' on them) a religious tradition. Only half of boomers in the United States exposed their children

> to formal religious training of any kind, compared with 86 percent who themselves had received religious training as children. Significant exposure was even lower: only 34 percent were sending their children to Sunday school classes, whereas 63 percent had themselves attended such classes. (Wuthnow 1998, 76)

In Britain, Brown records the 'unprecedented rapidity in the fall of Christian religiosity amongst the British population' (2001, 188) between 1956 and 1973. People started to give up baptising their children and sending them to church and Sunday school.

The church tried to respond in a number of ways to make itself more attractive to young people, including adopting elements of popular culture into its worship liturgies. Choruses substituted for hymns, guitars for organs. Indeed, boomers and GenXers who retained contact with the church pioneered the creative and sophisticated use of pop culture in the 'alternative worship' movement. Moreover, they have also developed a burgeoning Christian (often evangelical) pop culture industry. Christian consumers can now enjoy Christian TV and radio stations playing Christian music by Christian bands; they can watch Christian films and read Christian books ('Chri-fi'), comic versions of the Bible and so on. Still, the church has failed to connect with many GenXers who inherited the boomer suspicion of institutions. And yet the social and political uncertainties in which GenXers found themselves provoked questions of a religious nature and left many with a broad interest in spirituality. Popular culture was one way to engage with this spiritual inclination:

> During our lifetimes, especially during the critical period of the 1980s, pop culture was the amniotic fluid that sustained us. For a generation of kids who had a fragmented or completely broken relationship to 'formal' or 'institutional' religion, pop culture filled the spiritual gap. (Beaudoin 1998, 21) ✓

Virtual faith

Tom Beaudoin, a cultural-theologian, has developed the concept of 'virtual faith' to consider North American GenXer's relationship to religion and popular culture outside the church. His starting point is the proliferation of religious representations and artefacts found in mainstream popular culture. Often these sit on the edge of legitimate religious expression, but are not quite themselves religious. One example is chart-topping 'sacred music', another is the wearing of religious symbols as fashion items. Potentially these artefacts could be used in a straightforwardly religious way (i.e. as 'real' religion) to help in meditative prayer, for example, or as an outward indicator of real personal piety. On the other hand, it is equally possible for somebody to use them in a straightforwardly secular manner simply for entertainment or decoration with no attention necessarily paid to the religious symbolism at all. Between these two extremes is 'virtual faith'. Engaging with religious artefacts to catch the 'rumours of angels' (to borrow a phrase from Berger 1971) without actually being religiously obligated in any way. In this respect there is some play between the virtual and real since what might be virtual religion in one context can become real religion in another. It is Beaudoin's thesis in *Virtual Faith* (1998) that GenXers use these representations in mainstream pop culture to explore and express (often in a heavily ironic way) their own religious-cum-spiritual ideas and identities. By considering the virtual faith objects in pop culture that GenXers' create and consume, Beaudoin suggests we can get a sense of GenXers' religiosity and also learn something about the nature of 'real' religion.

In *Virtual Faith* Beaudoin analyses three types of popular culture – fashion, cyberspace and MTV – as they played out in the 1980s and 1990s when GenX were teenagers and young adults. From these he draws out four themes that pertain to GenX's lived theology.

The first is the suspicion of institutional religion (particularly Catholicism) inherited from the boomers and a concomitant irreverence towards the church. This is displayed in the critical and ironic use of religious imagery in music videos such as REM's *Losing My Religion*, Soundgarden's *Black Hole Sun* and Nirvana's *Heart-Shaped Box*. Like music videos, cyberspace provides opportunities for GenXers to mimic and ironise real religious institutions and symbols thereby showing them up for the social constructions that they are; emptying them of their original meaning only to inject them with new meanings that come closer to representing GenX religious sensibilities.

A second theme Beaudoin identifies, again inherited to some degree from boomer spirituality, is the importance of experience as the key to authenticating religious meaning. In this respect Beaudoin draws attention to the Catholic idea of *sacramentals* ('miniature, personal signs of God and God's grace in the world', 1998, 74) that lie in the space between official religious sacraments and the ordinary material world (1998, 75). Beaudoin argues that pop culture can provide sacramentals for GenXers. He gives the examples of the GexX fashions for body piercing and tattooing. Marking the body carries meaning which can be interpreted religiously. Tattoos might symbolise identification with the outcast in society for example. Naval piecing draws attention to the belly which has religious associations with the centre of selfhood and fecundity. As such, 'it implies finding the spiritual in the sensual' (1998, 79). Similarly, the blending of sexual imagery and religious symbolism in music videos such as Madonna's *Like a Prayer* could in the manner of the mystics be regarded as representing an ultimate desire for God.

Third, Beaudoin considers the theme of suffering. As we have suggested above, the social legacy inherited by GenXers was not an easy one to bear and suffering is a part of their experience. This suffering, Beaudoin suggests, 'sparks GenX religiosity' (1998, 99). It begs the question 'why?' and it seeks expression and healing. The fascination with Jesus and the cross in pop culture, however trivialised, can be taken as evidence of GenXers working through their suffering and, indeed, protesting against its dismissal as whining by American society in general. The grunge fashion of the 1990s is taken as another example of the expression of suffering and spiritual poverty; a retort to the excesses of the 1980s and a resignation to the reality of aloneness experienced by GenX in their childhood. Gothic fashions fulfil a similar function, in a typically ironic, excessively funereal manner.

Ambiguity is Beaudoin's forth identified theme of GenX lived theology. The juxtaposing of the sacred and profane in popular culture draws attention to the ambiguities and uncertainties of GenX life and to the doubts inherent in real faith. Beaudoin considers on-line versions of scripture as one example. Hotlinks embedded in the text take the reader to numerous websites which provide commentary on, but also contest, the meaning of sacred text. In this format it is harder to understand scripture as the permanent Word of God since it is so clearly under review by 'co-authors'. This provides GenXers with a different, more fluid relationship to scripture than was possible for generations before them. Ambiguity and uncertainty were represented in GenX fashions too – ripped jeans, oversized clothes, underwear as outer garments all suggest meaning cannot be take for granted. The internet goes even further to the heart of matter. In cyberspace individuals can take on multiple selves and in so doing may lose their 'real' identity if indeed there ever is a 'true' undivided self. Born out of this ambiguity Beaudoin suggests that the most fundamental question GenXers ask themselves is not 'What is the meaning of life, of my life?' which boomers asked, but rather, 'Will you be there for me?'

> We [GenXers] ask this of our selves, bodies, parents, friends, partners, society, religions, leaders, nation and even God. The frailty that we perceive threatening all of these relationships continually provokes us to ask this question. (1998, 140)

From cultural-theology to sociology

In this short chapter we cannot do justice to Beaudoin's erudite analysis of virtual faith. Nevertheless, it is enough to illustrate the multiple and creative ways in which pop culture can be used to simulate, explore and critique religion and as such to provide media through which GenXers can express their own religiosity.

Beaudoin's reading of popular culture and the sense which can be made out of it is, however, dependent on his sophisticated knowledge of theology. It might be argued that the average GenX pop culture consumer would struggle to draw quite so much religious meaning from music videos, fashion and so on, especially in Britain which tends to be more secular than the United States. Lynch (2002) considered British clubbers' perspective in this respect.

Club culture contains a degree of religious imagery and various commentators have described the clubbing experience, often enhanced by taking Ecstasy, as reminiscent of religious experience – a deep connection with others, 'oceanic' or 'ecstatic' experiences (Malbon 1999). Given these apparent religious features and the commitment some individuals have to the clubbing scene, Lynch interviewed a small group of GenXers to see if they drew specifically religious meaning from their clubbing. He concluded that although they did derive personal meaning from their experiences of club culture they did not see this in religious or even spiritual terms, and in fact rejected the association or saw it in a negative light. The meaning and value of clubbing for his GenXers were variously concerned with social connectedness, fun, sexuality and self-expression. Whilst these meanings may be interpreted in a theological way by somebody with the language and inclination to do so, the clubbers themselves in this instance did not. It may be that the religious interpretation of clubbing and other elements of pop culture is therefore a minority pursuit (see Moore, chapter 11).

Legacy to Generation Y

Generation Y are the inheritors to Generation X. GenY youth were born during the 1980s and 1990s and are reaching their teens and early adulthood as we write. The events that will shape Generation Y and their approach to life in their adult years are yet to be fully determined. However, it is evident that immersion in pop culture is continuing apace for them. A recent study conducted in Britain makes the point:

> Children up to 19 spend a remarkable £12 billion from their own pocket money or part-time jobs. They wear a hefty measure of this as £1.53 billion is exchanged in shopping centres for clothes and shoes . . . The record labels and software houses take nearly another £1 billion with £440 million going on music and £340 million exchanged for computer software. (Mayo and Nairn 2009, 5)

To this Mayo and Nairn add the money spent by parents on their children and calculate the total child-oriented market in the UK is worth £99.12 billion. And religion? Immersion in religious culture is rather more muted. Only around 6% of English 11–14 year-olds and 5% of 15–19 year-olds are to be found in church on an average Sunday (Brierley 2006). Some 45% of 16–24 year-olds in the UK say they have never been to church and are unlikely to do so (Ashworth and Farthing

2007, 9). The legacy of Christianity passed on to British GenYers is therefore even more slight than for GenX. This is reflected in young people's day-to-day life and their engagement with popular culture.

Savage et al. (2006) explored the shared world view of Generation Y by interviewing them about their engagement with films such as *Lord of the Rings* and *Harry Potter*, soap operas, adverts and cultural icons, dance music and clubbing. They found that young people used popular culture as a source of meaning. It helped them to make sense of their everyday lives and provided them with a glimpse of what an 'ideal' life might be – a happy, socially connected and authentic existence. Savage et al. (2006, 39) summarise this GenY world view as the 'happy midi-narrative' (2006, 39). Young people use popular culture to mediate between real life and the ideal. Religious concepts concerning God, sin and death, however, were largely absent from this work-a-day worldview. In other words, according to Savage et al., Generation Y derive meaning from popular culture but not religious meaning.

The relationship between youth, popular culture and religion is a growing area of academic interest and one which promises to reveal some fruitful insights into religious change and development. This chapter provides just a hint of the directions in which such theorising and research might take us, other chapters in this volume provide further clues. One thing at least is certain, with rapid developments in media technology, a growing recognition of the importance of religion on the world stage and Generation A on the horizon (Coupland 2009), the legacy of research is likely to be a long one.

Chapter 3

Explaining Change over Time in Religious Involvement

David Voas

Background

The social and personal significance of religion has declined in most developed countries during recent decades. Religious institutions, leaders and norms have become less influential, and at the same time individuals are participating less in religious activities and giving religion a less important role in their lives (Norris and Inglehart 2004).

There are large differences between the young and the old in various key indicators of religious involvement, in particular the willingness to identify with a religion, to attend services or to assign an important role to religion in one's life (Voas and Day 2007). Age is far more important than any other characteristic in the strength of its association with religious commitment, easily trumping gender, education, employment, place of residence, denomination and so on.

Some scholars maintain that although old forms of institutional religion are fading, spirituality itself is merely being transformed: belief (of some sort) persists and new forms of religious involvement will emerge (Houtman and Aupers 2007). Young people may not like the existing institutional forms of religion, but they will transform religion to fit their requirements. I do not find strong evidence for this hypothesis either in quantitative data or qualitative studies (Smith 2005; Savage et al. 2006; Mason et al. 2007). Nevertheless the debate is one that can be seen as parallel to the issues I address below. My question is why young people are different: whether that difference consists in being less religious/spiritual than their elders or in being religious/spiritual in new ways is a separate issue.

The challenge, then, is to discover why age matters. The search for answers will take us to a core issue in the sociology of religion: the explanation of religious change.

Age, period and cohort effects

Society may change because people change, or because of a change of people; it may stay the same even if everyone changes. Some illustrations may help to explain what I mean.

Imagine that a prophet comes to town and persuades a significant number of people, young and old, to convert to a new faith. The change is rapid and potentially enduring. Such a shift is an example of a 'period' effect, because it is specific to one particular point in history.

cohort effect

Imagine next that as children emerge into adulthood they adopt distinctive creeds and forms of religious behaviour, much as they do with music and slang. Society would alter even if no individual changed once he or she reached maturity, because older people would gradually be replaced by younger people who did things differently. Here we have a 'cohort' effect: people who were born around the same time (or were at school together or fought in the same war) share certain characteristics by virtue of their common formative experience.

Finally, imagine that people tend to have little interest in religion in youth but gradually become more religious with age. This pattern would be an 'age' effect. Perhaps the change occurs on reaching key stages in life, such as marrying and having children, or maybe it results from an awareness of personal mortality or an evolution in priorities. In this instance every single individual might change without society changing at all, because at any point one would always find the same mix of old and young, more or less involved with religion.

Age, period and cohort effects are important, but other demographic changes and their interactions might also affect the religious trajectory of modern societies. Immigration will offset decline to a degree dependent on its scale and the religiosity of immigrants relative to the native population. Because religious characteristics tend to be inherited from parents, decline may be slowed if religious people have more children than others.

The findings

Our first task is to try to understand what combination of age, period and cohort effects are at work. Is society becoming less religious because of forces that have an impact on everyone? Or do those forces have their effect by undermining religious upbringing, so that some generations come to be less religious than their predecessors? And if (as we tend to suppose) people become more religious with age (Greeley 1991), how far does this factor compensate for the other influences?

Even with the best available data and methods, unfortunately, it can be difficult to distinguish between these three types of change. Each of these three effects can be expressed as a combination of the other two. For example, an individual's age is simply the difference between the date at a given time (period) and an individual's year of birth (cohort), and with sufficient ingenuity all purported effects of one kind could be explained in terms of the others. Plausibility and parsimony will generally lead us to favour certain interpretations, however (Harding and Jencks 2003).

Presenting and interpreting the evidence would require more space than is available here. It seems clear, though, that the major changes observed in religious adherence arise from differences between cohorts. Religious involvement does not tend to change during adulthood, despite the impact of lifecycle and historical events. Age and period effects are therefore small, to the extent that they exist at all (see Voas and Crockett 2005; Crockett and Voas 2006; Wolf 2008).

Birth cohorts versus generations

Before going further it is worth examining the terms 'birth cohort' and 'generation' more closely. Some scholars use them interchangeably, while others prefer to apply them in different ways.

'Cohort' refers to people who have undergone a particular experience during the same period. Demographers typically analyse birth cohorts: that is, people born in a certain year or range of years, but we are also interested in cohorts of other kinds. For example, one might wish to compare the first cohort of women to be ordained in the Church of England (in 1994 and the years following) with those who joined the clergy more recently.

In studying differences between birth cohorts we might decide to compare people born in the 1920s, 1930s, 1940s and so on. These ten-year bands are obviously a classification of convenience, and they may or may not coincide with whatever social and historical forces shaped the formative experiences of each cohort. If World War II (1939–45) had a crucial impact on the psyches of young people who were aged between 10 and 16 during some part of that period, for example, then ideally we would want to look at people born between 1923 and 1935.

A birth cohort defined in this way is often called a 'generation'. (Note that the term 'generation' is used in a different way when we talk about children, parents and grandparents, or again when we think of how long it takes a population to reproduce itself.) The best known designation is the 'baby boom' generation, referring to people born during a post-war period of comparatively high fertility in Western countries.[1] The popularity of this categorisation led to labels such as 'Generation X' and 'Generation Y' for people born subsequently, and to a variety of terms including the Greatest Generation, the Lost Generation, the GI Generation, and the Silent Generation for those born during various periods earlier in the century (Strauss and Howe 1991; Brokaw 1998).

Such names imply that people born during the relevant periods share some common experiences and hence characteristics, and that these experiences and characteristics make them different from those who preceded or followed. In practice it is rarely the case that people can be so neatly partitioned, and the differences

---

[1]   It is conventionally defined as 1946–64 in the United States, but the demographic picture produces slightly different ranges in other countries: in Canada one tends to use 1947–66, in Australia 1946-61, and in Europe the pattern was more erratic; it's common to see twin peaks at the end of the War and then in the 1960s.

within a generation are likely to be far greater than the average differences
between generations. Karl Mannheim, who provided the classic exposition of the
concept in 1928, took pains to point out that not everyone qualified by date of
birth actually belongs to a generation defined by shared experience. Contemporary
sociologists have tended to ignore his distinction between people from a particular
period and those who are *of* the period in a fuller sense, but we should be aware
that broad-brush descriptions of one generation or another risk being caricatures.
Comparing averages is important; it is also important to remember the variability
of the individual characteristics being averaged.

Explaining generational differences

The evidence points to something that seems paradoxical. For decade after
decade in most developed countries, people have become less religious (at least
in a conventional sense) than their parents. To put it another way, there are many
families in which parents continue to identify with a religion and to practise it
while their adult children do not. (There are some families, but far fewer, where the
reverse is true.) If these parents regard religion as important – and one presumes
that they do – why have they failed to pass it on to their offspring?

Even posing the question makes us aware of other issues. One concerns
the ages that are most important for religious socialisation. If the years 6–10
are crucial, for example, then parents are clearly implicated if their faith is not
transmitted. By contrast, it is far less likely that the responsibility is wholly theirs
if the key period in religious development is 16–20. What makes the problem
especially challenging is that formative experiences may be concentrated in early
adolescence (e.g. 11–15), when the relative influence of parents, peers and the
wider world is far from clear.

The fact that religious involvement may only stabilise when people reach
their mid-20s does not necessarily mean that we should focus our attention on
young adults. Children living with their parents tend to pay at least lip service to
their values and are more likely to participate in joint activities (such as attending
religious services). Once young people have set up homes of their own we can
see where they are going, but their trajectory might have been determined some
years previously.

The generational nature of religious change is consistent with a close connection
between religion and personal values. Inglehart and associated scholars (Norris
and Inglehart 2004; Inglehart and Welzel 2005) have argued that the evolution of
society from agrarian through industrial to post-industrial stages tends to produce
corresponding shifts in how people are orientated: towards survival, rationality or
self-expression. Religion does best in traditional societies, though in their view
an emphasis on self-expression can promote interest in spiritual matters (where
spirituality is very broadly defined to include interest in the meaning of life).

I suggest that we need to look at three possible explanations for the changes in religious involvement between generations. The challenge is not only to measure the relative importance of these factors but to explain what produces them. These factors are:

- value changes among parents (reducing the priority they give to transmission of religion)
- value changes among young people (reducing the importance of religion to them)
- social changes that may have an impact on religion even if values remain the same.

Parental value change

It is natural to suspect that parents have not been trying as hard as previously to pass on their religion. (There are alternative explanations, of course: perhaps the environment has become less supportive of their efforts, or children and teenagers are now more resistant to parental socialisation.) One possibility is that their commitment to religion has declined, but then we would expect to see some declines in religious identification or attendance for their birth cohort, and such trends are generally absent.

It seems more likely that parental values have become more liberal or relativistic, so that transmitting religion no longer seems critically important. The idea that children should develop to be independent and autonomous makes it harder to enforce religious values. If people no longer much care whether others go to church, in other words – even if they attend themselves – then resistance from children may override parental preferences.

Participants in the famous 'Middletown' study were asked to choose three qualities that were most important for children to have. In 1924, strict obedience and loyalty to church were named by roughly half of parents; independence by only a quarter and tolerance by very few. In 1978 the first two of these rated only about 20 per cent while independence shot up to three-quarters, with tolerance named by about half (Alwin 1996, 122).

Parents have become less committed to conformity in their children. One possible explanation is that the value attached to autonomy (rather than social embeddedness) has increased, giving adolescents the option of avoiding church. Another possible explanation is that the practical utility of religious affiliation and values has declined, and so parents feel less need to socialise their children religiously.

new and creative maybe doesn't involve church

Change in young adults

To the extent that changes in religious involvement are the result of values shifts in the younger generation, we might consider two types of explanation:

- Compositional change: perhaps there has been little change in people *with given characteristics*; what has changed is the relative frequency of those attributes (e.g. higher education, employment for women, childbearing).
- Contextual change: arguably people have not changed, but the *environment* in which they make choices has changed (e.g. ethno-religious diversity, physical security).

Compositional change

One might try to explain recent changes in religious participation by reference to changes in the composition of the population (the approach taken by Wuthnow 2007). For example, people are spending longer in education, and if education undermines religious involvement, it follows that religion may suffer. As it happens, though, churchgoing is often positively correlated with education.

More women than before are now economically active, and churchgoing is lower for women in paid employment. Because the number of hours worked seems to have little influence on the probability of religious participation, we might speculate that employment has an effect because of how it changes social networks, identity or values rather than because it imposes time constraints.

Married people are more likely to attend church than the unmarried, and having children is thought to encourage churchgoing. People are now marrying later, some never marry and some remain childless. But family formation is a lifecycle effect, and if the proportion of people who start families is not in the end very different than in previous times, the impact on the cohort's ultimate attendance levels will not be very great.

Contextual change

Direct cultural effects may be more difficult to identify than compositional effects. Here we are looking for a general shift in values, away from tradition and respect for authority and towards the ethos labelled secular-rational by Inglehart. The boundaries with compositional changes (discussed above) and changes not directly affecting values (see below) are blurred. Increased access to higher education (which is a matter of context), for example, might have a compositional effect (if more educated individuals are less religious than others), which could in turn create a contextual effect (if the prevalence of non-religious worldviews had an impact on the common culture).

Contextual factors include:

- incentives to believe and belong (such as material insecurity or lack of meaning)
- the kind of education available (especially the balance between religious and secular instruction)
- the uses of time available (especially the balance between religious and secular activities)
- the kind of worldviews available (and promoted by the media or opinion leaders)
- the diversity of worldviews
- religious norms about required commitment (determining the cost of involvement and whether disengagement can be gradual)
- social norms about women working, the importance of family formation and so on.

Other factors

We should not focus exclusively on values in trying to explain changes in religious participation; other factors might also have an influence.

A number of (mainly American) scholars argue that the supply of religion (and in particular its breadth and quality) is crucially important to the level of religious involvement (Iannaccone 1991; Stark and Finke 2000). Other scholars in the same 'rational choice' tradition (Gruber and Hungerman 2008; Stolz 2009) emphasise the role of secular competition (including television, music, the internet, DVDs and so on) for time and attention. Such competition might reduce religious involvement without directly affecting values. In the longer term, of course, shifts in choices are likely to translate into shifts in preferences.

If divorce is commonplace, religious transmission may be disrupted. The extent of religious diversity can affect the proportion of people choosing a partner with a different religion (though value change will also have an influence on the willingness to enter into a mixed marriage). There are good reasons to believe that religiously mixed marriages tend to undermine religious involvement. A joint choice not to attend services may help to avoid disagreement about where and how much to participate. If parents have different religious backgrounds, it may be less likely that they will try to socialise their children in one or the other.

Geographical mobility may have positive or negative effects on churchgoing. On the one hand people may join a church following a move in order to become better integrated in the community. On the other hand people who have been churchgoers will lose their old ties and may not replicate their previous habits in the new location. With young adults it seems likely that the latter effect will dominate; moving away from the parental home frees people to make their own choices.

Social incentives to identify or attend may exist. The church may be a good place to meet potential partners (for marriage or business). The church may operate as a gatekeeper to preferred schools. Religious participation may affect one's reputation in the community.

Summary

Society is changing religiously not because individuals are changing, but rather because old people are gradually replaced by younger people with different characteristics. Much remains to be understood, though, about *why* recent generations are different. Parents may be partly responsible, by giving children more control over their own lives. The composition of society has changed, but so has the context in which people are raised. Young people acquire different values and face new conditions. The relative importance of the various factors mentioned here remains to be determined.

Chapter 4

'Generation X' Religion:
A Critical Evaluation

Gordon Lynch

The 1990s saw a growing interest in the concept of 'Generation X', the post-baby-boomer generational cohort born between the mid 1960s and early 1980s. The term 'Generation X' had itself become widely used by social commentators in that period as a result of the popularity of the work of the novelist Douglas Coupland, whose acclaimed novels *Generation X* (1992) and *Life After God* (1994) led to him being heralded as a spokesman for a new generation. As Coupland has since argued, the idea of Generation X as a cohort formed by challenging social circumstances of economic decline, failure of public institutions and family breakdown, and characterised by a distinctively ironic view of the world, largely emerged as the construct of media and marketing organisations who sought to define the traits of young adults for their own commercial needs (Lynch 2002, 25–6). But if the associations that became attached to the concept of 'Generation X' were more of a media and marketing narrative than the result of careful social analysis, they nevertheless found a receptive public audience amongst those wanting to understand the lives of post-boomers as they came into adulthood.

Books on religion and 'Generation X' began to emerge as the decade progressed. The first wave of these were more popular than academic, and addressed pastoral and missiological challenges associated with a cohort of young adults who were perceived as sceptical of institutional religion whilst at the same time craving meaning and community (e.g. Mahedy and Bernadi 1994; Bonacci 1996; Celek et al. 1996; Starkey 1997; Cox 1998; Schieber and Olson 1999; Cunningham 2006). The question of how to make it possible to connect Christian community and tradition with the needs and experiences of a new generation of questioning adults, shaped by their immersion in media and popular culture, subsequently found wider expression in the burgeoning movements of alternative worship, the emergent Church and post-Evangelical Christianity. Towards the end of the decade, a second phase of texts began to be published which adopted a more academic approach. Tom Beaudoin's (1998) *Virtual Faith: The Irreverent Spiritual Quest of Generation X* represented a landmark in this regard, combining the desire for effective pastoral engagement with young adults with a more nuanced theological argument concerning the ways in which media and popular culture formed a new context for the construction and practice of Generation X religiosity. Beaudoin's text was soon followed by more purely sociological studies of Gen X religion

(Flory and Miller 2000; Lynch 2002). Critiques of the broad generalisations associated with the label 'Generation X' have led some writers more recently to abandon the term in favour of more open descriptors such as 'post-boomer' religion (Flory and Miller 2008) or the religiosity of those in their twenties and thirties (Wuthnow 2007). But the effects of the interest in Generation X religion persist in studies which retain cohort terms to define their field of study (including the term 'Generation Y': Savage et al. 2006; Mason et al. 2007), as well as in those which begin with the implicit or explicit assumption that there is something distinctive about post-boomer religion in comparison to previous cohorts.

This chapter is premised on the idea that 'Gen X' or 'post-boomer' religion is a theoretical construct, developed initially in Christian pastoral contexts, and subsequently in academic contexts, which seeks to give identifiable form to broad patterns of religion amongst young adults. Motivations for the use of this concept vary, but its uses tend to encourage broad sociological typologies that account for religious and spiritual patterns across the whole of society. As with all theoretical concepts in the study of religion, it is important to be reflexive not only about the origins of concepts but also the ways in which they help or hinder research in this field. I argue here that interest in Generation X over the past ten years has had some very positive effects on the study of religion, but that the concept of 'Gen X' or post-boomer religion may obscure as much as it reveals. By taking this approach, I am suggesting that there is not so much a legacy of 'Generation X' religion out there in the 'real world' which teenagers and young adults are today inheriting, as much as a way of thinking about young people and religion that academics have constructed through the 'GenX' literature. It is this latter legacy that I critically assess.

To begin with, then, I argue that there have been two significant benefits arising out of the study of Generation X religion. The first of these is that it has made a significant contribution to the integration of the study of religion, media and popular culture within the sociology of religion more generally. The study of religion and media, and religion and popular culture were both becoming established during the 1990s with the creation of the regular international Media, Religion and Culture conferences (Hoover and Lundby 1997; Hoover and Clark 2002; Mitchell and Marriage 2003), specialist journals such as the *Journal of Religion and Media* and the *Journal of Religion and Popular Culture*, and the publication of landmark texts such as Forbes and Mahan's *Religion and Popular Culture in America* (2000). Whilst this foundational phase was crucial in establishing the study of religion, media and popular culture as having some credibility within the academy, it was not generally characterised by substantial engagement with debates in the sociology of religion. Important exceptions in this regard have been research conducted by the Centre for Media, Religion and Culture at the University of Colorado, Boulder, under the direction of Stewart Hoover, which has focused particularly on uses of media in the context of the family (Clark 2003; Hoover 2006; Hoover et al. 2004) and a range of projects on religion and media conducted at the University of Amsterdam under the direction of Birgit Meyer (eg.,Meyer and Moors 2006; Meyer 2008). The research undertaken out of Colorado and Amsterdam has played an important role in thinking about media uses in everyday religious life-worlds. The case material presented in Beaudoin (1998) and Flory and Miller (2000) similarly focused on the uses of media and popular culture in everyday religious practices, but understood this as a necessary component of studying religion amongst young adults rather than treating the study of media per se as their starting point. The meeting of interest in media and popular culture in lived religion amongst sociologically-minded media scholars such as Hoover and Clark, and culturally-minded theologians and sociologists such as Beaudoin and the contributors to Flory and Miller's (2000) *GenX Religion*, has had a significant impact on both the study of religion, media and popular culture and the sociology of religion. In the former, it has encouraged a shift from the analysis of media and cultural *texts* towards the study of the *uses* of media and popular culture in specific social contexts (Lynch 2008, 2009). In the latter, it has contributed towards a cultural turn in the sociology of religion, in which it is increasingly recognised that serious sociological analysis of contemporary religious phenomena will usually have to engage at some point with issues of media use and cultural practice.

A second important achievement of the literature on 'Generation X' religion was to reopen sociological discussion of sources of meaning and value beyond institutional religion. It is now more than forty years since Thomas Luckmann (1967) argued for the growing social importance of a new 'invisible religion' beyond the boundaries of traditional established religion, which focused on the importance of the authentic, autonomous and expressive self. Paul Heelas (1996, 2000) has since pointed to the importance of such an expressive humanism as an alternative source of meaning and value within Western culture beyond institutional religion, and interest in Heelas' work on alternative spiritualities has at times missed his broader point that such spiritualities represent only the sacralised fringe of a broader humanist turn to concerns of wholeness, intimacy and well-being. With the exception of Heelas, few sociologists of religion have accepted Luckmann's challenge to identify sources of meaning and value beyond institutional religion in increasingly de-Christianised Western societies. Indeed it has fallen to social scientists from other disciplines, such as Zygmunt Bauman (1993), Ronald Inglehart (1997) and Richard Sennett (1998) to offer major contributions to this debate. Whilst sociological interest in Western religion since the 1960s has broadened out to include the study of new religious movements and alternative religious traditions such as neo-paganism and Wicca, the numbers of active adherents in these religious movements remains a small fraction of Western populations. The study of meaning and value for those who have little meaningful contact either with established or alternative religious traditions and communities has therefore remained largely undeveloped within the sociology of religion. By focusing on the values and beliefs of a generational cohort seen as alienated from institutional religion, however, work on Generation X religiosity opened up new possibilities for work in this area. Beaudoin's *Virtual Faith* can be seen as playing a key role in this regard. Although his specific analysis of the forms and sources of meaning for young adults invited more rigorous sociological study, the very discussion of the idea that young people might form their own theologies from cultural sources beyond institutional religion such as books, films and popular music validated religious scholarship into what might be termed secular life-worlds. This has opened up new areas of enquiry into the role of media in the construction of secular identities (Clark 2007; Lovheim 2007), as well as the possibility of particular cultural spaces, such as the club scene, acting as significant sites of meaning and community within secular life-worlds (Lynch and Badger 2006).

Two key benefits from the scholarship on Generation X religion were therefore to draw attention to the importance of media and popular culture in lived religion and to reopen the study of people's meanings and values beyond established and alternative religions. These benefits are not specific to understanding religion in the lives of young adults, however, reflecting the fact that there are considerable shortcomings of the concept of Generation X religion as a framework for analysing the lives of young people. I briefly mention three of these here.

Firstly, the idea that there is some kind of broad cohort effect which leads to people in the West in their mid-twenties to mid-forties demonstrating similar patterns in relation to religion is too generalised to be of genuine analytical value. Cohort-based theories of religion risk obscuring both the similarities that members of a particular cohort share with members of other cohorts, and can also obscure significant differences within a specific cohort (Wuthnow 2007, 3–6). Indeed the notion that a shared cohort experience of economic uncertainty, institutional failure, media immersion and family breakdown provides a shared horizon for young people's engagement with religion fails to take adequate account of the ways in which such broader social trends are experienced unevenly across different social groups. As Amy Wilkins (2008) has recently argued, gender, class and ethnicity play a fundamental role in shaping the life chances of young people as well as providing the cultural repertoires through which they can attempt to negotiate the challenges of their social worlds. Gender, class and ethnicity also have a significant bearing on the ways in which young people do, and do not, engage with religion. Far from there being any broad cohort effect on young adults' engagement with religion, it is becoming increasingly clear that young people's lives reflect the increasing religious pluralism and fragmentation of Western societies. In Great Britain, a minority of young people have any active engagement with religious institutions, and the nature of this engagement can be shaped by a wide range of factors such as experiences of migration and degrees of identification with 'mainstream' British society, contact with trans-national media and movements, and the resources and ethos of the particular religious sub-culture they inhabit. Cohort-based theories of patterns of engagement with religion tend to generalise commonalities across social groups, but at this point we need more urgently theories that make sense of how the inter-play of agency and structure in varied social contexts produces different forms of engagement with religion (i.e. why are we likely to see this particular kind of religious performance or subjectivity in this particular social context?). We also need theoretical tools to help us to understand the lives of young people with little apparent engagement with established or alternative religions, for whom concepts of religion, relations with sacred others, and forms of cultural myth and ritual may remain important. Using categories of class, gender, ethnicity, migration and sexual orientation can help us to understand these differences more clearly, as may research methods that involve more in-depth engagement with young people's life-worlds.

A second shortcoming of concepts of 'Generation X' religion is that the emphasis on cohort-effects has tended to obscure other factors that may be more salient in shaping young people's engagement with religion. For example, more attention needs to be paid in the sociology of religion to the ways in which the negotiation of life-stages and life transitions have a bearing on the religious and secular lives of young people, particularly as these transitions become more extended and complex (Wuthnow 2007, 20–50). This would involve thinking about how religious sub-cultures provide norms, cultural resources and social networks that address the challenges that young people experience in negotiating the transition from adolescence to imagined adult lifestyles, as well as what resources young people draw on to negotiate this transition in secular life-worlds. More attention might also be paid to processes of value transmission in families. Growing up with religiously-committed parents and amongst peers who participate in a shared religious sub-culture is a strong predictor of future religious involvement. This raises questions of how such processes of the transmission of values and beliefs operate through intimate relations, how transmission breaks down, and how parents decide whether or not to provide a particular religious up-bringing for their children. In Great Britain, the transmission of conventional Christian beliefs and practices has grown progressively weaker in the decades since 1945 which raises questions of why this is the case, and what the implications of this might be for the future religious landscape of Britain if conservative and minority faiths prove more adept at transmitting their beliefs to their children.

A third shortcoming of the 'GenX literature', particularly in its more populist pastoral and missiological forms, was its uncritical assumptions about the importance of meaning and belief in individual's lives. The Augustinian maxim (refracted through humanist and existential psychology) that the human heart is restless and unfulfilled unless it finds some core meaning in life can be seen in the assumption that if members of Generation X tended to be alienated from institutional religion then they must necessarily be looking for sources of meaning elsewhere (i.e. in media and popular culture). Underlying this assumption – and much contemporary literature on spirituality – is an unquestioned view of the importance of metaphysical belief for individuals. The idea that all individuals have a need for a core set of metaphysical beliefs – whether drawn from formal religious traditions or elsewhere – can be challenged both by arguments about the historical and cultural specificity of such a concept of belief and more complex views of the motive-forces that influence our lives as social agents (see, e.g., Coleman and Lindquist 2008). To give primary emphasis in the sociology of religion to the frameworks of meaning that young people construct for themselves can obscure the possibility that issues of existential meaning may only become important for young people in specific moments, that young people may only learn to become 'believing subjects' through particular social contexts, and that assent to metaphysical or existential beliefs may play a relatively unimportant role in the day-to-day conduct of many young people's lives. The discovery by a succession of studies that young people tend to be 'incredibly inarticulate' about their beliefs, unless socialised into particular ways of articulating faith within specific religious communities, suggests that we still need more nuanced concepts of the nature and significance of meaning and belief in young people's lives.

The legacy of the study of Generation X religion has therefore proven highly influential in opening up new areas of study within the sociology of religion more generally, but cohort-based theories have proven less useful in helping us to make sense of the very different ways that young people engage with religion today. What is needed are new ways of thinking about how, where and when religion becomes important in the lives of young people, how factors such as gender, class, ethnicity and the specificities of religious sub-cultures are bound up with different religious practices and subjectivities, and how we might understand the sacred in the life-worlds of young people with little involvement in established or alternative religions. All of these questions are framed in the wider context of how globalisation, late capitalism, and the ever-growing extension of media sources and technologies provide a cultural ecology for contemporary religious life, and are to be addressed more adequately if sociologists of religion can engage in constructive dialogue with research on the lives of young people from other areas of social science. Theory plays an important role in helping us to make sense of this complex and evolving religious landscape. For a time the concept of Generation X was helpful in generating new perspectives on contemporary religion which have had a lasting effect in opening up new areas for study. But as a concept for helping us to understand the specificities of the lives of young people, Generation X has proven to be of limited value and the search for more adequate theoretical models continues.

PART II
The Big Picture:
Surveys of Belief and Practice

Gaining a comprehensive picture of young people's religious beliefs and practices is not easy. Three studies which have successfully provided a national picture of youth religiosity in different parts of the world are the focus of this section. These surveys are the National Study of Youth and Religion (NSYR) in the United States; the Teenage Religion and Values survey in England and Wales and the Spirit of Generation Y survey in Australia. The NSYR interviewed 3,370 teenagers and their parents. Smith describes an implicit form of faith that was apparent amongst the young people in the survey which he calls 'Moralistic Therapeutic Deism'. This faith bears some similarity to Collins-Mayo's account of the 'happy midi-narrative' world view implicit amongst English youth (Part I, chapter 2). Francis and Robbins built up a sample of nearly 34,000 13–15 year-olds during the latter half of the 1990s. Such a large sample enabled the researchers to gain a meaningful picture of young people from non-Christian world faiths which form a minority population in England and Wales, as well as the larger Christian and 'no-faith' groups. Their chapter maps the patterns of belief and practice they found. They conclude by drawing attention to alternative, non-institutionally based 'spiritualities' which some theorists have argued are beginning to take the place of institutional religion. Mason picks up the spirituality theme and explores it through a nationally representative study of 1,219 Australian young people aged 13–24.

Chapter 5

On 'Moralistic Therapeutic Deism' as US Teenagers' Actual, Tacit, *De Facto* Religious Faith

Christian Smith

My book, *Soul Searching: The Religious and Spiritual Lives of American Teenagers* (Oxford University Press, 2005), co-authored with Melinda Lundquist Denton, follows over hundreds of pages a variety of topical trains of thought and sometimes pursued diversions and digressions. But what does the bigger picture of the religious and spiritual lives of US teenagers look like when we stand back and try to put it all together? Here we re-summarize our observations in venturing a general thesis about teenage religion and spirituality in the USA, tentatively advancing this thesis as something between conclusive fact and mere conjecture. We suggest that the *de facto* dominant religion among contemporary teenagers in the USA is what we call 'Moralistic Therapeutic Deism' (MTD). This 'religion', which emerged from hundreds of interviews with US teenagers, consists of a God who created and orders the world, watching over human life on earth. This God wants people to be good, nice, and fair to each other, but does not need to be particularly involved in their lives, except when he is needed to resolve a problem. Being happy and feeling good about oneself is the central goal in life. When they die, good people will go to heaven. These tenets form a *de facto* creed that is particularly evident among mainline Protestant and Catholic youth, but is also more than a little visible among black and conservative Protestants, Jewish teens, other religious types of teenagers and even many 'non-religious' teenagers in the USA. Note that no teenager would actually use the terminology 'Moralistic Therapeutic Deist' to describe himself or herself and very few would lay out the main points of its creed so clearly and concisely. Rather, it is our summarizing term for the religious viewpoint that emerged from hundreds of interviews on matters of religion, faith, and spiritual practices. While quotes illustrating MTD are aplenty, suffice it here to examine merely a few that are representative of this religion's core components

First, MTD adherents believe that central to living a good and happy life is being a good, moral person. That means being nice, respectful, responsible, at work on self-improvement, taking care of one's health, and doing one's best to be successful. One teenager said this very clearly: 'I believe in, my whole religion is where you try to be good, and if you're not good then you should just try to get better.' Or, as more than one teenager summarized morality for us, 'Just don't be an asshole, that's all.' Highlighting the inclusive nature of this moral vision, another teenager said:

> Morals play a large part in religion, morals are good if they're healthy for society. I think every religion is important in its own respect. It's just whatever makes you feel good about you.

Feeling good about oneself is thus also an essential aspect of living a moral life, according to this dominant *de facto* teenage religious faith.

MTD is, secondly, about providing therapeutic benefits to its adherents. This is not a religion of repentance from sin, of keeping the Sabbath, of living as a servant of a sovereign divine, of steadfastly saying one's prayers, of building character through suffering, and so on. Rather, it is about attaining subjective well-being, being able to resolve problems, and getting along amiably with other people. One teenager expressed the therapeutic benefits of her faith in these terms: 'God is like someone who is always there for you. He's just like somebody that'll always help you go through whatever you're going through.' Making a similar point, though drawing it out from a different religious tradition, another teenager described her faith in this way: 'I guess for me Judaism is more about how you live your life. Part of the guidelines are like how to live and be happy with who you are, cause if you're out there helping someone, you're gonna feel good about yourself.' Thus, service to others can be one means to feeling good about oneself. Other personal religious practices can also serve that therapeutic end, as this teenager observed, 'When I pray, it makes me feel good afterwards.' It is thus no wonder that so many religious and non-religious teenagers are so positive about religion. For the faith many of them have in mind effectively helps to achieve a primary life goal: to feel good and happy about oneself and one's life.

Finally, MTD is about belief in a particular kind of God, one who exists, created the world, and defines our general moral order, but not one who is particularly personally involved in one's affairs – especially affairs in which one would prefer not to have God involved. Most of the time, the God of this faith keeps a safe distance. He is often described by teens as 'watching over everything from above' and 'the creator of everything and is just up there now controlling everything'. Like the Deistic God of the eighteenth-century philosophers, the God of contemporary teenage MTD is primarily a divine Creator and Law-Giver, but unlike the older version, Deism here is revised by the Therapeutic qualifier, making the distant God selectively available for taking care of needs. As this teenager said, 'I believe there's a God, so sometimes when I'm in trouble or in danger, then I'll start thinking about that.' God is something like a combination Divine Butler and Cosmic Therapist – he is always on call, takes care of any problems that arise, professionally helps his people to feel better about themselves, and does not become too personally involved in the process. As one teenager, in response to our inquiry about what is God like, said 'God is a spirit that grants you anything you want, but not anything bad.' Similarly, this teenager told us, 'God's all around you, all the time. He believes in forgiving people and whatnot and he's there to guide us, for somebody to talk to and help us through our problems. Of course, he doesn't talk back.' This last statement is perhaps doubly telling: God, being distant, does not directly verbally answer prayers, according to this girl, but he also does not offer any challenging comebacks to or arguments about our requests. Thus, one teenager complained with some sarcasm in his interview that, 'Well, God is almighty, I guess [yawns]. But I think he's on vacation right now because of all the crap that's happening in the world, cause it wasn't like this back when he was famous.' But few teens we talked to end up blaming God for failing them, since MTD usually seems to be effective in delivering its promised benefits to its many teenage believers in the USA.

To be clear, we are not saying that all US teens are adherents of MTD. Some teens are simply disengaged from anything religious or spiritual, and other teens embrace substantive religious beliefs and practices that effectively repudiate those of this revisionist faith. We are also not saying than anyone has founded an official religion by the name of MTD, nor that most US teenagers have abandoned their religious denominations and congregations to practice it elsewhere or under another name. Rather, it seems that the latter is simply colonizing many established religious traditions and congregations in the USA. Its typical embrace and practice is *de facto*, functional, practical, and tacit – not formal or acknowledged as a distinctive religion. Furthermore, we are not suggesting that MTD is a religious faith limited to teenage adherents in the USA. Our religiously conventional adolescents seem to be merely absorbing and reflecting religiously what the adult world is routinely modeling for and inculcating in its youth.

Moreover, we are not suggesting that MTD is a religion that teenagers (and adults) adopt and practice wholesale or not at all. Instead, the elements of its creed are normally assimilated by degrees, in parts, and mixed with elements of more traditional religious faiths. Indeed, this religious creed appears in this way to operate as a parasitic faith that cannot sustain its own independent life, but must attach itself to established historical religious traditions, feeding on their doctrines and sensibilities, and expanding by mutating their theological substance to resemble its own distinctive image. This religion generally does not and cannot stand on its own, so its adherents may be either devout followers or mere nominal believers of their respective traditional faiths. But they often have some connection to an established historical faith tradition which this alternative faith feeds upon and gradually co-opts if not devours. Believers in each larger tradition practice their own versions of this otherwise common parasitic religion. The Jewish version, for instance, may emphasize the ethical living aspect of the creed, while the Methodist version stresses the getting-to-heaven part. Each then can think of themselves as belonging to the specific religious tradition they name as their own – Catholic, Baptist, Jewish, Mormon, whatever – while simultaneously sharing the cross-cutting, core beliefs of their *de facto* common MTD faith. In effect, these believers get to enjoy whatever particulars of their own faith heritages appeal to them, while reaping the benefits of this shared, harmonizing, inter-faith religion. This helps to explain the noticeable lack of religious conflict between teenagers of apparently different faiths. For, we suggest, very many of them actually share the same deeper religious faith: MTD.

One way to gauge people's interest in different matters is to track their language use. The idea behind this approach is that people's discourse roughly reflects their concerns and interests. We used this method as one means of assessing US teenagers' relative orientations to religious and therapeutic concerns. We systematically counted in our interview transcripts the number of teenagers who made reference to specific subjects or phrases of interest. We found, first, that relatively few US teenagers made reference in their interviews to a variety of historically central religious and theological ideas. We counted less than 50, and often less than 10, counts of concepts such as personally sinning or being a sinner, obeying God or the church, righteousness – divine or human, the kingdom of God, and loving one's neighbor.

For comparison with these tallies on religious terms, we also counted the number of teens who made reference to the key therapeutic ideas of feeling happy, good, better, and fulfilled. What we found is that US teenagers were much more likely to talk in terms broadly related to therapeutic concerns than in the religious terms examined above. We found at least 20, and often close to 100, counts of the following concepts: personally feeling or being made happy, feeling good about oneself, and feeling personally satisfied or enjoying life satisfaction.

Our interviewed teenagers used the single, specific phrase to 'feel happy', for instance, more than 2,000 times. The interview transcripts reveal that the language of happiness dominates US adolescent interests and thinking about life – including religious and spiritual life. That is what defines the dominant epistemological framework and evaluative standard for most contemporary US teenagers – and probably for most of their baby boomer parents. This, we think, has major implications for religious faiths seriously attempting to pass on the established beliefs and practices of their historical traditions.

What we are theorizing here is the real existence of a shared American religion that is analogous to the American civil religion that Robert Bellah astutely described in 1967, yet which operates at an entirely different level than civil religion. While people may think of the USA comprising a variety of diverse religions that coexist more or less harmoniously, the reality is actually more complicated than that. 'Religion' in the USA in fact separates itself out and operates at multiple levels in different ways. American religion is most obvious at the level of formal organizations, the plane on which denominations, seminaries, religious congregations, publishing houses, and other religious organizations operate. But religion also often operates distinctively at a level 'below' the organizational plane, at the level of individual belief and practice. Here religious faith is often eclectic, idiosyncratic, and syncretistic, mixing together elements as diverse as belief in infant baptism, interest in horoscope predictions, and the collection of religious kitsch. This is the dimension that some scholars have called 'lived religion' or 'popular religion.' Beyond these two levels, Robert Bellah's major contribution in 1967 was to reveal civil religion operating in the USA at yet another level, 'above' the plane of formal religious organizations. Bellah insightfully showed how religious symbols and discourse – appropriated and abstracted from the Judeo-Christian tradition – are mobilized at a national civic level for purposes of national order, unity, and purpose (1967).

What we are suggesting here in our observations about MTD is that, to understand the fullness of US religion, we need to come to see yet another level or plane of religious life or practice operating in this social order.[1] At the 'bottom' exist the eclectic, idiosyncratic faiths operating at the level of individual religion. 'Higher up' abide the more coherent, systematized faiths operating on the plane of organizational religion. Even 'higher' is the nationally unifying political faith of American civil religion. But situated between the individual level at the 'bottom' level and the organized religions and civil religion on planes above that, there operates yet another distinct level of religion in the USA – the widely shared, inter-faith religion of MTD. Like American civil religion, MTD appropriates, abstracts, and revises doctrinal elements from mostly Christianity and Judaism for its own purpose. But it does so in a 'downward', apolitical direction. Its social function is not to unify and give purpose to the nation at the level of civic affairs, but rather to foster subjective well-being in its believers and to lubricate interpersonal relationships in the local public sphere. MTD exists to help people succeed in life, to make them feel good, and to help them get along with others – who otherwise are different – in school, at work, on the team, and in other routine areas of life.

Finally, to suggest that 'religion' in the USA operates complexly and distinctly on different levels, however, does not mean that those levels never interact or influence each other. They do. Purely individual beliefs, for instance, are shaped in part by the teachings of organized religion – as well as by horoscopes, advice columns, talk show hosts, and so on. And American civil religion is affected both by liberal religious activism and by the Religious Right operating at the level of formal religious organization. The same observation about inter-level interaction and influence is also true of MTD. It helps to organize and harmonize individual religious beliefs 'below' it. It also both feeds upon and shapes the religious doctrines and practices at the organizational and institutional level 'above' it. And it mirrors and may very well interface with American civil religion at the highest level by providing the nation's inhabitants a parallel and complementary common, unifying, functional faith that operates at a more apolitical, private and interpersonal level of human life. The cultural influence of MTD may also be nudging American civil religion in a 'softer', more inclusive, ecumenical, and multi-religious direction, making suspect those who believe that only the born again go to heaven who are justified by the spilled blood of Jesus Christ, or that the Angel Moroni really did appear to Joseph Smith with a new and commanding revelation, or that God's chosen people really must faithfully observe his laws.

---

[1]   As shown in Figure 2, *Soul Searching*, p. 169.

The flock of sheep is diversified and expanded, but certain goats remain part of the picture nonetheless.

Adults in the USA over the last many decades have recurrently emphasized that which separates teenagers from grown-ups, highlighting things that make each of them different and seemingly unable to relate to each other. But our conversations with ordinary teenagers around the country made clear to us, to the contrary, that in most cases teenage religion and spirituality in the USA is much better understood as largely reflecting the world of adult religion, especially parental religion, and is in strong continuity with it. In many ways, religion is simply happily absorbed by youth, largely, one might say, 'by osmosis' – as one teenager stated so well: 'Yeah, religion affects my life a lot, but you just really don't think about it as much. It just comes natural I guess after a while.'

However, it appears that only a minority of US teenagers are naturally absorbing by osmosis the traditional substantive content and character of the religious traditions to which they claim to belong. For, it appears to us, another popular religious faith – MTD – is colonizing many historical religious traditions and, almost without notice, converting believers in the old faiths to its alternative religious vision of divinely underwritten personal happiness and interpersonal niceness. Exactly how this process is affecting American Judaism and Mormonism we refrain here from further commenting on, since these faiths and cultures are not our primary fields of expertise. Other more accomplished scholars in those areas will have to examine and evaluate these possibilities in greater depth. But we can say here that we have come with some confidence to believe that a significant part of 'Christianity' in the USA is actually only tenuously Christian in any sense that is seriously connected to the actual historical Christian tradition, but has rather substantially morphed into Christianity's misbegotten step-cousin, Christian MTD. This has happened in the minds and hearts of many individual believers and, it also appears, within the structures of at least some Christian organizations and institutions. The language – and therefore experience – of Trinity, holiness, sin, grace, justification, sanctification, church, Eucharist, and heaven and hell appear, among most Christian teenagers in the USA at the very least, to be being supplanted by the language of happiness, niceness, and an earned heavenly reward. It is not so much that Christianity in the USA is being secularized. Rather more subtly, either Christianity is at least degenerating into a pathetic version of itself or, more significantly, Christianity is actively being colonized and displaced by a quite different religious faith.

Acknowledgement

This chapter is an edited version of 'On "Moralistic Therapeutic Deism" as US Teenagers' Actual, Tacit, *De Facto* Religious Faith' from *Soul Searching: The Religious and Spiritual Lives of American Teenagers*, Smith, C. with Denton, M. (2005), Oxford: Oxford University Press. Reprinted by permission of Oxford University Press, Inc., www.oup.co.uk.

Chapter 6

The Teenage Religion and Values Survey in England and Wales

Mandy Robbins and Leslie Francis

Introduction

The Teenage Religion and Values Survey (TRVS) was established in the 1990s in order to provide an in-depth study of the part played by religion within lives of young people in England and Wales. This chapter presents some of the main findings from this survey and introduces the new study that is testing these findings among the next generation of young people.

Ways of collecting the data

As this book illustrates, empirical research concerning the place of religion in the lives of young people draws on both qualitative (often using interviews) and quantitative (often using questionnaires) traditions within the social sciences. Both traditions have their unique strengths. The TRVS belongs to the quantitative tradition since our aim was to survey a large sample of young people and to make clear generalisations on the basis of our data.

Questionnaires can be used to collect either open-ended responses or closed responses. The open-ended approach invites young people to write answers in their own words. The closed approach invites young people to indicate their view by selecting from a range of predetermined responses. The TRVS employed the closed approach since our aim was to provide a crisp statistical profile of the views of young people.

Within this closed approach, the Teenage Religion and Values Survey employed three types of questions. General factual information was gathered by forced-choice questions. For example, sex could be indicated by ticking one of two categories: male *or* female. Some clear-cut issues could be assessed on a simple dichotomous scale. yes *or* no. Most issues, however, were assessed on a standard five-point scale following the method originally proposed by Likert (1932). Well-phrased items could be evaluated on the continuum: agree strongly, agree, not certain, disagree, and disagree strongly.

Designing the survey

Drawing on our previous studies (Francis, 1982, 1984; Francis and Kay 1995) and a series of focus groups in which young people discussed their concerns in life, we developed a map of values concerning 15 areas: personal well-being, worries, counselling, school, work, politics, social concerns, sexual morality, substance use, right and wrong, leisure, the local area, religious belief, church and society, and the supernatural. Each area was represented in the questionnaire by at least six items.

A values map of this nature means that a broad canvass can be covered, but also that inevitably each aspect of the canvass is only thinly covered. We recognised that each of our 15 areas could have deserved many more items, but that to have extended the scope in this way would have made the questionnaire too long.

The TRVS was designed to enable sophisticated statistical modelling to explore the associations between the different kinds of information that we were able to collect. Such analyses were nested within the individual differences approach to social psychology. Overall, we are concerned with the cumulative influence of a range of individual differences, including factors like age, sex, socio-economic background and personality (Eysenck and Eysenck 1991). Such factors have to be taken seriously before we can ask questions about the potential influence of religion, since individual differences in religion may themselves be associated with these very factors.

Finding the young people

The TRVS was an ambitious project not only in terms of the scope of the issues covered but also in terms of the sample frame. The aim was to collect data from a sample of young people large enough to make the religious minorities visible. In order to ensure that we had full access to sufficient young Jews and young Jehovah's Witnesses (to name just two of the groups specified) we settled on a target of 34,000 young people representative of England and Wales as a whole, stretching from Cornwall in the South to Northumberland in the North, from Pembrokeshire on the west cost to Norfolk on the east coast.

The young people were accessed through schools. In defining the sample we recognised that we needed a proper mix of rural and of urban schools, of state maintained and of independent schools, of schools with a religious foundation and of a secular foundation.

Our main aim was to be able to talk about adolescents coming toward the end of the period of compulsory schooling, but at the same time we recognised the problems of approaching Year 11 pupils (15–16 year-olds) in view of the pressures from the GCSE examinations. We settled, therefore, on Year 9 pupils (13–14 year-olds) and Year 10 pupils (14–15 year-olds). The survey was given scrutiny from the appropriate ethics committee and deemed suitable for the age group.

Each participating school was asked to administer the questionnaire throughout their Year 9 and Year 10 classes to avoid any self-selection of pupils by the schools. Pupils were assured of confidentiality and anonymity, and that their replies would not be inspected by teachers within their school. Pupils were given the chance not to participate in the survey, although surprisingly few opted out.

Schools were recruited by the technique of snowball sampling. We found that once schools had participated in the survey and perceived the benefit of the enquiry for the participating pupils, then schools were generally keen to commend the project to other schools. All told, 163 schools took part in the survey during the second half of the 1990s, giving rise to 33,982 thoroughly completed questionnaires.

Listening to the findings

A survey of this magnitude takes considerable time and resources to carry out and to prepare for analysis, but the richness of the database has then generated a wide range of publications following the initial overview of the data presented in *The Values Debate* (Francis 2001a). The present brief overview of some of the findings recognise that religion is a multi-dimensional construct and examines one by one the correlates of different aspects of this complex area of scientific enquiry. Attention is given in turn to: religious affiliation, denominational affiliation, religious belief, belonging without believing, church attendance, church leaving, prayer, religiously affiliated schools, and alternative spiritualities.

Religious affiliation

Self-assigned religious affiliation is (from different perspectives) both a straightforward and a problematic dimension of religion. This is the dimension of religion routinely gathered in many countries within the context of the national census. The question was included in the Census in England and Wales for the first time in 2001, deliberately focused on religious affiliation rather than on denominational affiliation, and distinguished between the eight categories of none, Buddhist, Christian, Hindu, Muslim, Jewish, Sikh, and another religion (Francis 2003). The TRVS enabled the usefulness of these categories to be explored among young people.

Analyses reported by Francis (2001b, 2001c) identified significant differences across a number of domains. For example, in terms of personal values 50% of young people who belonged to no faith group reported that their life had a sense of purpose, compared with 51% of Sikhs, 61% of Christians, 62% of Hindus, 64% of Jews and 68% of Muslims. In terms of family values, 47% of young people who belonged to no faith group found it helpful to talk about their problems with their mother, compared with 45% of Sikhs, 40% of Hindus, 52% of Muslims, 53% of Christians and 71% of Jews. In terms of divorce, 17% of young people who belonged to no faith group took the view that divorce was wrong, and the proportions rose to 20% among Christians, 21% among Jews, 28% among Sikhs and 42% among Muslims.

In terms of school-related experience, 25% of young people who belonged to no faith group were worried about being bullied at school, and the proportions rose to 30% among Christians, 31% among Muslims, 32% among Jews, 34% among Sikhs and 39% among Hindus. In terms of sexual practices, 11% of young people who belonged to no faith group considered it wrong to have sexual intercourse outside marriage, and the proportions rose to 15% among Christians, 23% among Jews, 27% among Sikhs, 29% among Hindus and 49% among Muslims. In terms of substance-related attitudes, 17% of young people who belonged to no faith group took the view that it is wrong to become drunk, and the proportions rose to 21% among Christians, 21% among Jews, 33% among Sikhs, 33% among Hindus and 68% among Muslims.

Clearly, knowledge about self-assigned religious affiliation conveys important information about personal and social values.

Denominational affiliation

While the 2001 Census in England and Wales chose to distinguish only between major religious traditions, the census conducted at the same time in Scotland distinguished between (certain) Christian denominations, and this has remained the case in many other national censuses (Francis 2003). The TRVS enabled the significance of denominational affiliation to be explored among young people.

Analyses reported by Francis (2008a, 2008b) identified significant denominational differences across a number of domains. For example, in terms of personal values, 50% of non-affiliates felt that their life had a sense of purpose, and the proportion rose to 58% among Anglicans, 59% among Presbyterians, 63% among Roman Catholics, 64% among Methodists, 65% among Baptists, 73% among Jehovah's Witnesses and 75% among Pentecostals. In terms of family values, 23% of non-affiliates found it helpful to talk about their problems with their father, and the proportion rose to 25% among Methodists, 26% among Anglicans, 26% among Roman Catholics, 28% among Baptists, 31% among Pentecostals, 31% among Presbyterians and 46% among Jehovah's Witnesses.

In terms of attitudes toward sex, the view that homosexuality is wrong was taken by 20% of non-affiliates, 18% of Presbyterians, 19% of Anglicans, 20% of Roman Catholics and 21% of Methodists, but the proportions rose to 27% among Baptists, 59% among Pentecostals and 81% among Jehovah's Witnesses. In terms of attitudes toward substances, while 35% of non-affiliates and 35% of Roman Catholics maintained that it is wrong to smoke under the legal age the proportions rose to 40% among Anglicans, 43% among Baptists, 47% among Methodists, 52% among Presbyterians, 54% among Pentecostals and 78% among Jehovah's Witnesses.

Clearly, knowledge about religious denomination conveys important additional information about personal and social values. It may be mistaken, therefore, to regard all Christians as the same.

Religious belief

Unlike religious and denominational affiliation, religious belief tends to be seen in much more personal terms. This is not the kind of questions that is likely to find its way into the public census, although the issue has a well-established place in many social attitudes surveys. The TRVS provided opportunities to explore both the factors that are likely to influence religious belief and the correlates of such belief. Taking the straightforward belief question, 'I believe in God', the TRVS enabled levels of belief in God to be explored against such factors as age, sex, social class, parental separation and divorce, television viewing and church attendance.

According to the data published by Francis (2001a), 41% of the total sample of young people believed in God. While 43% of Year 9 pupils believed in God, the proportion dropped significant to 40% among Year 10 pupils. A significantly higher proportion of females (45%) than males (38%) believed in God. A significantly higher proportion of young people from professional and semi-professional backgrounds (47%) than from semi-skilled and unskilled manual backgrounds (38%) believed in God. A significantly higher proportion of young people from intact homes (43%) than from broken homes (36%) believed in God. Young people who watched more than four hours television a day were less likely to believe in God than those who watched less television than that (38% compared with 42%). The chapter on church attendance demonstrates that not all churchgoers believed in God and that not all non-churchgoers did not believe in God: 82% of weekly attenders believed in God, but so did 21% of those who never attended.

Clearly, levels of religious belief are associated with a range of personal and demographic factors.

Belonging without believing

So far, the preceding sections have examined religious affiliation and religious believing independently one of the other. Francis and Robbins (2004) suggest that the real social significance of religious affiliation could be best examined if religious belief were held constant. They proposed, therefore, to make a comparison between two groups: those who do not believe in God and claim no religious affiliation, and those who do not believe in God but describe themselves as Anglicans. The data clearly demonstrate the significant differences in the values held by the two groups.

For example, in terms of social concern, non-believing Anglicans were more inclined than non-believing non-affiliates to express concern about the risk of pollution to the environment (66% compared with 58%) and more inclined to express concern about the poverty of the Third World (52% compared with

44%). In terms of attitudes toward substance use, non-believing Anglicans were more inclined than non-believing non-affiliates to believe that it is wrong to use marijuana (49% compared with 44%) or to believe that it is wrong to use heroine (70% compared with 65%).

Church attendance

Like religious belief church attendance is generally regarded as a personal matter, not as a matter of public concern appropriate for inclusion in a national census. Like religious belief, however, measures of church attendance are often included in social surveys. The present data demonstrated that nearly half of the young people (49%) never attended church or other place of public worship. However, the analysis reported by Francis (2001a) made it clear just how important frequency of church attendance is in predicting personal and social values among young people.

For example, in terms of personal values, 70% of weekly churchgoers felt that their life had a sense of purpose, compared with 49% of the non-attenders. In terms of family relationships, 38% of weekly churchgoers found it helpful to talk about their problems with their fathers, compared with 30% of non-attenders. In terms of school, 57% of weekly churchgoers considered that teachers do a good job, compared with 37% of non-attenders. In terms of social concern, 78% of weekly churchgoers were concerned about the poverty of the Third World, compared with 50% of non-attenders.

In terms of sexual practices, 39% of weekly churchgoers considered that it is wrong to have sexual intercourse under the legal age, compared with 18% of non-attenders. In terms of substances, 28% of weekly churchgoers considered that it is wrong to become drunk, compared with 16% of non-attenders.

Church-leaving

As well as collecting information about current levels of church attendance, the TRVS also collected data about regular attendance at church or Sunday school during earlier phases in life. Robbins (2000) employed these data to compare the profile of four groups of young people: those who attended church regularly at the time of completing the survey (attenders); those who used to attend church regularly, but now do so only occasionally (partial leavers); those who used to attend church regularly, but now no longer attend church (total leavers); and those who have never attended church regularly (non-attenders). Across a number of values domains, the findings demonstrated that the young church-leavers differed from those who have had no contact with the churches.

For example, the section on sexual morality demonstrated that young church-leavers maintained a significantly more traditional view compared with non-attenders, although the difference remained quite small. While 17% of non-attenders considered that it is wrong to have sexual intercourse under the legal age, the proportion rose significantly to 20% among total leavers. While 32% of non-attenders considered that abortion is wrong, the proportion rose significantly to 37% among total leavers.

Personal prayer

While questions on church attendance access the public dimension of religious practice, questions on prayer access the personal dimension of religious practice. The question on prayer in the TRVS was used by Francis (2005b) to illustrate how public church attendance and personal prayer are by no means perfectly overlapping variables: 12% of young people who attend church weekly never pray, while 29% of the young people who never attend church pray, at least from time to time.

Dividing the TRVS database into several different segments, Francis (2005b) went on to demonstrate how prayer frequency was a significant predictor of levels of purpose in life both among young people who attended church weekly and among young people who never attended church. This finding suggested that personal prayer was associated with positive psychological benefits for young people growing up outside the churches as well as within the churches.

In a subsequent analysis of these data Francis and Robbins (2006) went on to demonstrate the positive association between frequency of personal prayer and pro-social attitudes among young people who never attended church. The finding holds true over three areas: attitudes toward school, attitudes toward law and order, and attitudes toward substance.

Religiously affiliated schools

Within England and Wales the role of the churches (particularly the Anglican Church and the Roman Catholic Church) in the provision of schools within the state-maintained sector was consolidated by the 1944 Education Act (Dent 1947). The TRVS provided an ideal opportunity to examine the connection between religiously affiliated schools and pupil values.

In an analysis that focused on Anglican schools, Lankshear (2005) distinguished between three religious groups: non-affiliates, Anglican and those affiliated with other Christian denominations. The data demonstrated that Anglicans attending Anglican schools recorded higher levels of religious values and comparable levels of moral values, in comparison with Anglicans attending non-denominational schools. Non affiliates attending Anglican schools recorded higher levels of personal dissatisfaction, lower levels of moral values and comparable levels of religious values, in comparison with non-affiliates attending non-denominational schools.

In subsequent analysis Francis (2002a) examined the values of pupils attending Catholic schools and Francis (2005a) examined the values of pupils attending independent Christian schools.

Going deeper

The TRVS has enabled a number of other issues concerning the place of religion in the lives of young people to be examined in depth. Detailed studies have been offered on the influence of religion on attitudes toward smoking (Robbins 2005), on attitudes toward religious education and school assemblies (Kay and Francis 2001), on attitudes toward science (Astley 2005), on spiritual health (Francis and Robbins 2005) on attitudes toward abortion (Francis 2004), and on suicidal ideation (Kay and Francis 2006). More complex multi-variate analyses have been employed to identify and isolate the influence of Bible reading on purpose in life and attitude toward substances (Francis 2000, 2002b); and to model the influence of God images on personal well-being and moral values (Francis 2001d).

Alternative spiritualities

While the original TRVS was established in the 1990s to examine the role of traditional religiosity in the lives of young people, the new TRVS survey currently underway has been broadened to reflect a much wider view of spirituality. One of the first papers to emerge from the new study has explored the association between the spiritual revolution and suicidal ideation among young people (Robbins and Francis 2009). These data make it clear that alternative belief systems are not fulfilling the same psychological function as conventional Christian beliefs. While conventional Christian beliefs were associated with lower levels of suicidal ideation, paranormal beliefs were association with higher levels of suicidal ideation. The preliminary findings from the new study, therefore, seem to be suggesting that the ways in which young people view the transcendent are not merely a matter of academic curiosity, but that they are in fact a matter of considerable concern for society as a whole. Research that is concerned about the future of young people needs to take both conventional religiosity and alternative spiritualities firmly into account.

Collaboration

The TRVS has throughout been a collaborative venture between the research groups that we lead, the sponsors who have made the research possible, the schools that have participated, and students and colleagues who have worked with us. Now that we are in the process of conducting a new study of comparable dimensions, we welcome collaboration from teachers, postgraduate and postdoctoral researchers, and undergraduate students who may wish to work with us in gathering new data, in testing new theories and in challenging old conclusions.

Chapter 7

The Spirituality of Young Australians

Michael Mason

Almost a century ago, Emile Durkheim observed: 'The old gods are dying or dead, and others are not yet born' (2001, 322). As the deicidal virus has seeped from Europe to permeate Western cultures, the religion and spirituality of young people has changed profoundly.

This chapter outlines, on the basis of recent research, what young people's spirituality is like today in one multicultural but increasingly secular Western society: Australia, and how and why it has changed, and why this matters.

What is spirituality?

Until recent times, 'spirituality' was used mainly to refer to the 'interior' dimension of a traditional religion – people's personal religious experiences and practices. Nowadays, with once-dominant Christianity on the wane in Western culture, some scholars claim that spirituality has become part of the creative construction of the self: it may borrow elements from religious traditions, but stands independent of them, and at times defines itself in opposition to religion (Marler and Hadaway 2002; Fuller 2001). Wade Clark Roof (1999) popularized the idea of a 'spiritual marketplace' in which consumers could 'mix and match' components of spirituality from a wide range of sources, rather than having to 'buy' one complete 'package' (see also Hughes et al. 1995; Lyon 2000; Bruce 2002; Heelas and Woodhead 2005; King 2008).

So according to these writers, a contemporary spirituality is a personal construction which could include any of the following:

- a major Western or Eastern world-religion;
- a 'new religious movement' such as Scientology;
- a blend of elements from different traditions – e.g. Christianity and Buddhism;
- a reappropriation of animism or shamanism as in Native American spirituality;
- a revival of an ancient religious form such as Paganism or goddess worship;

- an esoteric or occult practice like Wicca, spiritualism (contact with the spirits of the dead), channelling, divination (foretelling the future) by astrology or the 'reading' of tarot cards or palms or other signs;
- a non-religious life-vision such as self-realization, holistic health, feminist or men's spirituality; ecological spirituality / environmentalism, understandings of human life based on science or psychotherapy.

Some spiritual themes like ecology, healing or feminism are found in both religious and non-religious forms; but there is no contradiction in the idea of 'secular spirituality' – some who adopt non-religious spiritualities, especially those based on philosophy or science, expressly reject belief in any kind of supernatural beings or powers.

'Spirituality' has survived as an inclusive name for all of these diverse outlooks because it can easily be understood to refer to whatever *inspires* someone – the vision of reality from which they derive their zest for life, their sense of meaning and purpose, their basic worldview and fundamental values. It can also be stretched beyond its religious origins to cover non-religious sources of inspiration such as the vision of care for the earth or the search for the true self.

Reactions to the alleged 'new spirituality' range from enthusiastic advocacy (Tacey 2003; Heelas and Woodhead 2005) to its sceptical unmasking as fraudulent pseudo-religion (Carrette and King 2005).

The spirituality of young Australians

A research project entitled *The Spirit of Generation Y* was undertaken to explore the varieties of spirituality among Australian youth.[1] The study's findings supported some of the conjectures about spirituality described above, but found little evidence for others.

The expectation of a decline of traditional religion among youth was strongly confirmed. But only a very small proportion of Australian youth were turning to the kinds of alternative spiritualities described above.

While everyone had heard of the wide variety of spiritual options available, and many agreed with major themes like care for the earth, and most had also experimented with astrology or tarot readings or Buddhist meditation, few had taken up any of these as a spirituality – a source of inspiration that gave meaning to their life and shaped their decisions and lifestyle.

---

[1]   Mason, Singleton and Webber, 2007. The project team comprised M. Mason, A. Singleton, R. Webber and P. Hughes. Generation Y was defined as those born 1981–95. The research made use of extended interviews, and a survey in 2005 of a nationally representative probability sample of youth aged 13–24 (N=1219) with an additional sample aged 25–59 (N=400).

The level of interest in and involvement with religion or spirituality of any kind among Gen Y was generally low: most of those who still identified with mainstream Christian denominations were only nominal or marginal adherents; only 27 per cent of the age group were actively practising any traditional or alternative form of spirituality – 17 per cent were engaged with Christianity, 6 per cent with another world-religion, 4 per cent with an alternative spirituality.[2]

The things young people considered most important were close relationships with friends and family, an exciting life and helping others. They also wanted a peaceful, cooperative, just and secure world and care for the environment. Very few rated 'spiritual life' as significant.

The activities favoured as sources of peace and happiness were listening to music, work or study, but not spiritual reflection, prayer or meditation.

Young people said they felt that their lives had meaning and purpose; they felt a sense of belonging, and except for a small minority, were free of any deep feelings of hurt or alienation.

Most had no overarching vision, whether religious or secular, inspiring them and shaping their lives, but seemed content to pursue short-term goals like passing exams, getting a job, finding a relationship. On a more general level, their view of the world seemed to consist of a collection of fragmentary ideas and values from a wide variety of sources, tentatively held, not necessarily consistent with each other nor put into practice in any planned or regular way.

Except for a core of committed members, Christians held religious *opinions* rather than beliefs, convictions or commitments – they manifested neither belief nor belonging in any strong sense, contrary to Davie's thesis that belief continues even as belonging declines (1994). A majority of members of all denominations agreed that it was 'okay to pick and choose your religious beliefs, rather than having to accept the teachings of your religion as a whole' and a majority of Gen Y agreed (although less than half of conservative Protestants and Anglicans) that 'morals are relative, there are no definite rights and wrongs for everybody'.

These findings raise further questions:

- Does the 'spiritual marketplace' approach assume that as people move away from the spiritual traditions of the world-religions, they will find at hand alternative spiritualities which are coherent, reasonably comprehensive sets of beliefs, values and practices? Such systems are complex, and in the past were worked out over centuries by religious specialists. They are like a warehouse of outfits for all occasions, available in all sizes. 'Alternative spiritualities' are often no more than shreds and patches: a few fashionable ideas and values; hardly an adequate wardrobe.

---

[2]   Younger interviewees were not sure what was meant by 'spirituality', guessing it was related to religion. However those over age 30 (especially women) were more likely to be interested in alternative spiritualities.

- Has it been taken for granted, on the basis of past patterns, that youth are 'spiritual seekers' – that they still feel the need for a coherent story or master narrative for their lives, and that if traditional religion holds no appeal, they will search for a new vision or construct one for themselves? On the contrary, they seem happy to go spiritually near naked – with a scrap of covering here and there, but no well-woven spirituality to provide overall warmth. All very well while the sun is shining; but perhaps the hard frosts and long snowbound winters yet to come will compel them to either find or make some more substantial 'spiritual garments'.
- Is this state of affairs peculiar to youth because they are not yet fully mature, still moving towards developing a coherent view of life? There is more interest in alternative spiritualities among those in their thirties. Will today's youth, as they mature, move in this direction, or even back towards traditional spiritualities? Or is *bricolage* the way of the future for all? One indication: the baby boomers' worldviews appear as uncertain and fragmented as their children's.
- Has there been a 'spiritual revolution' – a fundamental change to a new type of spirituality, or is young people's spirituality so fragmented and chaotic largely because they are uninterested in it and give it little attention? The second seems the more parsimonious explanation.

Further light is shed on these issues by describing the spirituality of young Australians in a little more detail. Then we consider how it has changed, and inquire into the causes and consequences of these changes.

Traditional spirituality

Fifty-one per cent of Generation Y said they believed in a God, 17 per cent said they did not believe and 32 per cent were unsure.

Just over half identified with a traditional religion: 46 per cent considered themselves Christian, 6 per cent belonged to other world-religions (Buddhism, Islam, Hinduism, Judaism) and 3 per cent believed in a God, but did not endorse any particular religious tradition. Almost half of Australian young people between the ages of 13 and 24 did not belong to any religion or denomination.

Gen Y Christians (46 per cent of Gen Y) hardly differed on most measures of religiosity from Christians of their parents' generation – the baby boomers.[3] But there were also major differences: a high proportion of the baby boomers were raised as practising Christians in a quite strongly traditional environment, while Gen Y are starting out where their parents have ended, with a low level of religious involvement, in an aggressively secular society.

---

[3]   'Baby boom' refers to the period of high birth-rates after the Second World War, 1946–65. Most of Generation Y's parents were 'baby boomers'.

Gen Ys from conservative Protestant denominations manifested much higher levels of religious belief and practice than Catholics or Anglicans.

It is especially significant that young women are now no more traditionally religious than young men on a wide range of measures.[4]

There is a strong drift away from Christianity among Generation Y: some have ceased attending worship services; others no longer believe in God. Before they reach the age of 25, about 18 per cent of those who used to belong to a Christian church are already ex-members.

Alternative spiritualities

There was a much lower uptake than expected among Generation Y Australians of forms of spirituality drawn from non-traditional sources.

Of the 17 per cent of Gen Y who were classified as 'New Age' in their spirituality, almost half (8 per cent) were 'New Age Believers' – who held a mix of New Age beliefs: in reincarnation for example,[5] or astrology, or communication with the dead, but were not seriously involved in any New Age practices. Only about 9 percent were 'New Age Participants', who both held New Age beliefs and engaged in one or more forms of practice. The majority of the New Age spiritual type were not involved in a traditional religion, but many did retain some traditional religious beliefs.

In summary, despite a few New Age beliefs having very wide currency, only a small proportion of Gen Y are seriously involved in New Age spiritualities.

Secularity

Of the 28 per cent of Gen Y who reject religious and quasi-religious options, and follow an expressly secular path in life, 10 per cent can be classified as nonreligious – they never believed in God and reject New Age beliefs. Four per cent are ex-religious, having once believed in God but now rejecting both traditional and New Age beliefs. Fourteen per cent are undecided, unsure about whether God is real, but also not accepting New Age beliefs.

Seventeen per cent of Gen Y do not believe in a God, 19 per cent hold that there is very little truth in any religion and 23 per cent believe that there is no life after death.

---

[4] Yet women show more interest than men in alternative spiritualities. For a discussion of possible explanations of the decline of gender difference in traditional spirituality see Mason et al. (2007, 207–10).

[5] Thirty-one per cent of Gen Y said they 'definitely' believed in reincarnation, which they understand, not in its Hindu or Buddhist sense, but in a Westernized, New Age mode. Perhaps they find comfort in the prospect of renewed existence after death rather than extinction.

What has changed and why

As noted above, there is a significant drift away from Christianity among members of Generation Y who are still in their teens. The kinds of changes in belief and practice which used often to take place after finishing high school, moving out of home and entering university or the workforce, now commonly occur around the transition from primary school to high school.

In the year of our survey, 2005, when Generation Y were aged 10–24, and the Boomers 40–59, the two groups were remarkably similar in their level of belief in God (Gen Y 51 per cent; Boomers 56 per cent), their identification with religious denominations, their agreement with their church's moral teachings and their patterns of church attendance (Mason et al. 2007, 84, 101). At first sight, there appears to be very little decline across the generations.

However, when the Boomers were in their teens and twenties in 1981, 68 per cent of them affirmed belief in God, so there has been considerable decline across the period.[6]

And when we compare the Boomers, in turn, with *their* parents, we see an even larger decline: unbelief was much less common in that generation. In 1981, those born 1932–51 were aged 30–49; 81 per cent of them responded 'Yes' to belief in God; of those born before 1931, 90 per cent gave the same reply. So belief in God declined by almost half from those born pre-1931 (90 per cent) to Generation Y (51 per cent).

We have examined responses to only one question, but other studies have shown that the decline from the pre-Boomers to the Boomers extended to religious identification, beliefs and practices (Bouma and Mason 1995, 39–53).

These findings provide empirical support for the theory that a 'cultural revolution' took place in Australia in the 1960s and 1970s – a rapid and major advance in the 'secularization of consciousness', and that this process is continuing.

International comparisons (Mason et al. 2007, 316–19) show that similar changes have taken place in continental Europe, Britain, Canada and Australia, and are even impacting on the youngest age cohort in the United States. The thesis of 'European exceptionalism' (Davie 2002) – that secularization is confined to Europe, and is due to its unique history – is implausible in the light of similar changes outside Europe.

Theoretical explanations of the causes of the major changes in religion among youth throughout Western societies[7] need to take into account influences such as the following:

- Demographic: the baby boomer generation was so massive in numbers and so idealized by marketers and opinion-makers that the generation's

---

[6]   From online analysis of the 1981 and 2005 World Values Surveys, available at: http://www.worldvaluessurvey.com, last accessed 22 September 2009.

[7]   The literature on secularization is vast: for an overview, see Taylor (2007).

attributes took on the status of norms for the whole culture. The authority of personal experience superseded that of parents, the state, the church, tradition.

- Political: the student revolutions of the late 1960s and 1970s, the Vietnam war and the polarization around it, further divided youth from their elders.
- Technological: television, computers, the communications revolution and its offspring the internet and the mobile phone, were mastered first by youth and enhanced their cultural and social authority; they also greatly decreased the incentive for young people to gather in groups.
- Cultural: the increased influence of science and 'scientism', the more secular style of public cultures and most of all, the very high level among youth of the 'spirit of individualism', which has been steadily growing in Western cultures since the Reformation, hastened the privatization of religion – its increasing exclusion from the public sphere and reduction to a 'lifestyle choice' in the private zone of individual and family life (Bellah et al. 1985; Mason et al. 2007, 323–34).
- Social-structural changes are fundamental to the process of secularization: continued social differentiation, globalization, economic restructuring, the collapse of 'mediating structures' between individuals and the State, the decreased stability of the family.

Why does it matter?

We conclude this brief overview of changes in the religion and spirituality of youth in Australia and elsewhere by questioning their significance. Young people have largely abandoned old-style religion and not replaced it with any systematic, overarching, comprehensive worldview and value-system – so what? Why should anyone care?

There are political and social consequences from the individualism which has decimated organized religion. Voluntary associations of all kinds are suffering the same fate. But these 'mediating structures' which stand between the individual and the state are fundamental both to the health of democracy and to a culture of mutual care and responsibility. In the Australian Gen Y study, while social concern was generally low, practising Christians were much more likely than others to have positive civic attitudes, to demonstrate high levels of social concern and to be actively involved in service to the community.

Finally, there are indications that the individualist's 'freedom' from communal memberships, with their consequent norms, ties and obligations, comes at a high price: young people's personal identity now rests on the fragile foundations of family of origin, friendship networks and unstable sexual partnerships, no longer sustained by the massive support of church, neighbourhood and voluntary associations.

Today's young people will require more than the usual level of support and assistance from older generations, but we cannot help admiring the courage and joy with which they confront the unique challenges society has placed before them.

PART III
Expression

The expression of religiosity and spirituality in young people's lives is the focus of this section. The six chapters taken together show something of the diversity of expression that young people in different parts of the world display. They highlight the fact that spiritual expression is by no means confined to church and temple, synagogue and mosque and thereby encourage us to broaden our religious imagination. Equally, they show how traditional religious expressions might atrophy or be appropriated and adapted by young people to give expression to personal concerns, longings and values. The importance of belonging and connectedness as part of young people's wider spiritual expression comes through in several of the chapters. The section opens with Tacey's reflections as an educator on the meaning of spirituality to undergraduates. Based on his observations of teaching encounters with students in Australia he draws out various dimensions of the spiritual inclinations of young adults. Virtanen, Cush and Moore explore different forms of embodied expression. Virtanen describes the *ayauasca* ceremony practiced by indigenous youth of the Brazilian Amazonia. The young people's use of psychoactive substances as part of this shamanic practice has some resonance with a very different context for potential spiritual expression, namely the electronic dance music cultures of Sheffield, England, where euphoric drugs can contribute to transformative experiences (Moore). Cush considers the meaning and ethic of witchcraft practiced by teenagers in Britain. Day and Cooksey and Dooms focus our attention on the complex relationship between belief, moral outlook and behaviour that is also hinted at in the earlier chapters. Day notes that moral reasoning for young people in England has little connection with traditional church-based obligations and sanctions, yet young people 'believe in belonging' and demonstrate a sense of moral awareness based on social rather than religious authority. Cooksey and Dooms echo these points in their analysis of American and South African young people's religiosity and its impact on their sexual behaviours.

Chapter 8

What Spirituality Means to Young Adults

David Tacey

Spiritual longing in secular society

In the year 2000, sensing a need in the student community to explore spiritual questions, I set up an undergraduate subject called 'Spirituality and Rites of Passage'. The subject is a freestanding elective at first year level, and is not a core subject of any discipline. It would have to draw its enrolment from students attracted by the content of the course. My university is state-funded, secular and non-religious, with historical ties to Marxism. It does not teach theology and I am based in a literature department. I was taking a risk by setting up a spirituality subject in this climate. When the idea for the new subject came to me, I did not know what kind of students I would attract. My colleagues were suspicious, and said I would probably attract two kinds: the 'very religious', and I would have difficulty with their rigidity, and 'New Agers', who would present a different sort of trouble, flakiness. As one colleague remarked, 'The religious right and the New Age fringe will come to your lectures.'

This almost unnerved me as I turned up to my first lecture to face the assembled audience of 150 students. Who were they? What did they want? What did 'spirituality' mean to them? I was on a steep learning curve, and discovered a great deal about young people in a short period of time. The first thing I discovered was that my cynical colleague was wrong. To think about 'youth spirituality' as an entirely marginal, eccentric activity is a cliché that suits secular and humanist prejudice, but is far from the truth. There were a few actively religious students in my classes, and a sprinkling of advocates of the New Age. But they were very much in the minority. The majority were secular and relatively 'normal' students who were interested in the search for meaning. They represented at least 80 per cent of the student body. Many of these had no religious background or affiliation. Nor were they, as my colleagues had supposed, interested in New Age esoterica such as spirit travel, channelling, astrology or crystals.

In my view, the attractiveness of the New Age to youth is overestimated by social researchers. The spirituality of my students was not 'New Age' but *postmodern*, since we now know that the postmodern also includes the post-secular (Caputo 2001). The postmodern era brings with it a loss of 'belief' in secularism and scientism, and a hunger for the more traditional needs of the spirit. However, these needs are mostly not being expressed in traditional ways, but in ways that are just being explored (Tacey 2004). The fact that many students are not part of any established religion, and yet find themselves on a search for meaning, is no reason to suppose that they belong to any ideological movement with an esoteric agenda. Researchers need to differentiate between a narrow and ideological New Age movement, and a broad-spectrum, non-ideological and post-secular spirituality movement (Tacey 2001). The misconception that they can be placed in the 'New Age' category arises in some religious research which does not read the signs of the times.

It suits some academics to construct the broad interest in spirituality as 'New Age' or 'Aquarian', as they can then stigmatise this interest as cultic and reprehensible. This means vast numbers of youth can be characterised as lost, wrong or fallen by the wayside. To religious sociologists, they are 'lost' until they find their way 'back' to the traditional religious expressions (despite the fact that they were never in these expressions in the first place). To secular academics, they are lost because they look toward the spirit at all. What religious and non-religious academics need to understand is that we live in momentous times, and the values of the past no longer apply. Nothing is as it appeared in the *traditional* era of religion, or in the *modern* era of science (Berger 1999). The postmodern is outside religion and science, and neither category can understand where youth are at today (O'Murchu 1997). The traditional religious container has broken, but so too has the rationality of the modern paradigm, which kept the spirit away. Spirit is back, much to the surprise of religious and nonreligious commentators, and it looks like being here to stay. Spirit is back, but in a radically free, unbounded and undefined state. Apparently this was the original human condition, until formal religions decided they held a monopoly on the spiritual, and declared everything outside their orthodox precincts to be heretical or wrong. To Paul Heelas and Linda Woodhead, it seems that human society is 'reverting to type', and spirituality appears today to be more dominant than formal religion, especially in young people but by no means confined to them (2005).

Those of us who are free of religious or secular prejudice and who are receptive to the signs of the times can see that spirituality is innate in the human person and does not necessarily belong to any specific tradition. Some of us have been brainwashed into believing that religion produces spirituality, but it seems that it works the other way around. Spirituality is the primary element in human society and personality. The research of Robert Forman and David Hay, among others, has shown that spirituality belongs to our innate human anthropology and needs to be conceived as a category in its own right (Forman 2004; Hay 2006). This is only being revealed to us now, in our socially unstable times, and the appearance of spirituality brings anxiety to religious scholars, who find the priority of spirituality to be a threat to traditions, and it brings anxiety to secular scholars, who do not like to think that postmodern society might have to make some concessions to the life of the spirit. It is almost as if a new continent of human experience has emerged in the last couple of generations, ironically propelled into our awareness by the demise of formal religions.

The majority of my students cannot be characterised as anti-religious; it is just that they know nothing about it. Many come from families that have been secular, humanist or atheist for at least three generations. Their only exposure to religion is what they see represented in the media, and formal religion is only in the media when bad or atrocious things have been committed. Hence they don't hold a very good opinion of 'religion' in general. But they are not anti-religious so much as pre-religious, or pre-theological. They have felt the inward stirrings of the spirit, but have not had the opportunity to relate these stirrings to any cultural tradition. They stand somewhat naked before the numinous realm they seek. Often, I find their parents are puzzled by the 'outbreak' of spiritual interest. Some worried parents contact me, assuming I am running some kind of sect on campus. Students describe their struggles with their parents in essays, and on Open Day at my university I am questioned by concerned parents. Sometimes the conversation goes along these lines: 'I have brought my child up to be a good modern citizen, but now he or she claims to be spiritual! Where have I gone wrong?'

Students profess an interest in spirituality because they want to find meaning in life, or discover a deeper kind of truth. They talk about meaning as if it were a precious commodity, as if society does not possess meaning, or if it does, they are not aware of it. Most students report that a sense of absence or loss – in society and self – has inspired them to become interested in spirituality. They often declare 'something is missing', and say they have felt this most of their lives. I am delighted to hear this, because this is the nature of the call to religious experience throughout the ages. The great mystics and visionaries were often encouraged into spirituality, not because they felt God's presence, but on the contrary because they sensed God's absence. Ironically, the spiritual wilderness of secular modernity sets up the ideal conditions for many to become mystics in search of truth.

Absence of meaning and mental instability

I have long known that the younger generations are aware of a spiritual emptiness at the heart of society. It is this emptiness that drives their journey toward what they call 'spirituality'. A few of them have suffered acutely from a sense of emptiness. Over recent years, I have been aware that a number of my students have suffered from depression, anxiety, panic attacks, eating disorders or personality problems, and are looking to spirituality as a form of healing. This fully accords with recent medical research, which indicates that up to half of the patients suffering from mental health problems consider that spirituality is important for their recovery (Faulkner 1997). Students in this category are not driven into spirituality by mere curiosity or academic interest, but by a sense of urgency, often sparked by a crisis in the home, family or personal relationships.

When I taught this subject, 'Spirituality and the Rites of Passage', in 2007 I became markedly aware of the 'mental health' issue in spirituality. I noted from student introductions in tutorials and from written statements in the 'special comments' section of their record sheets, that many of them had suffered or continue to suffer from mental health problems. For instance, a few requested they would like to sit beside the door, in case a panic attack came upon them and they had to rush outside. Some declared they were recovering from drug addictions, and hoped they would be able to keep up with the course and attend as many classes as possible – but if they had to miss classes, would I please understand? When I read the first essays, in which I asked them to respond to the question: 'What is spirituality?' – a few wrote that spirituality was paramount in their attempt to overcome depression, which had burdened some of them since early adolescence. I realised that a significant proportion of the students were wounded, vulnerable and fragile. They had gravitated toward a spirituality course as if for therapy and recovery. I decided to survey the group, and found that just on 50 per cent of students had experienced a mental illness, drug addiction, eating disorder or personal trauma that motivated their enrolment. So one answer to the question, 'What kind of student is attracted to a spirituality course?' would be: 'those in need'.

I found this moving and to me it was unexpected. I had read in books and journals that mental illness is afflicting people at ever-younger ages, but I had not noted this among my own student body because, until recently, I had not considered prying into this sensitive area of student life. I am normally reticent to cross the border into personal experience, but I was encouraged to do so because the students seemed keen to disclose this as a relevant aspect of their enrolment. It was as if their vulnerability was a qualification for embarking on a spiritual search. Although I am not a therapist, my background in psychoanalytic theory was useful at this point, as the barrier between academic education and personal experience appeared to want to come down. It helped to steer me away from a highly intellectual approach toward a focus on the healing capacities of spirituality. They looked to spirituality as a sign of hope and faith in their future.

The God-shaped hole

Students often report that the sense of emptiness in society is so strong that it has the capacity to drive them to take action. They conjecture that in a former time, positive thinking and idealism may have protected us from our existential plight, but in this postmodern era, things are different. One student wrote:

> Attitudes to spirituality have changed in recent times, and have become more receptive. I don't think that it is seen as a weakness any more to admit to the feeling that there is something missing in our lives. In the modern era, to refer to the spirit, and to call attention to what was missing in modernity, might have raised the ire of those of us who felt they were getting along nicely without 'religion' or 'spirituality'. Today in the postmodern world, it is more obvious that

we are missing something, and to point this out is no longer seen as offensive or impolite. – Amber 2005[1]

This is typical of the intelligent kinds of reflections I find in their essays. Students perceive society is running on empty, and that it pours enormous material resources into this emptiness. Consumerism or 'retail therapy' may be society's answer to the problem of emptiness but many students demand something more from experience.

Beginning the journey

I often find students grappling with the issue of whether they can begin a spiritual journey at all, and if so, whether they can trust the interior forces that urge them in this direction. Is such a journey real, or a flight into fantasy?

> What is spirituality? The idea excites but also terrifies me. If I go in this direction, if I take this path seriously, then I have to know that it is right and true. What if I invest so much of my self, my energy, my identity in something that proves to be completely false or unreal? That is a scary feeling. But I always come back to what feels right, even though my intellect fails to provide me with the rational answers. It cannot tell me why I need spirit at all. Sometimes, when I have doubts, I remember that the spirit is ultimately a mystery, and we can never conceptualise or understand it. If I could define God once and for all, I believe God would really be dead then. – Ambika 2006

It is a miracle that students embark on such journeys at all, given that they get so little support for this quest from society, education or family. As we can see here, there is an innate trust of the inward voice which is hopeful. The student seems aware that an important part of experience cannot be grasped by reason, and this does not mean that this part has to be rejected or declared unsound. They are demonstrating Keats's 'negative capability' (1817), as well as an attunement to the intuitive origins of spiritual experience.

A popular theme in student writings is that the inwardness of their experience is more trustworthy than external tradition:

> I trust my own experience above all else. I cannot trust outside authorities, which might be right or wrong, but I cannot afford to believe in them in case they are wrong, or right in theory but corrupt in practice. In my view, if I have not experienced something, it does not exist. – Melissa 2007

---

[1] All students quoted are between the ages of 19 and 24. I have sought permission from each student to use their comments in my published research.

> My spirituality is far too important to be gambled on a religion which I feel
> suspicious about, or unable to fully endorse. I have made my spirituality my
> religion. I realise it is a hodge podge of various ideals and moral standards, but
> it is all I have to go by. – Carrie 2008

I find these statements moving, and see the sacred at work in these young lives.
The light of tradition has gone out for them, and a new light is being kindled in the
foul rag-and-bone shop of the heart.

Hope, renewal and utopian dreams

At risk of sounding critical of youth spirituality, I want to mention a potential
down side to this new universal interest. I have noted that 'spirituality' has become
a carrier of utopian dreams and fantasies. I am often astonished by what some
students say about spirituality, as if it were a panacea to cure all ills and solve all
problems. For instance, one student wrote:

> Secular nonreligious spirituality offers us infinite possibilities for our spiritual
> lives. As a secular spiritual person you can practise as little or as much as you
> want to fulfil your spiritual needs. – Louise 2004

Here the student wants to contrast nonreligious with religious spirituality, arguing
that the former has more benefits and positives, because it is flexible and styled
to personal needs. Yet this seems unreal to me and I have become suspicious of
this kind of discourse. Something appears false in this idealisation, as if an idol is
being worshipped or a new kind of addiction is being proposed. Some students talk
about spirituality as if it were on tap and dispensable at a moment's notice. Some
appear to relate to it like an ecstasy-producing pill, and speak of it in ways which
remind us of drug-addicts extolling the virtues of their addiction. Sometimes the
boasts about spirituality, about what it can do and deliver, are tell-tale signs about
what is *not* happening in students' lives. In other words, spirituality has become
an idealised myth or construct which compensates for what is absent – namely,
happiness, fulfilment and satisfaction with life.

However, when I realise that spirituality is a new myth that promotes hope
and idealism in broken or suffering lives, I am forced to soften my criticism. I
become aware that my own generation had many sources of hope and idealism,
such as left-wing politics, radical social movements, feminism, the revolutions
in sexuality and relationships. These were important in my undergraduate years,
as sources of hope in a society that, as with today, produced a sense of emptiness
and lack of meaning. Each generation needs its sources of hope and idealisation,
even if one generation's hopeful vision becomes the next generation's source
of disillusionment. What do young people have to fervently believe in today?
Left-wing politics has failed, so has feminism and the sexual revolution.

The only comfort is to soak oneself in music, entertainment and technology, which are surely the stimulants of our time, but where is hope to be found if not in the spiritual search itself?

The rational adult world continues to be wary of youth spirituality, and concerned parents often worry about the health of their children. They are concerned that a spiritual focus might lead them to self-centredness. In a worldly, extraverted culture such as ours, spirituality is often seen as negatively inward and introverted. It is often feared that it will lead to emotional isolation and an inability to function in the world. However, genuine spirituality will always seek fellowship and community. True spirituality never shuts us off from the world, but rather gathers the world to ourselves.

Chapter 9

Shamanic Practices and Social Capital among Native Youths in the Brazilian Amazon

Pirjo Kristiina Virtanen

Introduction

Shamanic practices continue to be carried out among many indigenous peoples in both rural and urban areas. This article deals with young Indians aged between 14 and 24 in Brazilian Amazonia and the social networks created by collective shamanic rituals. Specifically, it focuses on the ritualistic use of ayahuasca (*Banisteriopsis caapi*), a hallucinogenic concoction, among the Manchineri living in Acre state, in the western part of Brazilian Amazonia. The results show that for young Indians shamanic practices are linked to the making of the sacred, morality, as well as social and cultural differentiation, contributing to the creation and maintenance of social networks and trusting relationships. Furthermore, shamanism produces personal relationships and relatedness not only within an individual's native community and its spirit world, but also with representatives from other native groups and non-native participants.

The Manchineri number some 900 people occupying the Mamoadate reserve by the Yaco River and 150 living in Rio Branco, the capital of Acre state. From the end of the nineteenth century, the Arawak-speaking Manchineri were forced to work in the rubber industry. Their indigenous reserve, 2–3 days' travel from the closest urban centre, is currently the largest in the state. Besides hunting and gathering, people engage in small-scale agricultural activities and animal husbandry. In Rio Branco, Manchineri families live dispersed among several different neighbourhoods, and their young people either study or work in indigenous organizations, security, healthcare or receptionist positions. They have also faced economic obstacles that prevent them from entering schools and, consequently, from finding employment.

The ritualistic use of ayahuasca is the most important shamanic practice among the Manchineri. To explain it, I draw on ethnographic data: interviews, participant observation, photographs, video recordings, and drawings made by young indigenous people. The fieldwork carried out between 2003 and 2005 focused on the lived worlds of young Manchineri people in both the indigenous reserve and in Rio Branco. Included are the interviews with 90 young Manchineris (72 in the reserve and 18 in the city; 42 females and 48 males) and an additional 48 Apurina and Cashinahua youths in the city.

Here the principal analytical tool employed is the concept of social capital as an actual or potential resource of a mutually recognized durable network that provides 'credit' among the group's members (Bourdieu 1986, 248–9). The concept of social capital as immaterial wealth has been popular in the social and economic sciences since the late 1980s when it was observed that individuals in Western countries no longer lived communally, yet that communal living contributes to the well-being of individuals. Social capital has been measured, for instance, by voluntary work, association membership and networks of obligation among certain communities (see Coleman 1988; Putnam 2000). For Pierre Bourdieu (1984, 1986), social capital refers to social networks, trust, memberships, friendships, honour and respectability, all of which are essential to social life both for collectives and individuals as a way of controlling their own lives.

Shamanism and ayahuasca ceremonies in Amazonia

Shamanism is a cosmological system that focuses on the well-being of the community and the control of the vital forces of the universe. The universe is believed to have visible and invisible elements and forms of energy that are related to all the processes of production and reproduction in life. These energies can be harnessed in altered states of consciousness through psychoactive plants, dreams, dances and chants (Langdon 1996, 26–8; Chaumeil 1983). Among other aspects, shamanism involves ritualistic activities, natural medicine and a knowledge of different shamanic songs, techniques and the past of the native community. In the Amerindian context, shamans have the special capability to adopt the perspectives of animals or spirits and see the world from their normally invisible 'human' viewpoint and intentionality (Viveiros de Castro 1996, 117–18).

It has been pointed out in relation to indigenous children that learning shamanic practices is an essential part of growing up (Overing 1988, 169; Lopes 2002; McCallum 2001, 55–7; Lagrou 2001, 120–1). Peter Gow (1991, 241) in his studies on the Piro (Yine) noted the fundamental significance of shamanism, besides the school education of indigenous youth. Today spirituality is acknowledged and promoted in the multicultural education of indigenous schools of Brazil (Conselho Nacional de Educação 1999), but there is a need for a deeper analysis of what shamanic practices offer for today's native adolescents. I have addressed the meaning of shamanism for the young native people and shamanic practices as one of the rites of passage elsewhere (Virtanen 2006, 2007, 2009).

In North Western and Western Amazonia, the use of ayahuasca is one of the most traditional spiritual and healing practices among many Arawakan, Panoan, and Tukanoan speaking natives (e.g. Gow 1991; Reichel-Dolmatoff 1996; Luz 2002; McCallum 2001; Lagrou 2001). The hallucinogenic liquid ayahuasca is also commonly known as *gahpí*, *yagé*, *cipó* and *daime*, the latter the name by which it is consumed today in the Santo Daime Churches. In Manchineri this concoction is called *kamalampi* (meaning vomiting). Manchineri shamans take ayahuasca to cure illnesses, seeing its cause in the resulting hallucinogenic visions. It is also used in collective rituals as a means of receiving spiritual guidance, protection and knowledge from the spirits. Young Manchineri people consume ayahuasca for the first time somewhere between the ages of 11 and 19 with their own portion of the liquid. Some young men also know how to prepare ayahuasca: this process involves collecting vines (*Banisteriopsis caapi*) and leaves (*Spycotria viridis*) and the special herbs and roots used by the Manchineri, and then boiling the resulting concoction for several hours.

The use of ayahuasca is strictly ritualized but not secret. The ritual usually starts at dusk in a house, in the forest or on a riverbed. In the city, everything takes place in a very similar manner to the reserve. The ritual has its own special rules concerning how it should proceed, as well as its own roles, sacred objects and pace. The ritualistic nature of the event opens up its own sacred time and space through the performance of certain practices. Sacralization (see Anttonen 2005) is produced by creating a visible place for a specific use, the control of everyday behaviour (such as a preference for silence), and socially internalized prohibitions and rules that mark the entry into the temporal and liminal space of the sacred. The sharing of informal conventions that determine specific objects, roles and the participants' actions marks out a sacred and 'timeless' ceremonial space. A special form of speech – chatting quietly as one arrives at the place – is one of the ways of marking ritualistic space and time (see Hill 1993; Seeger 1987). Usually the leader of the ritual – who is the best singer, a shaman or an elder person – serves a cup of the ayahuasca concoction to those wishing to partake. Usually the men smoke a pipe while waiting for the ayahuasca to take effect.

When the leader of the ritual feels the first effects of ayahuasca, he starts singing the ayahuasca chants, calling the ayahuasca spirit and certain plant and animal spirits. The ritual chants usually tell of natural spirits such as the boa constrictor or the mother spirit of ayahuasca itself. The singer controls the encounter with the spirit world through music by singing chants that either invigorate or calm the hallucinations.

The sense of affinity in the native community

Today younger Manchineri, especially boys, are actively training in shamanic practices through the use of ayahuasca; they have learned many ritual songs in the indigenous language and are also learning new chants. As in the reserve, young people in the city have also assumed important roles in ayahuasca ceremonies and are interested in strengthening Manchineri spirituality. In the rituals, the focus is on the ancestors and the jungle, and its ritualistic objects convey not only memories but also imagery of the past. According to young Manchineri in the reserve, most animals and plants have their own song and if a participant learns this music under the effect of ayahuasca, he or she also learns the secrets of the animal or plant concerned. Hence one can suddenly 'receive' secret instruction from an animal or plant spirit and subsequently use its power in one's own life. Ayahuasca songs help the person to 'see' a certain animal and thus receive its powers. They therefore work as spells and charms similar to those used by shamans in various parts of the world. Singing is an important way of expressing feelings and creative activity (see Seeger 1987, 65), thereby making forest spirits, the past and the present more concrete.

Young people who had taken ayahuasca usually said that its consumption allowed them to 'see better' or to 'see everything', meaning that they could see spirits, the future, distant relatives, and generally acquire a better vision of the world and the things in it. Many authors have shown how ayahuasca ceremonies help a person to receive solutions to personal conflicts, to interpret their current situation and to find the appropriate way of coping with future events (Reichel-Dolmatoff 1996). According to Manchineri youths, ayahuasca helps to show the participant how he or she should proceed, and to foresee the future in general – for instance, whether the person is about to take up a position in the community, or who his or her future partner will be. It helps in decision-making and provides an important source of knowledge for personal development. However, many young people of both genders in the reserve and the city explained that they did not want to consume ayahuasca due to the change of consciousness provoked and the visions of the spirit-world.

Certain preparations are required to ensure that a positive effect is obtained from the ayahuasca: these include avoiding the consumption of salt, alcohol, greasy food, and abstaining from sexual intercourse for a few days before and after taking ayahuasca. The youth said that if they had not been *mirando*, having visions, it was due to their failure to adhere to these regulations. Some young people also explained that the spirits had appeared to them as evil ones, and they had been horrified. Nevertheless, during the ritual, the participant has to concentrate and wait for any nausea to pass: only then can he or she discover what the female spirit of the ayahuasca plant has to teach. Consequently, young people are habituated from an early age to understanding that their acts are both controlled and punished. For the youths, the use of ayahuasca in their community transmits moral values and codes for proper behaviour (Virtanen 2009).

People can also participate in the ritual without consuming ayahuasca. In the city especially, the ritual offers a place for Manchineri families to encounter other Manchineri people and to listen to their own language and ritual chants. As the ritual is usually held on the occasion of an important visit from one of the villages, it also brings together Manchineri from both urban and rural areas. The event is important for the Manchineri who live in distant suburbs or far away from each other. Shamanic rituals make the young people feel that 'we are all here', 'this is like it used to be' and 'this is my community'. Shamanic practices instil an idea of place and placelessness, corporeality and non-corporeality, and thus allow young people to leave behind the responsibilities and roles essential to contemporary society and its social system. The same idea of leaving social categorizations behind is universally found in music, art and sports, and explains the experience of the transcendent associated with these domains (Anttonen 1999, 38). When the hallucinogenic effects have passed, the visions and experiences are discussed within the ceremonial group. Elders provide younger participants with explanations and interpretations within the framework of their history. Sharing rituals turns urban and rural dwellers of the same native group into real kin: ayahuasca ceremonies are one of the most important ways of uniting single native groups on reserves and in urban areas through communication with the most commonly known non-human beings and the sharing of similar cosmological knowledge and 'beliefs'.

Sharing the ritual with other native youths

Ayahuasca rituals may also unite several indigenous groups, and young people in the city especially may look for remote places to take ayahuasca with other young Indians living in urban areas. The use of ayahuasca compels them to take a particular stance, representing what they are and are not, and with what and whom they wish to relate. Their shamanic practices and beliefs represent ways of acting and knowing that differ from the dominant society (including its Santo Daime Churches, see e.g. MacRae 1992). According to the youths, consuming ayahuasca is an integral and ancient part of the religious practice of their people, a ritual they therefore wish to preserve. I once asked two Manchineri young men whether they went to a church. The younger one answered simply: 'We take ayahuasca', and the other one: 'Sometimes I go to those Evangelical churches. But the religion of the Indian is ayahuasca.' For young natives, the practice of shamanism is also a way of displaying pride in their own indigenous traditions. The ayahuasca ritual is a representation of Indian lifestyles, their knowledge, spirituality, traditions and ritual practices.

For Amazonian native youths, shamanic practices offer both non-materialistic and, through the shamanic objects used, materialistic ways of continuing to reproduce their indigenous cultural traditions. Through the use of certain concepts, manners, speech and forms of avoidance, young Indians are able to confirm that they have not been acculturated into the dominant society, but that instead their traditions continue in the present, despite the discrimination sometimes experienced by native populations. This produces a social space in which religious ideas and practices, in the words of Kim Knott (2005, 165), 'allow this group to live with the imposed order, to challenge it with a non-racist narrative, and to transcend it by allowing something different and more just to be imagined'.

However, not all native participants are completely equal, since there are certain roles observed in the ritual, such as those of the ceremonial leaders, and only a few young people have managed to learn ayahuasca chants. Often other indigenous groups are also accused of practising sorcery, causing afflictions and sometimes death. All these destructive practices are believed to be revealed in ayahuasca ceremonies, though, and trusting and non-harmful relationships constructed that can be profited from in the future. Due to the need to act together in indigenous politics and revitalize indigenous cultures, there is also an increasing interest in comparing different traditions and learning new shamanic chants and methods from other native peoples. However, all groups have their own sacred knowledge, transmitted between kin only.

Enabling interactions with non-natives

Non-natives are also occasionally invited to take part in the ritual, especially in urban areas. However, the ceremonies are not open to all, but shared only with the people the natives think are worthy of showing their way of being. In the nocturnal periods of the ayahuasca ceremonies, liminality is real and offers experiences of being beyond time as well as being autonomous from the group. Sharing similar spiritual experiences caused by the hallucinogen and music is especially effective in generating trust between participants. Shamanic acts are sometimes recognized as legitimized spaces of communication with non-natives, where the 'others', non-natives, may turn into 'us', even if just temporarily.

Meanwhile, for contemporary young Indians who are increasingly seeking out their traditions, ayahuasca ceremonies offer cultural capital, such as knowledge of spiritual matters, medicinal plants and healing practices. This can facilitate new friendships and respectful relations beyond social and cultural boundaries since knowledge, skills and qualifications can be converted into social capital: friendships and memberships. In general, the change in Acre state's local politics has also gradually influenced the way indigenous cultures are valued by non-natives.

The non-natives invited to take ayahuasca may be male and female representatives of non-governmental organizations, government officials or other educated people with a higher social status – people with whom young natives would not otherwise have the chance to interact. These non-natives support and are interested in the philosophy of the local traditional peoples, and are usually respected by the indigenous population for contributing to the recovery and documentation of indigenous traditions, such as music, iconography and mythologies. These people may have economic and cultural resources that can also be acquired through new networks (see Bourdieu 1986, 248–9). Social credit may thus take the form of cooperation established by sharing knowledge and experiences, as non-natives may help publish material, find project funding and so on.

Young indigenous people may have a strong psychological feeling of reciprocity and interaction between people who understand their culture, share a common interest and believe in the same non-human beings and phenomena. However, this social space also has its own power struggles, especially where authenticity is concerned. After ayahuasca ceremonies, for instance, non-native participants are very often criticized for not being quiet or still enough, while Indians in the city are sometimes accused of not knowing the right way to practise the ritual. Overall, becoming involved in shamanic practices offers the possibility of acting within a new social space beyond ethnic, gender, urban and rural boundaries.

Conclusions

Among today's young Amazonian Indians, shamanic practices are the most important instruments in creating and building social networks at three different levels: between the members of the native community, sometimes gathering together members from both rural and urban areas, with other native groups, and with non-natives. Shamanic practices comprise an interethnic field of action, since they are experienced in relation to a larger social group than one's own native community. Spiritual knowledge and attitudes reproduced in the social environment of the youths are closely involved in the production of social capital. Particularly in the case of indigenous populations in cities where a multitude of different social and ethnic groups reside, and where people become aware of different religions, ideas and sub-cultures, shamanic practices offer a means of maintaining trusting relationships. The social networks with natives and non-natives are produced and maintained by sharing experiences of non-human beings and beliefs in a similar cosmology that are made visible in the acts of sacralization. Trust and membership are manifested by similar moral values that also produce social capital. Thus any future research designed to understand the composition of social networks must take into account the production of different forms of immaterial symbolic capital.

Chapter 10

Teenage Witchcraft in Britain

Denise Cush

A growing phenomenon

In the last decade or so there has been a growth of interest from young people in Britain (as well as elsewhere in the Western world) in 'witchcraft' and other forms of Paganism. The Pagan Federation have recently brought the age of membership down from 18 to 16 and have appointed a youth officer, in response to the many enquiries they have from teenagers (Pagan Federation 2009). Although the 'teenage witch' phenomenon has only attracted media and academic interest in recent years (for media, see, for example, the Channel 4 documentary *Teenage Kicks: the Witch Craze* aired 28 August 2002, and for academic publications, Berger and Ezzy 2007; Cush 2007a, 2007b), the interest of young people in Paganism was certainly present among students in the late 1980s (see Cush 1997), and many of today's adult Pagans first became interested as teenagers in the 1960s and 1970s (Harrington 2007). It is however the third generation of teenage witches that has hit the headlines. In a similar time period, Paganism has begun to establish itself as a new/revived/reconstructed 'world religion' appropriate for inclusion in university Religious Studies degrees (see, for example, York 2003).

Defining terms

Words such as 'witch', 'Pagan' and 'Wicca', are often used loosely and have different meanings in different contexts. In this chapter, 'witch' refers to someone who practises ritual magic within a generally Pagan worldview, drawing upon powers believed to be present within nature and oneself. 'Pagan' in this context follows the Pagan Federation definition of 'a polytheistic or pantheistic nature-worshipping religion' (Pagan Federation 2009). I tend to reserve 'Wicca' for the more organised initiatory traditions stemming from the teachings of Gerald Gardner (see Pearson 2002a, 2002b), but acknowledge that many young Pagan witches may use the term more generally as synonymous with 'witch'.

Commercial publications

One reason why the third generation of teenage witches has attracted more attention than their predecessors is the wide availability, since the 1990s, of commercial publications aimed specifically at them. RavenWolf (1998) is perhaps the most well-known. Although criticised by many 'serious' adult Pagans, this book is not just a collection of handy spells for dealing with parents and teachers, but sets out a clear theology, described as Wiccan, which would be recognisable to adult Pagans, and can form the basis of a personal spirituality. Girls' magazines, such as *Mizz* and *Sugar*, often contain items related to teenage witchcraft. These present spells and other 'mystic stuff' as an ordinary interest, no more sensational than fashion or the latest 'boy band' star.

Two films released in the 1990s (*The Craft*, 1996 and *Practical Magic*, 1998) were responsible for a flurry of interest in witchcraft. Some of the girls featured in the 2002 documentary admitted to having copied rituals they had seen in the films. However, my focus group were quite clear that there was a difference between such films which were clearly 'just entertainment' and what they saw as 'real witchcraft'. They considered themselves to be media-literate as a result of their education, and not easily manipulated by magazines, films or television programmes.

Interviews with female students aged 18–24

Interviews with individual young witches were undertaken between 2003 and 2007. To date in-depth interviews have been undertaken with seven young women and three young men identifying as witches and/or Pagans, two 'ex-teenage witches', three 13 year-olds who did not identify as witches but were 'interested in spirituality' and a focus group discussion with a class of 16 year-olds. Not all of the young people would use the term 'witch', but all would subscribe to a generally Pagan worldview and engaged in rituals that would place them squarely within the definition of 'witchcraft' above.

The initial focus was on young women, as the 'witch' label is more readily associated with women and most of the commercially produced materials are aimed at girls. From the interviews with young women aged 18–24, several common themes emerged. One of the strongest reasons for the attraction of witchcraft seemed to be the sense of self-esteem and sense of control over one's own destiny gained from identifying as a witch. The witch concept, as well as the positive valuation of the female in Paganism more generally, had provided an empowering identity not found in more mainstream religious traditions, which were viewed as patriarchal. The practice of rituals (or 'magic') provided a sense of being able to take action to transform both the world and the self. Whether this worked by drawing upon external energies or 'psychologically' was not considered important. Most practised as individuals, and saw the self and personal experience as the main source of authority. Information about witchcraft and Paganism was mainly gained from books, and to some extent the internet. They were very well informed and had read academic as well as popular literature. However, this literature served to confirm an existing worldview and provide a vocabulary for articulating it rather than being the cause of that worldview.

In one case the sense of identity as a 'witch' was related to a 'goth' identity, and there is some overlap between the two. Although there is some preference for black clothes and pentagram earrings, a more common opinion was that 'real witches tend not to wear outward symbols'. To some extent the taking on of a witch identity was a way of marking oneself out as different and special, and in some cases was a response to or a cause of bullying by other pupils at school (Hall 2004).

Other attractions of witchcraft and Paganism included the libertarian ethic of 'an it harm none, do what thou wilt'.[1] All strove to live morally positive lives but wished to make ethical decisions for themselves rather than having a set of commandments or precepts imposed by someone else. Pagan witchcraft was viewed as having a positive and realistic attitude to sexuality, and as being welcoming to gay and lesbian teenagers, unlike their experience with more mainstream religious traditions.

The growing popularity of Paganism has often been attributed to the obvious link between a tradition concerned with the worship of nature and environmental concerns. The young witches interviewed viewed their Pagan witchcraft as including concern for the natural world. All were familiar with the cycle of eight festivals common to many contemporary Pagans, whether or not they actually celebrated them by themselves or with others. Although all were happy with the label 'Pagan' for their worldview, they did not feel comfortable with the label 'New Age' which either meant nothing to them, had negative associations, or was seen as something referring to previous generations. Doug Ezzy, however, (2003) has argued that much 'popular witchcraft' could be characterised as 'New Age'.

They reflected that girls more than boys would be attracted to Pagan witchcraft for a number of reasons. The image of the witch is of a powerful female, girls tend to enjoy books about fairies, witches and magic from early childhood more than boys, and generally to be more imaginative. Practices such as sewing a bag to keep herbs in would appeal more to girls and, crucially, most of the marketing is aimed at girls. Whereas some adult Pagans are irritated by what they see as the trivialising of their religion by the 'little girl' version, the young women interviewed considered that the material in some of the popular publications could actually be a useful first step towards a serious interest in Paganism, and was at worst harmless: 'twee but cool'.

The actual theological beliefs of these young women were quite varied. They included belief in the existence of many gods and spirits or in the one power underlying all things, thus fitting with the Pagan Federation definition. Only

---

[1]   'As long as you harm no-one, do what you will.'

one was happy to employ the term 'God' for the divine within all things. They also disagreed on how literally 'deity' language is meant, varying from realist to metaphorical with shades in between.

Interviews with female students aged 13–14

One of the most impressive features of the accounts of younger witches was how well informed they were. They had considerable theoretical knowledge of witchcraft and Paganism, and were articulate in expressing their views. Two examples of this are the definition of a witch given as 'one who recognises what is beyond face value in what you see around you' and of a 'spirit guide' as 'an idealistic vision of yourself which looks after you'. In contrast, the three 13 year-olds who were 'interested in spirituality' but not witches talked about their beliefs in ghosts, spirits, fairies, prediction, astrology, reincarnation and karma, but with far less clarity. The reason given for their interest in such things was notable though: 'because logic and science are too boring'.

As with the older students, being a witch gave personal confidence, a sense of being special and a sense of having some control over events. They seemed to have a more negative view of the state of the world than the older students. One answer to the question as to why young women become witches was 'because they don't like the world around them'. Witchcraft is thus a form of protest and resistance but also transformative: a method for 'changing the world and yourself'. Self-chosen ethics was an attraction for these girls who were seen by parents or teachers as to some extent rebels. Concern for the future of the planet emerged, and as with the older students, theology varied. One expressed a clear pantheistic monism, believing in 'the essence of everything', whereas another saw the crucial factor as being that 'there is no deity above humans', and wondered aloud if this view should be labelled 'Satanism' rather than 'Paganism'.

Interviews with male students aged 18-22

Interviews with male students were expected to reveal clear gender differences, but in fact their responses were very similar to those of the young women. They did not call themselves 'witches', partly because of the female images associated with the term, but definitely rejected the label 'wizard', preferring just 'Pagan'. Yet both the theology and the practices they described seemed very similar to those of the young women. All practised magic(k) rituals, mostly in private. They gained a sense of identity, empowerment and control from their practice. As with the young women, this identity might or might not be signalled by outward symbols such as black clothes, long hair or 'occult' jewellery. The Pagan ethic was considered to be life-affirming in contrast to the world-renouncing tendencies of some major world faiths. The material world is good, to be enjoyed, and to be looked after as sacred.

In addition to the books and internet resources mentioned by the young women, they noted a rock band and a shop as being their first encounters with the tradition. They were all as committed as the young women were to the perception of gender equality, or even the superiority of the female, both divine and human.

Attempting to find some differences was difficult and may reflect only difference between individual young Pagans rather than a gendered distinction. The young men seemed to be more interested in particular ancient forms of polytheism such as the Norse, Egyptian, Aztec or Mayan pantheons. As well as mentioning polytheism, they also spoke monistically or pantheistically about 'pure consciousness' or 'divine energy'. They also admitted the possibility of using ritual magic for negative ends, something that they tried when younger. Unlike the young women, one of whom claimed to be both Christian and Pagan, they were explicitly negative about Christianity, and saw Paganism as standing in opposition to Christian beliefs.

Comparison with other recent research on teenage witches

In 2007, a major study by Berger and Ezzy was published, as well as an edited volume by Johnston and Aloi, including chapters by both academics and practitioners. Berger and Ezzy interviewed 90 young witches between 2001 and 2004 in the USA, Australia and the UK. Their findings, whilst based on a much larger sample, were very similar to mine. Witchcraft gave the young people self-esteem and increased confidence. It helped them deal with difficult life circumstances. Often those attracted were a bit 'different' and witchcraft enabled them to celebrate this difference. Books were their main resource, followed by the internet. Berger and Ezzy comment on the explosion of materials available from the 1990s which enabled Wicca to expand from an esoteric initiatory coven-based tradition into a 'generic' practice followed by individuals. Their young witches, though rarely using the label 'feminist', were committed to gender equality, and to harmony with nature, if not eco-activism. They were individualistic in seeing the self as authority, but not selfish. Magic ritual was rarely 'results magic' but a religious practice, focused on self-transformation. Their ethic was open, tolerant but responsible, with a positive attitude to the body and material world. Berger and Ezzy argue that much of the 'witch' worldview fits very well with the current cultural milieu of individualism, gender equality, environmentalism and self-spirituality. They found that the young people were more serious, religious and responsible than some of the commercially available materials would suggest.

Recent research on the worldviews and spirituality of young people

Research such as Blaylock and Williams (2005, 2007), Mikkola et al. (2007, 123) and Savage et al. (2006) on youth spirituality, echoes similar themes to the research on teenage witches. All found that the young people they studied were committed to tolerance and the rights of all to respect and to their own beliefs and opinions. This includes tolerance of diversity in religious beliefs and of sexual orientation as a matter of individual choice. Savage et al. comment that 'belief in God is an optional matter, a consumer choice' (2006, 21). Individual choice is almost sacred, and subjective experience is the authority relied on. This recalls the individualism of the young witches, and their appreciation of the tolerance of Paganism.

The stress on individualism and the self as authority does not mean that young people are selfish or narcissistic. They have a strong concern for others, so that Mikkola et al. call them the 'MeWe' generation (2007, 36). This links to the concern for human rights and the environment noted by researchers. The young people questioned prefer to develop their own personal ethics, rather than having them imposed by 'organised religion'. This was an attraction of the Pagan ethic for young witches. Religion, however, can be an important part of identity, especially for minorities, including young Muslims, and young Christians in black-led and the newer evangelical churches, as well as the Pagan minority. For others, friends, family, music and other lifestyle choices play a similar role (Savage et al. 2006, 85).

According to Blaylock, more 16–19 year-olds in England would accept the label 'spiritual' than 'religious', but this is still only a minority. Savage et al. concluded that 'Generation Y' (those who were 15–25 in 2006) were not generally on a 'spiritual quest' but happy with the meaning in life provided by friends, family and leisure activities. This they dubbed the 'happy midi-narrative' (2006, 37). With the stress on individual autonomy and subjective judgement, Heelas' 'spiritual revolution' is evidenced, but, the majority are more 'secular' than 'spiritual'. Belief in God is a minority choice, but atheism an even smaller minority, with an important middle group of 'positive agnostics' (Blaylock and Williams 2005, 12). Interest in the 'supernatural' in the media is not a sign of a spiritual quest, but generally categorised as entertainment, including by teenage witches. Blaylock and Williams found that there was a lack of knowledge of Christian doctrines and concepts, and of vocabulary to articulate individual beliefs. It has been suggested that this is the outcome of a parental generation that did not wish to impose religious beliefs on their children (e.g. Mikkola et al. 2007, 10).

Youth spirituality, teenage witchcraft and the role of religious education

The numbers of young people who would actually call themselves witches or Pagan is relatively small, nevertheless the number who are aware of or interested in similar issues is larger, and I would argue that the 'teenage witches' represent an acute case of themes found in youth spirituality more generally. These include a commitment to the right to individual beliefs, tolerance and respect for the beliefs of others, self-chosen ethics, an interest in the mysteries of life and death, concern for others and a desire to improve the world and the self. They can, and do, draw on a wide range of sources and, although there is some evidence of a turn from the 'religious' to the 'spiritual', a majority appear to be neither committed to mainstream religions nor to scientific atheism. The self as the source of authority, and the right to choose, are extremely important. There is some evidence that an immanent concept of the divine is more attractive than a theistic deity.

However, the teenage witches appear to have gained some helpful resources from their involvement in Pagan beliefs and magical practices. Their identity as witches and/or Pagans gave them self-esteem and self-confidence so that their status as 'different' or 'special' was positive rather than a source of anxiety. Pagan theology enabled them to see their female gender or sexual orientation as something to be proud of. The ability to engage in magic ritual gave them a sense of being able to take some control over events rather than passively experiencing them. This gave them a resilience that the 'happy midi-narrative' identified by Savage et al. was not always able to do. The Pagan theologies which they were able to discuss gave them a vocabulary with which to articulate their individual beliefs and values. As a religious educator I conclude that perhaps one of the most important roles of religious education might be to draw upon the wide diversity of religious traditions, including Paganism, not to persuade young people to adopt any particular one of them, but to give them access to languages with which they can articulate their individual spirituality.

Chapter 11

Exploring Symbolic, Emotional and Spiritual Expression amongst 'Crasher Clubbers'

Karenza Moore

Introduction

This chapter positions British trance[1] clubbing as a form of emotional and alternative spiritual expression produced by youthful participants 'committed' to heterogeneous electronic dance music (EDM) club cultures (Moore 2004) within the context of the British night-time economy's (NTE) 'commercial exploitation of pleasure' (Measham and Brain 2005, 277). Forms of alternative spiritual expression in 'dubious' NTE contexts such as trance club spaces have tended to be downplayed or dismissed due to young people's illicit drug consumption and the ongoing commercialisation and criminalisation of EDM cultures (Measham and Moore 2008). The historical and contemporary problematisation of 'youth at play' has meant the various significances of EDM forms of expression for some young leisure consumers are typically interpreted as examples of the denigrating processes of market seduction and state repression, which supposedly renders contemporary EDM club cultures symbolically, emotionally, spiritually and politically meaning*less*, and physically and mentally harmful.[2] Through the lens of contemporary Religious Studies scholarship such conceptualisations may be disputed and disrupted. By exploring young people's articulations of the emotional and spiritual significance of a local trance space, via work on contemporary rave and EDM club configurations which is open to their transformative possibilities yet avoids overly celebratory conceptualisations, a greater understanding of youth cultures and ultimately youth spiritualities, may spring.

Gatecrasher One in Sheffield, UK, formerly The Republic, was razed to the ground in June 2007. The site of hundreds of trance music parties, drawing capacity

---

[1]   See http://www.moodbook.com/music/trance.html for a brief history of trance music, including the various sub-genres. The 'Gatecrasher' sound tended towards euphoric (vocal) trance, progressive trance and tech trance.

[2]   For a conceptual review of 'rave culture' literature, including public health research on raving and clubbing which focuses on the 'risks' and 'harms' viewed as inherent to club drug use, see Anderson and Kavanaugh (2007).

crowds of young people consuming illicit club drugs, 'Crasher' was considered by some as the 'spiritual home to a generation of trance lovers' (message posted by P on www.gatecrasher.com, 25 June 2007). Through an examination of the fiery demise of this British nightclub it is argued that there remains scope for young club-goers to create positive local and global 'experiences of connectiveness' (Ovaleson 2004, 100) with others in the face of their ongoing positioning as public order 'menace' (Squires 2008), criminalised, drug-taking 'Other' (Measham and Moore 2008) and targeted leisure consumer cohort (Measham 2004a, 2004b).

Branding the gods of trance: commercialised, criminalised, yet meaningful forms of youthful Expression

How can we best capture the emotional and alternative spiritual significances of a commercial trance music club, including its impact on a young person's orientation towards others in spaces and times beyond the club through practices which may create 'revolutions of everyday lives' (Moore 2004, 462) or new 'morality sensibilities' (Jackson 2004, 152)? Celebrations of EDM clubbing based around inclusionary 'Peace, love, unity, respect' (PLUR) discourses tend to ignore the ways in which such collective connections and individualised expressions remain stratified by the exclusionary discourses and practices of youth consumer culture. These produce enduring divisions on the club door and dance floor according to gender, sexuality, 'class', race and ethnicity, disability and nationality (Bose 2005; Chatterton and Hollands 2002, 2003; Hollands 2002; Hollands and Chatterton 2002; Hutton 2006; MacRae 2004). Overly celebratory EDM clubbing discourses also obscure the commercialisation of EDM clubbing exemplified by the global multi-million pound success of large-scale trance clubs such Gatecrasher and Godskitchen. Both clubs incorporate 'euphoric drug-high' and PLUR references within their brand imagery, which could be perceived as the commercial 'incitement' of emotionally significant 'altered states of consciousness' (ASC) through the ultimately money-generating exultation of trance club 'drug styles' (Manning 2007). This includes the commercially-productive deployment of religio-spiritual discourse, as in Crasher's Easter 2008 trance event promotional material with its advertising strap-line, 'Feel the rush. Punch the sky. Behold the Resurrection' (http://www.gatecrasher.com/crasher).

The most relevant recent contribution to debates surrounding religio-spiritual discourses, practices and experiences associated with EDM club cultures is Lynch and Badger's (2006) work on (British) 'mainstream' post-rave events such as those run by *The Ministry of Sound, Cream* and *Gatecrasher*. Drawing on Luckmann's (1967) work on novel non-institutionalised forms of social religion, Lynch and Badger (2006; see also Lynch 2002) conceptualise British commercial EDM club events as 'secondary institutions that facilitate the processes of self-realisation and self-expression that characterise the new social form of western religion' (2006, 28). Lynch and Badger's concern with commercial EDM clubs acts as a useful (empirical) point of departure from a concentration on 'underground' raving and free festivals in much existing work on alternative religio-spiritual, revolutionary and countercultural dimensions of EDM cultures (Partridge 2006, St John 2003). Lynch and Badger's analysis of interviews with 37 young adults participating in high-profile commercial British post-rave dance events dominated by hard house, trance and techno genres (2006, 32) highlights the *absence of explicitly religious or spiritual discourses* in participants' articulations of their clubbing (and club drug) experiences. However, despite this absence, Lynch and Badger note a 'basic shared framework' (2006, 34) structuring participants' understandings of their clubbing experiences. This framework consists of:

> … an emphasis on the post-rave dancing event as a welcoming and accepting community, the association of the clubbing community with values of personal autonomy, authenticity, self-expression and tolerance, and the importance of clubbing experiences in promoting self-development. (Lynch and Badger 2006, 34)

Alongside a critical engagement with ('mainstream') EDM clubbers' discourses through an empiricism often lacking in early rave and club scholarship (St John 2006, 15), Lynch and Badger's work is strengthened by their recognition that whilst EDM clubbing provides a significant minority of young people in Britain with what is perceived as a tolerant, diverse, friendly 'extended family' (2006, 34) or 'welcoming and accepting community' (2006, 34), this sense of unity and most notably diversity 'may be as much imagined as real, but is no less powerful for clubbers by being imaginary' (2006, 34).

Two points of departure from, or perhaps additions to, Lynch and Badger's (2006) informative work have become apparent in the course of my research on British trance club and club drug cultures. The first involves the suggestion that *at specific EDM club culturally-symbolic moments*, post-rave dance scene participants *do* express their involvement in, and commitment to, EDM clubbing in *explicitly* religio-spiritual terms. Capturing such culturally-symbolic moments involves engagement with the assemblage of chemical, audio-visual and, importantly, virtual technologies which enable 'the global flow of new spiritual lifestyles' (St John 2006, 14, see also Davis 1998; Greener and Hollands 2006; Mattar 2003), best exemplified by the transnational location of those posting web forum dedications to the now defunct Gatecrasher One.[3]

The second extension to Lynch and Badger's (2006) work is further critical engagement with notions of 'undergrounds' and 'mainstreams' (Thornton 1995, Hutton 2006) and concomitant patterns of legal and illegal drug use. 'Recreational' drug use in the context of EDM scenes within the British NTE

---

[3] For further examples of the use of explicitly religio-spiritual expression in promotional material by, and online dedications to, a commercial EDM club following its demise, see http://www.turnmills.co.uk.

relates to the potentialities of (here trance) clubbing as a form of emotional and alternative spiritual expression. Within 'mainstream' post-rave club spaces alcohol consumption continues and indeed is heavily marketed to young EDM clubbing consumers.[4] Yet within these same spaces, 'determined drunkedness' (Measham and Brain 2005, 268; see also Measham 2004a, 2006) is not apparent as the main aim of a night out, nor apparent as a socially acceptable or desirable behaviour, although 'determined drugged-ness' through illegal club drug and EDM music consumption may be (Moore and Measham 2008; Smith et al. 2009). In the place of determined drunkedness, experiential consumption (Malbon 1999) of 'spiritual hedonism' (Davis 2004) is facilitated by the polydrug mix of psychoactive substances favoured by EDM clubbers (Measham et al. 2001), predominately ecstasy tablets and MDMA powder/crystal (Smith et al. 2009), but also alcohol, cannabis, cocaine, amphetamine, GHB/GBL, and the recently criminalised dissociative anesthetic ketamine (Moore and Measham 2008; Riley et al. 2008). It is suggested therefore that what *unites* seemingly disparate commercial 'mainstream' EDM clubs with 'underground' spaces is participants' disdain for the violent, 'binge-drinking' or 'extreme drinking' 'anti-social' 'Other' (Martinic and Measham 2008). It is assumed that the weekend leisure pursuits of 'those most thoroughly seduced consumers, to the tune of a dozen lagers' (Hobbs et al 2003, 273) remain largely devoid of emotional and alternative spiritual meaning. In sum, we cannot seek to understand the 'new social modalities' (Jackson 2004, 163) suggested by illicit drug-fuelled 'mainstream' *and* 'underground' EDM clubbing without engaging with the ongoing discursive creation of a (sub)culturally, emotionally, and spiritually moribund drunken 'Other' (MacRae 2004; Moore 2003), an 'Other' against which clubbers and ravers position themselves (Riley et al. 2008; Smith et al. 2009).

Marking and marketing the demise of Gatecrasher One

The importance of documenting the emotional and spiritual dimensions of participating in commercialised 'mainstream' clubbing 'playspaces' became apparent following my attendance at the post-fire Crasher 14th birthday event at Magna, Sheffield. The event was heavily marketed as a positive response to the Gatecrasher One fire, whilst coinciding with the release of the *Gatecrasher Immortal* CD. The following quotations highlight the ways in which the Crasher

---

[4]   This often occurs through alcohol company sponsorship deals, such as *Bacardi Rum's Bacardi B-Bar* at Southport Weekender, UK. Some commercial clubbing brands such as *Ministry of Sound* made much of the possibility of extended alcohol consumption (following changes to alcohol licensing laws in the UK in 2003) in the context of predominately illegal drug-orientated consumption amongst their customers. Alcohol then becomes another choice in clubbers' late-night/early morning poly-drugging 'repertoire'.

brand positioned itself as 'bravely' responding to the 'tragic' events of June 2007:

> Following a difficult year in which the flagship venue – GC1 – was destroyed by fire, this was a chance to forget the blaze and commemorate the Crasher birthday in style (from www.gatecrasher.com/crasher)

> Gatecrasher IMMORTAL is an EPIC compilation album! This is the ultimate, 3 CD, Crasher experience! Bringing you the big hitters that have narrated the history of Gatecrasher, underground classics and the FUTURE smashes. IMMORTAL is the album that every crasher kid needs to fill the void this summer …! In the wake of the unfortunate fire of legendary Sheffield nightclub in June 2007, IMMORTAL hits back with the return of SCOTT BOND to the label. Proving that Gatecrasher will not only live on but that it's bigger, badder and more banging than ever. (From www.gatecrasher.com/crasher/gatecrasherimmortal, capitalisation in original.).

At work here are processes of commercial production involving an invitation to feel sentimental attachment to space and place structured around the articulation of a 'micro-community', an elective 'vibe tribe' (St John 2006, 11; see also Hodkinson 2002, 2005) or 'trance tribe' (St John 2008) constructed within secularised contexts (Cohen et al. 1987). Of course EDM clubbers may decline such an invitation. From interviews with those attending 'mainstream' trance, techno and hard dance events, Lynch and Badger found, 'that participants tended to see the application of terms such as "religious" or "spiritual" to clubbing as naive, the consequence of over-use of recreational drugs or the expression of an over-idealised view of club culture' (2006, 33). They assert the 'clubbing-as-religion' metaphor deployed by mainstream club promoters often amounts to little more than a thinly-veiled marketing agenda aimed at reassuring young adults that their enthusiasm for the club scene is valid and healthy given that this is their 'religion' (Lynch and Badger 2006, 29). Despite these misgivings, Lynch and Badger (2006) conclude that researchers of contemporary forms of religion and spirituality need to be wary of dismissing the transformative potentialities of young people's involvement in EDM club cultures and the ways in which such involvement may offer participants a 'lived sense of meaningfulness' (St John 2006, 16) simply because it (necessarily) takes place within the problematised flows of Western consumerism. To further promulgate this orientation towards the study of EDM club and club drug cultures as popular sites of contemporary meaning production (Lynch 2002), 'Crasher clubbers'[5] virtual textual expressions of their participation in this particular 'trance tribe' are explored below.

---

[5] Or 'Crasher Kids' as attendees at Gatecrasher events became known in the late 1990s/early 2000s.

Articulating trance 'spiritualities of life' in commercialised club spaces

Tensions arising from attempts to articulate emotional and alternative spiritual commitment to EDM club and club drug cultures in the context of the broader commercialisation and criminalisation of rave – which over the past 20 years is thought to have severely undermined its ability to claim countercultural significance (Melechi 1993; Reynolds 1997) – were apparent in Crasher clubbers' responses to the demise of Gatecrasher One. Such tensions are made manifest when the act of consuming is presented as an integral part of the transformative, meaning-making process of becoming a committed trance clubber, club drug-taker and ultimately a global Crasher brand consumer, as the following quotation demonstrates:

> Gatecrasher was very important in my life and career. It's been one of the biggest influences in my life, and it was through it that I found my path in music ... I remember my first contact with 'the lion'[6] here in Brazil, when Gatecrasher hosted a colourful and mind-altering arena at our Skol Beats festival. Back then, trance was something close to a myth here, so people were enchanted with the new music. I remember my first time as a clubber at the Summer Sound System, it was such a journey! I just couldn't believe my senses. Everything was beautiful: the atmosphere, the music, the people ... Yes, the Crasher Kids! :o) I remember all the amazing Gatecrasher compilations that covered most of my life's soundtrack, from 2001–2003 ... I wish you all the best and hope to see 'the lion' stand once again. (Message posted by F on www.gatecrasher.com, 24 June 2007)

Through their responses to Gatecrasher One's demise, Crasher clubbers focus on a sense of meaningful belonging representing 'not so much an escape from somewhere as an escape to somewhere better' (Luckmann 2003, 25). The difficulty of expressing emotional and spiritual attachment to EDM clubbing spaces is apparent from another quotation from the Gatecrasher website:

> I've always tried to explain to people this place has something special which I have never in all 7 years of going there been able to explain, this place, the trance, the whole experience meant everything to me. Gatecrasher thank u and goodbye, u will always be with us, the legacy will live on. (Message posted by A on www.gatecrasher.com, 23 June 2007)

This creation of an (idealised, inclusive) community embedded within a particular material and symbolic space also involves the representation of an 'Other' who did not (and perhaps could not) know what it means to be a (globally-situated) 'Crasher Kid', as the following quotation demonstrates:

---

    6   This refers to the 'Gatecrasher Lion', the club's emblem present on all its marketing material.

On turning up Matilda Street I could see the devastation just as it had been depicted on the news and on the internet ... A few other people pulled up to look and an old couple asked me what I was doing. I know to most people it is just a building but to those who knew, as a lot of other people have already expressed, it feels just like the death of a friend. As I read the cards and messages pinned to the fence, my thoughts were articulated beautifully by a poem someone had written just after the release of the black album. It summed up the feelings that the club had generated in those who visited and the last part was about those people in their beds at the time who had no idea what was happening across town – of the power of the experience. Feel sorry not for us but for those who never knew it and as of this week never can ... I am glad I visited. I feel I have paid tribute to a building and a club and the memories that I will always hold dear. I draw strength from knowing that so many others out there understand. (Message posted by M on www.gatecrasher.com, 23 June 2007)

Again the articulation of the transformative, meaning-making, technologically enabled process of 'doing being a clubber' (Moore 2006, 222) is embedded in the act of consumption (of a Crasher compilation CD, of Gatecrasher Global events). In addition, inclusion and exclusion is articulated in the quotation above through 'those who had no idea what was happening across town – of the power of the experience', yet this exclusion remains tinged with sympathy 'for those who never knew it and as of this week never can', the implication being that such people would have been welcomed into the fold if they had so wished – although, not, one assumes, if they were the violent, extreme drinking, anti-social 'Other'. Ultimately, for the Crasher clubber to be able express emotional grief at the loss of the 'spiritual home to a generation' (message posted by P on www.gatecrasher. com, 25 June 2007) that was Gatecrasher One and all it symbolised, they must be able to imagine a community of those 'out there who understand', and by implication, those who do not.

Post-rave global EDM cultures, drug-taking trance clubbers and contemporary consumer culture: an unholy alliance?

In exploring trance clubber's responses to the historically and culturally significant moment of Gatecrasher One's destruction through fire, the problem clearly remains, as highlighted by Lynch and Badger (2006), of young people attempting to express the emotional and spiritual significance of EDM clubbing. Articulating such significances necessarily takes place in the context of the problematisation of rave's 'original' PLUR ethos (Reynolds 1997), the ongoing commercialisation and criminalisation of contemporary local and global club cultures, and the often media-driven anxieties about drug-taking youth at play (Measham and Brain 2005; Manning 2007; Murji 1998). Yet, as suggested in this chapter, for a significant minority of young people, post-rave EDM club cultures *do* remain profoundly emotionally and spiritually significant. Explorations of their significance for young people are possible however *only* if it is accepted that technologically-enabled meaning-making practices of EDM clubbers represent a 'new, more diffuse, social form of religion' (Lynch and Badger 2006, 37) which focuses on community, belonging, self-realisation and self-expression. Through such meaning-making practices, commercialised EDM cultures may produce 'revolutions of everyday lives' (Moore 2004, 464) for clubbers as constrained but active social beings. However, these 'revolutions' are unavoidably embedded within the possibly alienating flows of late modern capitalist consumer society, the concomitant exclusion and degradation of a (mythologised) 'Other', and the 'crime and control' governed spaces of publicly and privately regulated (alcohol-orientated) post-industrial night-time economies.

Chapter 12

'Believing in Belonging': An Exploration of Young People's Social Contexts and Constructions of Belief

Abby Day

The current generation of teenagers and young adults in Britain is less religious than previous generations (Brierley 2006; Garnet et al. 2006). Data about youth religiosity fit a general wider pattern of declining religious identification, affiliation and practice in Euro-American countries (Brierley 2006; Davie 1994, 2002; Hadaway et al. 1993; Heelas and Woodhead 2005) but theories vary about why this might be so.

Some people argue that such data only describe certain public behaviours and not private beliefs, that most people 'believe without belonging' (Davie 1994), privately maintaining beliefs in God or other 'spiritual' phenomena. Religion is thus described as implicit, invisible, individualised or transformed into spirituality (Bailey 1990; Garnett et al. 2006; Heelas and Woodhead 2005; Luckmann 1967; Warner 1993). Davie suggests belief transforms into private forms of belief: 'as the institutional disciplines decline, belief not only persists, but becomes increasingly personal, detached and heterogeneous' (2002, 8).

Alternatively, some scholars say that Britain is now a secular culture with traces of a Christian identity, where secular means a rational worldview without beliefs in supernatural powers (Bruce 1995; 2001; 2002). Some attribute decreasing religiosity to declining transmission from parent to child (Brown 2001; Inglis 2007; Regnerus et al. 2004; Voas and Crockett 2005).

Most debates are also typically sustained by references to 'belief' that remain strikingly unexplored. Large surveys sometimes ask overtly religious, closed questions using religious vocabularies that could force religious, and particularly Christian, answers (Hill and Hood, 1999). For example, asking people if they 'believe in God' would not tell us anything about what they might mean by belief or by God. Abercrombie et al. (1970, 106) found when they asked respondents if they believed in a god who could change events on earth; one person replied: 'No, just the ordinary one'. Even small-scale, qualitative studies tend to select people who are religious, or are interested in religion, and usually discuss overtly religious questions.

I attempted to resolve some of those methodological problems by probing belief without asking religious questions (Day 2009b, 2011). I concluded that most people 'believe in belonging', with human relationships being the main sites for sourcing and experiencing meaning, morality and 'transcendence'. If asked to self-identify with a religion, many may say 'Christian' to mark familial or ethnic identity (Day 2006; Voas and Day 2007).

Fourteen months of fieldwork involved discussions with more than 200 people aged 14–83, from a variety of ages and backgrounds, including 68 semi-structured, one-to-one interviews. I asked what they believed in: about their moral beliefs, what was important to them, how life began, how it might end, what, if anything, life means to them, what frightened or delighted them and where those emotions and beliefs came from. They responded with long, richly described stories, illustrating their points in reference to specific people, places and times. I was not listening to coherent, cognitively-based belief statements, but stories with real characters, plots and emotional content. These polyvocal, indeterminate stories, or 'belief narratives' as I prefer to call them, did not fit with the idea of a neatly constructed 'belief system' as envisaged by, for example, Borhek and Curtis (1975) and yet are typical of how people express their beliefs and identities (Good 1994).

Through three schools in the region, I facilitated class discussions and interviewed 25 young people aged 14–19. Here, I explore that data, arguing that young people are not devoid of beliefs in areas conventionally associated with religion – morals, transcendence or meaning – but they are locating those beliefs in places where we might not conventionally be searching for them: in the everyday and the social. I illustrate my points with specific references to individual informants who seemed to capture the mood and meaning of what many other young people were saying. All names have been changed to protect confidentiality.

Sociality of morality

The young people I interviewed shared, broadly, the same moral codes as older informants. Generational differences centred on where people located moral authority. None of the young people I interviewed, even those who described themselves as Christian or otherwise religious, believed they should behave morally just because their god or religion ordered them to do so.

Georgia, for example, an 18-year-old student living with her parents on a farm, in a rural area, said she had a strong idea about rights and wrongs: 'I feel I do. I think it's to do with my upbringing.' Knowing right from wrong did not prevent Georgia from making mistakes involving a boyfriend and brief foray into drug experimentation: 'I broke all my morals for him.' Once she finished with him, and the drugs, she felt wiser and does not regret the experience, she told me: 'Well, I feel now that it's a good thing that I've done it, got it off my chest.'

She was clear when I asked her at the beginning of the interview about her beliefs that she did not believe in religion: 'Nothing religious at all, anything like that. I believe in things like love and stuff like that, feelings, more so than religious things. I don't have any beliefs on that side at all.'

In talking about her moral beliefs, Georgia neatly summarised herself in relation to both public and private forms of belonging: 'I wouldn't class myself as a Christian. I'm not devoted. I don't live by the Ten Commandments. I don't attend, so I wouldn't define myself as Christian at all.'

Here, she conveyed her position on religious beliefs ('not devoted'), her self-identification ('class myself'/ 'define myself') and her approach to practice ('don't live by'/'don't attend'). Her reference to 'the Ten Commandments' is likely to refer to the first four commandments defining one's relation to God, with the comment 'I don't attend' being an elision of 'attend church' and indirect reference to the fourth commandment. This reminded me of another student who told me he lived by some of the commandments, but not the first four. They were clearly distinguishing between 'social code morality' and the obligation of a Christian, Jew or Muslim to love and obey God. (And, as an aside not to be explored here, they reflect a fluency with religious doctrine probably attributable to the UK practice of compulsory Religious Education.)

Even young people who told me that they believed in religion distanced themselves from what they considered to be prescriptive morality and obedience. Sarah, 15, described herself as a Christian who attends church regularly, but she now rejects some Christian morals, specifically those prohibiting sex outside of marriage: 'I used to be very judgmental, but now that I'm a teenager, I've learned not to be', she said. Sarah also seemed to be making a statement about asserting the rights of young people to determine their moral authority. Young people may be more in search of 'authenticity' than prescribed templates of morality (Lynch 2002).

Another girl I interviewed, Lindsay, 14, described herself as a Christian who believed in God and prayed regularly to Jesus. There were times, however, when she rejected the advice Jesus gave her, particularly when it concerned her friendships. When I asked her if it bothered her that she was not obeying Jesus' advice, she said, with calm confidence:

> No, not really. Sometimes it does when I know what he says is right and I don't
> do it, then that bothers me. But when I think I'm right, then, no, it doesn't bother
> me at all.

Although she is a practising Christian, she would not blindly obey a higher authority when she thinks her own authority is more legitimate in the context of her social relations with her friends. Divine he may be, but for Lindsay sometimes Jesus simply does not have the everyday, lived, social experience that informs her decisions.

Even the most radical amongst the young people I interviewed respected moral authority when they perceived it to be legitimate. Charles, 16, who described himself as an 'anarcho-communist', was interested in history and politics and

often referred to his parents, teachers and others as respected authorities. Charles
dismissed religion as inherently immoral, adding:

> As an historian, and looking back to times when people were more religious,
> morality wasn't higher. Now in this country I think it's less than one percent
> that people go to church every week, but we've got less crime, we don't have
> 12 year old prostitutes like we did a couple of hundred years ago, we don't have
> the same sort of immorality as then and yet religion has declined. So, I see no
> link between religion and being moral, necessarily.

What young people often seemed to be saying was not that they rejected morality,
but they rejected a form of morality that assumes strict adherence to a god or
a religion without allowing for a multiplicity of social influences and norms.
Looking at the wider social context, I found a general pattern of young people's
lack of obligatory respect for authority figures (Margo 2008).

Believing is belonging

Jordan, 14, initially confounded me. When I asked my usual opening question,
'What do you believe in?', He replied 'nowt' [Yorkshire dialect for 'nothing']. He
continued that: 'I don't believe in owt [anything]. I don't believe in any religions.'
I was confused, and simply repeated what he had said: 'You don't believe in any
religions.' He answered, 'No. I'm Christian but I don't believe in owt.'

In saying he is 'Christian' rather than 'a Christian', Jordan seems to have
internalised the term into his identity. It would be like saying, for example, that
he is 'English', rather than 'an English'. I began to understand how he viewed
his identity as something he was born into, with grandparents who were, as he
described them, 'really strong Christians' who believed in God, the Bible and
Jesus. He said he did not believe in those things. Christian was an identity he
believed he inherited through his family.

Most informants I talked to 'believed in' their relationships with other people,
most commonly friends, partners and family. What mattered was the emotional,
adherent, reciprocal and trusting quality of the relationship.

Adherent relationships helped define people's beliefs, with most people
identifying the source and reinforcement of their beliefs in their personal
relationships and the experiences they have had with those relationships. Belief,
therefore, is not limited to belief in a god or religion, although it tended amongst
my informants to imply 'faith'. Nadia, a 17-year-old Muslim student, described
her beliefs in terms of whom or what she had faith in and trusted:

> I believe in lots of things. I think my religion is really important to me. Helping
> me cope. And prayer is very important to me. I think my family is very important
> to me as well. Very important. And there's certain things in my life. I have

certain principles. I don't like – I don't like, I don't like hypocrisy. I hate it. You know, when people say something and don't do it, it really annoys me. I can get annoyed really quickly at people like that. Like my Dad. A big hypocrite, you know, he tells people not to do things then does them himself.

Other young people I interviewed firmly rejected religion and, with it, the idea of a pre-ordained plan or purpose in life. This lack of a big picture – a teleological universe, perhaps – did not seem to trouble them, however. Duncan, 14, said that although he was raised as a Christian, he never believed in God, he said, at least not after he 'started thinking'. Duncan does not think the universe was created by any higher being or intelligent design. He suggested that some people might like religion particularly because they want an organising principle, but he would not, mainly because such a power could be bad as well as good.

For young people like Nadia and Duncan, belief implies what or whom they could trust, not simply about what or whom could exist. As Gemma, 14, said: God may have created the universe but 'I don't, like, worship him or anything.' Gemma is making a distinction between propositional belief and faith-based belief, that others have theorised about in more depth (see Robbins 2003, 2007; Ruel 1982). Gemma might believe 'that' God exists, but she does not believe 'in' him. There is a tendency, amongst scholars and some of my older informants, to use unproblematically the term 'believer' or 'unbeliever' as if we are to understand implicitly that 'belief' means believing in God, or a specific faith. The connections between 'belief' and Christianity, in particular, have been explored in depth elsewhere (Needham 1972; Smith 1967, 1977, 1978, 1979; Ruel 1982). Ruel (1982) concluded that belief is best understood as 'faith' and it is in that context that most of my informants seemed to be using it. The faith-based belief form may reflect a return to a relational sense of belief, recapturing a former use of the term 'belief' as 'beloved' (Smith 1967; Lopez 1998).

Believing in bereaving

Young people may believe in the transcendent, but often only if they have relocated it to the social and temporal. Being religious did not mean that one's supernatural experiences are also religious, I found. Vickie, 14, told me that she believed in God, attends church and sometimes prays, although she converses more often with her deceased uncle than she does with a deity. When she feels upset about something she often imagines him talking with her and helping her.

Briony, a 19-year-old student and atheist, feels protected by her deceased grandmother, whom she describes as 'sort of there, and sort of looking'. She first sensed the presence of her grandmother when she awoke in hospital after a suicide attempt and, since then, has felt her grandmother watching over her, protecting her from harm or disappointment. (I treat the significance of gender in supernatural beliefs elsewhere, see Day 2008.)

As Collins-Mayo (2008) found in her study with young people, even those who do not attend church or have a religious affiliation often pray to some kind of spiritual entity. Amongst the non-religious youth in my study, the 'entity' was invariably a deceased relative. I suggest that most people's supernatural experiences allow them to continue a relationship with a deceased loved one. These are the relationships I have so far described as adherent, emotional, reciprocal relationships – relationships in which people feel they belong.

Discussion and conclusion

My small-scale case study complements large-scale studies in the sociology of religion that have generally found that young people derive meaning, happiness and moral frameworks from social relationships, not religion (Clydesdale 2007; Mason et al. 2007; Savage et al. 2006; Smith with Denton 2005). My findings, however, complicate some of their interpretations and conclusions, particularly as they all predict that young people's socially-rooted beliefs will be insufficient to support them in the future. Smith with Denton (2005, 143) describe teenagers being 'nearly without exception profoundly individualistic, instinctively presuming autonomous, individual self-direction to be a universal human norm and life goal'. The authors further suggest (156–8) that teenagers today live in a 'morally insignificant universe' where decisions are not guided by or grounded in larger, invisible, sources of either religion, philosophy or other supra-mundane moral forces. I prefer to conclude that young people are guided by social authority that they feel transcends religious authority. Situating the source of moral authority in the social rather than the divine therefore does not necessarily reflect an 'individualistic' tendency, but is, perhaps, a Durkheimian turn, where the sanctity of the collective is upheld over any one individual or religion. There is also evidence of decreasing nationalism amongst young people (Tilley and Heath 2007) and decreasing racism, which a recent study has attributed to improved education, increased social diversity and general societal discouragement of racist discourse (Ford 2008). These may reflect cultural shifts and a desire for more acceptance of pluralism and socially-diverse modes of meaning and authority.

The move towards the social here reflects my thesis' general findings about 'believing in belonging'. Increasing rates of youth irreligiosity may therefore more properly be seen as an effect from the wider culture rather than simply a passing phase marked by age or life-cycle effects. It remains to be seen what happens as the current generation ages, as little good longitudinal evidence is available. Most is either dated, focuses on specific religious groups, or consists of larger studies where religion and belief are not investigated in any depth (Smith et al. 2003).

With an understanding of 'belief as belonging' it is difficult to sustain the argument that belief has become more private. It is particularly through the social that beliefs are being sourced, tested, experienced and articulated. It is no longer, as Asad (1993) suggested, the case where beliefs are being officially legitimised and sanctioned by religious leaders and institutions. The argument about what young people believe today necessarily hangs on what is meant by belief.

My explanations in this chapter about why young people today are less religious than previous generations suggest a long-term trend towards the decline of religion. The reason for this, I suggest, does not lie with the traditional secularisation culprit of 'modernisation' but rather with the relocation of belief from the transcendent and spatial to the mundane and temporal. This may be occurring through a process of social differentiation, often seen as part of modernisation, but not as a product of modernisation's tendency to rationalise or bureaucratise. Rather, it is a feature of the way beliefs have become more diffused and more rooted in concepts like authenticity and legitimacy.

Chapter 13

The Role of Religion in the Sexual Lives of Teens

Elizabeth Cooksey and Tessa Dooms

Introduction

'Sex before marriage is a sin.' This message is commonly associated with religious voices when questions arise concerning young people, their sexual attitudes and behaviours. As a major world religion, Christianity in its various forms shares this stance, preaching the sacredness of bodily intimacy and sexual abstinence prior to marriage. But how effective is this message for today's youth in a modern and increasingly global world in which sex has become a public and pervasive feature of social life? Although many countries are witnessing the increase of both new religious movements or variants of more established ones, and reports of religious affiliation among adolescents remain high (Smith et al. 2002; Garner 2000), religious attendance does not necessarily equate with religious influence. Might the relevance of religion for teenagers, and hence its ability to impact their social lives and practices actually be diminishing as secularists suggest?

We approach how religion might impact the sexual practices of young people against this backdrop of pervasive sexuality juxtaposed against the continued existence and importance of religion in the contemporary world. To explore ways in which religion and sexuality intersect in the lives of youth, we draw on findings from both the United States and South Africa – two countries where religion remains important in the lives of individuals and communities. Clearly the adolescent cultures of the two countries differ as culture is a dynamic entity that incorporates the identity, practices and perceptions of young people in a specific social context. Religion and sexuality comprise two important components of social life in each nation, however. And while our specific examples are drawn largely from the Christian context, we explore theoretical issues that underpin links between religion and sexuality for young people in general.

Before we consider the contributions of religion in shaping the ways in which adolescents make decisions about how they express their sexuality, we present brief descriptive information on religious beliefs and behaviours among youth in both the United States and South Africa, along with an account of their sexual practices in order to illuminate the cultural contexts from which we draw our examples. Although we are unable to cover all aspects of the interplay between religion and sexuality among adolescents, we touch upon issues associated with sexual risk behaviour, religious power, and religion and the body, plus consider some ways in which religion might actually be able to impact sexual decision making among youth today.

Youth and religion: South Africa and the United States

Has secularisation led to a decline in religiosity among youth? Statistics suggest that this is neither the case in South Africa nor the United States. Although South Africa is considered a secular country, religious participation among South Africans is high. Approximately 75 per cent of all South Africans report a religious affiliation and 82 per cent of religious South Africans report a Christian denomination. Further, after sport, church is reported as the second most popular type of organisation that South African youth are affiliated with (Statistics South Africa Census 2001; Community Agency for Social Equity 2000). In many ways the United States presents a similar picture, as the USA is one of the most religious developed nations with only 15 per cent of adults reporting no religious affiliation. Again Christianity prevails: results from the 2008 American Religious Identification Survey showed close to 90 per cent of religious Americans identify with a Christian denomination, over half are Protestant and just under one third are Catholic (Kosmin and Keysar 2009). These statistics highlight the potential importance of religious influences on the lives of youth either directly or through the views and beliefs of their families.

Youth and sexuality: South Africa and the United States

In South Africa as a whole, sexual activity among young people is both high and risky in nature. According to the Reproductive Health Research Unit (2003), 48 per cent of youth aged 15–19 report having engaged in sexual intercourse, with, 67 per cent in the 15–24 age group. More striking is the risky nature of this sexual activity in light of the HIV epidemic. Studies, based on self-reported surveys, found the average age for sexual debut amongst South African adolescents to be 16.4 years for males and 17 years for females, with an alarming increase in sexual debut at ages 12 and 13. Moreover, adolescents report regularly having more than one sexual partner and the younger adolescents report a reduced likelihood of condom usage (King 2003). These and other risky sexual behaviours impact negatively on the sexual wellbeing of adolescents and reinforce the need to understand the roles that various social institutions, including religious institutions, may have in the discourse on sexuality to adolescents, as sex is the predominant mode of transmission of HIV.

Although the percentage of American teens who report having had sexual intercourse has declined since 1990, their levels of sexual activity, pregnancy, abortion, fertility and rates of sexually transmitted infections remain among the highest in the world: close to half of American teens report having had sexual intercourse at least once, and roughly one in seven initiated sex prior to age 15. When it comes to contraception, American teens are increasingly using condoms and hormonal methods, yet close to one third of American girls get pregnant by age 20, more than 80 per cent of teen pregnancies are unplanned, and just under half of unintended teen pregnancies end in abortion. And of those teen pregnancies that are carried to term, less than 20 per cent occur within marriage (Singh and Darroch 2000). Further, minority youth report both higher rates of sexual involvement and earlier timing of first sex than their white peers.

Sexual health risk behaviour and HIV/AIDS among young people

Any discussion about young people and sexuality today must highlight the health risks associated with sex. Nearly half of the global population today is less than 25 years old and these youth comprise a generation that has not known a world without AIDS (UNAIDS 2004). Sub-Saharan Africa has the highest prevalence of HIV in the world and contains almost two-thirds of all young people living with HIV – approximately 6.2 million people. Many youth-focused HIV/AIDS awareness and prevention initiatives have consequently been undertaken in South Africa through the education system and by tapping into youth culture and the media.

Although teens and young adults represent only 25 per cent of the sexually active population in the United States, again the peak ages for STIs are 15–24 as this age group accounts for nearly half of all STI diagnoses each year, including half of all HIV diagnoses (Weinstock et al. 2004).

Rates of HIV infection among American youth are much lower, although large racial/ethnic disparities exist in overall STI prevalence as black youth have rates of STIs that are 20–35 times higher than white youth. Again, the main mode of transmission is heterosexual intercourse and the burden of STIs falls not only on the infected individuals themselves, but also on society in general with associated economic and psychological costs. However, during the first few years of the twenty-first century, abstinence-only sex education programmes that reiterate the confinement of sex to marriage have flourished, and as of 2009, the provision of HIV/STI education is required in only 35 states (Guttmacher Institute 2009).

Youth, risky sexual behaviours and religion

In light of the sexual nature of the HIV/AIDs epidemic and the health risks associated with pregnancy and abortion, sexual behaviours among youth are risky behaviours. As Planet and Planet (2000) argue, adolescent risky behaviours are not isolated activities as much adolescent culture is based on risk behaviour being normative. According to King (2003), risky sexual behaviour among young people is fostered by contextual forces such as coercion, peer pressure, low self-esteem, pessimism, lack of parental communication, poverty and low education levels. As churches adapt to changes that occur in the world around them, they still have to 'maintain moral authority with respect to right belief and behaviour' (Ellingson et al. 2004). The sinfulness of sex prior to marriage is a strong moral tenet to hold onto, but religious organisations should also look to address a variety of issues related to the psycho-social and interpersonal needs of young people in order to replace the social meanings that produce risky behaviour with norms and values that do not.

Religious power and sexual practices

In *The History of Sexuality* Foucault (1978) argues for an understanding of sexuality not only as a series of individual sexual choices, but as a product of, and response to, socially discursive projects of power. Discourses of sex and sexuality are embedded in power relations, and it is these relationships that can either serve as aids or obstacles to the negotiation of the sexual practice of adolescents. It is therefore very important to understand the social structures that give meaning to these relationships, and for Foucault, religion is a vitally important structure.

With this is mind, the body becomes a central meeting place of religion and adolescent sexuality: sex is an act of the body, and religion commonly takes the view that physical bodies serve as vehicles for ritual and interaction. Foucault argues that religious institutions and practices exert power over sexual bodies by creating a culture of sexual silence and repression in which sexual discourse and practice are relegated to the private sphere, using sacred institutions such as marriage.

How can this power be accounted for in terms of the intersection between religion and sexuality? According to Weber, religious orientations and approaches toward sexuality polarise conceptions of sex either as a destructive and erotic force or as based on self-giving love and develop strategies for ensuring that the latter is reproduced through social interactions (Gane 2002). This indicates how religion is seen as sanctioning some meanings associated with sexuality while others are considered dangerous and undesirable.

Foucault, in his analysis of discourses of sexuality in modern Western societies reinforces Weber's assertion. Placing a strong emphasis on religion and particularly Christianity as a dominant factor shaping commonplace notions of sexuality, Foucault's 'repressive hypothesis' inextricably links the Victorian age of sexual secrecy to the dominant Christian discourse and institutionalisation of sex in marriage (Foucault, 1978). Not only does he argue that religion placed limitations on when and where sex is to take place, but also how and why it was to be engaged in. This is no different in contemporary religious experience, particularly for young people who are faced with a central abstinence message in religious contexts.

Does religion matter?

Key questions remain: Does religion matter when adolescents make sexual decisions? If the answer is yes, then how? What is it about religion and religious beliefs that affect the sexual attitudes and practices of youth? Religion *could* affect adolescent sexuality and its practice in a number of ways. In its quest to direct and preserve the internal self, religion has taken on the role of regulating the physical body. By providing individuals with rules, rituals and relationships, religion creates a structured social environment that people can be socialised through. Through teaching what constitutes morally acceptable behaviour and what does not, religion has the potential to shape both attitudes and practices (Germond and Dooms 2008).

Centrality of belonging

The feeling of belonging is a key concept. Adolescence is a time when individuals are impressionable, the opinions of others, particularly peers, become central to the process of identity shaping, and when religious conversion is likely to take place (Smith 2005; Rutenburg et. al. 2001). For youth who attend religious services, the religious institution serves as a social entity, poised to present a network of adults and peers that may influence them, aid in their identity formation, and provide a sense of group belonging. A prominent reason for attendance at Christian youth groups in Potchefstroom, South Africa was the desire to belong to the group and socialise. In their study of the impact of religion on the sexual perceptions and practices of South African adolescents, Germond and Dooms (2008) report the following as some of the reasons youth gave for attendance that illustrate this importance of belonging: 'I want to build relationships', 'To speak to trustworthy people', 'Friends encourage me' and 'To feel I belong there'. Belonging is a need expressed by young people but it is also central to the concept of religion. Through creating a feeling of belonging religious institutions can increase the likelihood that religious messages will shape and direct sexual practices.

Clear and relevant messaging

In order for religious institutions to succeed in regulating the physical, sexual body, their messages must be clearly stated, and, in response, teens must commit to the beliefs that are advocated. Using data from a recent national survey of youth and religion in the United States (NSYR), Regnerus (2007) found that religiously involved kids had a difficult time coming up with religious guidelines about dating and sexuality. Whereas teens are getting a lot of information from the Internet, educators and public health officials, they do not seem to be getting clear messages from religious leaders. Teens interviewed in the NSYR knew that their religious institutions encouraged saving sex for marriage but that was about the extent of the message received.

This message also fails to convey what constitutes 'sex'. In the movie named after her, Juno asks her friend: 'What does sexually active even mean?' This is a question Christianity rarely addresses. Readings of Christian discourses about sex equate sex with heterosexual intercourse. While most religiously involved youth do not report having had intercourse, many do report other sexual behaviours. For example, 35 per cent of youth attendees at a Pentecostal youth group in Potchefstroom, South Africa reported having had vaginal intercourse (Germond and Dooms 2008). Of those who had not, 81 per cent reported experiences of kissing and/or touching in a sexually arousing manner. These teens largely agreed that sexual intercourse was the only act that could be regarded as sex, and thus the only act that was prohibited by their church's teachings. However, even among young people who report no sexual intercourse, 47 per cent reported being uncertain of whether God approved of their sexual behaviour. This suggests that these teens are uncertain about the extent to which other sexual acts besides intercourse are also prohibited by the church's teaching.

Similar findings are evident from a study of primarily African American youth ages 13–19 attending 18 Christian churches in Columbus, Ohio (Steinman et al. 2005). Some 58 per cent of these youth reported having engaged in some intimate behaviours and 38 per cent reported having had sexual intercourse. Among those who had had intercourse, over 70 per cent also reported oral sex, and more than one in five reported anal sex. When pastors of these churches were asked to estimate how many of their congregations' youth they thought had had sex, their guesses were only in the 5–10 per cent range.

Evidence from national studies and our own localised research suggests that many religiously active teens are not committed to the message of abstinence until marriage. A problem with linking sex to marriage in today's teen culture is that the churches' position seems not just idealistic but even inapplicable. In recent decades, several important demographic changes have occurred that have weakened the authority of the official traditional teachings of the church for their youth (Smith 2005). For example, marriage now occurs at older average ages yet sexual maturity occurs earlier than in the past, resulting in prolonged periods of singlehood in the teen and early adult years. Additionally, many children are growing up in a cultural context in which marriage fails to play a prominent role: in the United States today, close to 70 per cent of black children are born outside of marriage. It isn't really surprising that marriage has been described as a 'white thing'!

Some concluding thoughts

Despite the abundance of articles written about adolescent sexual behaviour in recent decades, relatively little research has addressed the role that religion might play in affecting teen's sexual attitudes and behaviours. The predominant Christian message concerning sex for young people is that premarital sex is not permissible.

While this is a simple and direct message in some ways, it is also confusing to today's youth: what is sex and why should marriage be considered important? Messages from the pulpit, youth pastors, and church communities may instead require greater complexity to address the real decisions young people face today as they grapple with questions related to sexuality more broadly than just whether or not they should have sexual intercourse.

Religious institutions possess the tools to be successful, but in order for religion to be *consequential*, or as both Foucault and Weber would say, an entity that really holds and effectively directs power, religion must provide not only clear and relevant messages, but have salience for teens, and by recognising the centrality of belonging and social networks for teens, supply a strong support system that reinforces the religious perspective in order to compete with more sexually permissive scripts that youth are constantly exposed to in the rest of their lives (Regnerus 2007).

Religion can also indirectly affect sexuality through influencing friendship choices and dating patterns. Religion provides social capital via social networks and hence also functions as a source of social and individual control. Participation in religious activities can also affect how adolescents use their time: if religious pursuits take up time that could otherwise be spent hanging out unsupervised with a boyfriend or girlfriend then they reduce opportunities for sexual activity.

It should come as no surprise that although they are a world apart, teens in both South Africa and the United States who were the least likely to engage in any form of sexual activity were those with the highest levels of religious commitment, or put another way, those who had moved from growing up in the church to the 'church growing in them'.

PART IV
Identity

This section looks in particular at identity amongst religious youth. Minganti focuses on identity negotiated by young Muslim women in Sweden whilst Singh considers Sikh youth in Britain. Two other chapters focus on Christian youth, one on those who go as pilgrims to Lourdes (Harris), another on those who construct their identity through Christian youth groups (Shepherd). Heynes' offers a different angle on the relationship between religion and identity by exploring how teenage girls relate to representations of women and gender in religious education classes in Britain. In each chapter, whilst age is a key variable in identity construction, religiosity or ideas about religiosity forms the other critical dimension. In different ways the chapters in this section remind us that 'being religious' in religiously diverse late modern societies is a complex business which requires work on the part of the young person; it cannot be taken for granted.

Chapter 14

Islamic Revival and Young Women's Negotiations on Gender and Racism

Pia Karlsson Minganti

In today's Sweden with 9 million inhabitants there live an estimated 300,000 Muslims. Some perceive themselves as religious, some do not. This chapter focuses on young devout women engaged in Sunni Muslim youth associations in Sweden.

It illuminates the women's construction of an 'Islamic' identity, and further, its possibly beneficial implications for their agency, primarily in challenging racist and sexist oppression.[1] I do so by highlighting a key scenario in the women's narratives about their development as Muslims, containing the following three aspects (1) being born in a Muslim family with Islam as the tacit 'common sense'; (2) going through a teenage crisis when growing up and meeting with the world outside the home sphere; (3) being religiously awakened when enrolling in Muslim youth associations and, consequently, in the global Islamic revival. I claim that this key scenario reflects points of conflict for the women, in the intersection between gender, religion, 'race'/ethnicity and generation. I also claim that such a scenario indicates a distinction between 'religion' and 'cultural traditions', which is commonly used among adherents of the contemporary Islamic revival all over the world – a distinction which allows for some reinterpretation and change. Thus this chapter shows how the position as an awakened, 'practising' Muslim carries with it promises of empowerment for the women, making it more understandable why they would choose to engage in a seemingly gender-conservative religious movement.

Method and theoretical frame

This chapter draws on material collected during an extensive fieldwork among members in the Sunni-dominated national organisation Sveriges Unga Muslimer

---

[1]   My application of the term 'racism' includes different processes of othering and domination, that is, one based on the notion of 'race' as a biological fact, but also, for instance, those labelled as 'cultural racism' and Islamophobia (Runnymede Trust 1997; Larsson 2006). For 'sexism' I refer to processes of domination based on the notion of gender difference.

[SUM, i.e. Sweden's Young Muslims] and some of its local youth associations between 1998 and 2002 (Karlsson Minganti 2007, 2008). The method used was qualitative with participant observations and spontaneous talk (resulting in fieldnotes), along with in-depth interviews with nine women (resulting in audio recordings and printed transcriptions). When I first met the women, they were between 18 and 25 years old, still unmarried. Some were upper secondary school students, others had begun higher education or employment. They were born in West Asia, North and East Africa, to parents who, one way or another, defined themselves as Muslims, and they had all come to Sweden during childhood (at 4–11 years of age). This chapter focuses on their construction of a common Islamic subject position in Sweden, across the diverse backgrounds of their families.

A theoretical point of departure is that of the subject as a site of intersecting identifications and power orders, resulting in different experiences and interests, sometimes coherent and sometimes in conflict (see, for instance, Anthias and Yuval-Davis 1992). This chapter deals primarily with intersections between gender, 'race'/ethnicity, religion and generation. Another basic premise is that subjects, identities and power orders are socially and culturally constructed, and, thus, sites of contestation. To underscore this power perspective, I work with the concept of negotiation, that is, processes that lead to social or cultural reproduction or change. People struggle to have their actions (verbal and non-verbal) appear meaningful – a struggle for precedence of interpretation and, thus, agency (Thurén 1998; Khan 2002). Similarly religion is, in this context, understood as contested knowledge, providing people with frames of reference and means to deal with everyday life (Berger and Luckmann 1991; Mahmood 2005).

Experiences of sexism and racism

Regardless of the women's families' diverse backgrounds and degree of religiosity, they all transmitted to their daughters a firm belief in God and the basic pillars of Islam. For this the young women expressed gratitude. However, in their transformation into 'practising' Muslims they took a critical stance to the tacit character of this knowledge and strived for a conscious and reflexive faith as represented by their new Islamic community.

The women's growing up and shaping individual selves coincided with their encounter with non-Muslims in Swedish society and with Muslims of varying backgrounds and religious practices. Following this complexity, all the women's narratives contain descriptions of teenage crises that threatened their bonds to both family and religion. Besides all the possible conflicts that young people might endure, these women's narratives highlight problematic relations in association with gender and 'race'/ethnicity. As put by a woman whom I call Noor:

It's not easy to be young. And especially not a young *woman*. I mean, boys were allowed to do everything they wanted. But demands were on girls. For instance, that they weren't allowed to go out, that they shouldn't do this and that, that they shouldn't go to school parties. Just a thing like that, you were not allowed to go to school parties! And my brother, he never had to do the dishes at home. These are all just small matters, but they meant so much back then.

/.../

One does not know who one is, or where one should turn oneself. I mean, I already had a hard time getting into that ... what should I say, Swedishness. And then I discovered that: 'Nope, I cannot become Swedish either'. Or rather, I am not *allowed* to be. Just when the family noticed that: 'Okay, that's it, now she is becoming Swedish' ... then they put up even more severe demands and boundaries.[2]

The women were clearly critical of gender issues in their families, especially what they rated as unjust division of labour, and as unwanted control over their bodily behaviours, such as dress code and movements outside the home. Control over their female chastity seemed to increase as they entered puberty and as they came to live in a society dominated by the absence of what was perceived as Muslim morality. This role of women as symbolic bearers of community identity and purity is well researched and proven not to be Muslim-specific, but to increase in diasporas (Anthias and Yuval-Davis 1992; Sered 2000). The young women were certainly interested in guarding their modesty; yet meeting with the world outside the home they were alerted to criticisms against sexism and began to question the gender relations of their families and ethnic networks.

Confusingly enough for the young women, the hostility towards them as Muslims often drew on discourses that were critical to oppression of Muslim women. Amal reported explicit verbal abuse from peers in school: 'When I used the headscarf I got to hear: "Okay, so you are oppressed now?!" Or: "God, it smells like shit in here!" I got to hear such things when they passed by me. And... I thought it was horrible.' The young women suffered from different kinds of oppression under both patriarchal and racist power orders, and consequently they had a hard time making their own voices heard – as individuals, as women and as members of minority groups.

When the women were asked to speak, they found themselves pushed into the position of being representatives of 'the Muslims' and Islam. With Islam under attack, this position often turned into a defensive stance, as non-Muslims demanded elaborated statements about 'what Islam says' and 'what Muslims do'. Rather than giving an account of anything but the simplest elements in childhood faith they

---

[2]   In this chapter the interviews have been translated from Swedish into English by the author.

were urged to give theological explanations about social and political events in countries that they had never visited. Muslims, such as family or congregation members, on the other hand, often claimed to have the right answers and demanded from the young women that they represent collective truth and respectability.

To sum up, the women expressed the dilemma of living under pressures from different power orders, and – from a marginalised position – having to deal with the mismatches that sometimes occur and with the silencing of their subjective voices. They testified about how these experiences led to a youth crisis that made up a significant risk of splitting from their families and their faith. In the end these nine women did not make such a break, but chose to challenge prevailing norms from within, that is, by enrolling in the Islamic movement.

Becoming a 'practising' Muslim

The women described the way out of their youth crises in terms of religious awakening. Through Koran schools, siblings, or peers, they came in contact with the first and still largest national organisation for Muslim youth in Sweden – Sveriges Unga Muslimer (SUM), i.e. Sweden's Young Muslims. It was founded in 1991 and claims to have an estimated 5,000 members all over the country.[3] With the headquarters in Stockholm it also links several local youth associations in different towns – the main arenas for the activism of the young women in my study.

Latifa was enthusiastic when she described the friendly atmosphere in her local association. 'You must come and see for yourself!' The invitation was followed by a performance showing me how the girls run to greet and hug each other, and how the young ones call themselves 'sisters and brothers in Islam'. I deem her performance to express an important motive for the youth's engagement in the Islamic movement, namely the desire for identification and alliance. According to the cultural theorist Lawrence Grossberg, it is not necessarily rational and initiated consideration that guides the youth, but feelings of attraction or repulsion, likes and dislikes (1997, 13–14). The women's Islamic engagement coincided with their emerging self-definitions in wider societal contexts, and the questioning of their parents' norms. Similar to the narratives of other teenagers, this process was imbued with distinctions between I/Us and the Other(s). What makes me similar to others? What makes me different? Who am I and who will I become? Thus, in a situation which for the teenage women mostly appeared as 'chaotic', it seems they were not only motivated by Islamic doctrine, but also by finding a sufficient platform for identity construction. From this perspective, the young Muslims' achievement of religious ideology and community could be understood in terms of

[3]   *Sveriges Unga Muslimer.* Homepage http://www.ungamuslimer.se/, accessed 28 May 2009.

emotional investments and alliances that Grossberg labels *affective empowerment* (1997, 31–2, 76).

The women explained the way out of their youth crises in terms of a religious awakening or 'return to Islam', and this, according to my interpretation, involves the dimensions of affective empowerment and cultural contestation described above, but certainly also a dimension of religious conviction. When 'returning to Islam', they joined Muslims worldwide, following the call of the Islamic revival movement: 'Back to Islam!' With the Islamic revival I refer 'not only to the activities of state-oriented political groups but more broadly to a religious ethos or sensibility that has developed within contemporary Muslim societies' (Mahmood 2005, 3).

The revival movement's call for a return to Islam entails two aspects. Firstly, Muslims are urged to turn to Islam as the main guide for the individual and society, refraining from other interests and ideologies, including unrestrained 'Westernisation'. Secondly, Muslims are urged to turn back to the Koran and Sunna in search of the 'authentic' message free from human delusions. In the young women's everyday life, this call was expressed in their comprehensive practising of Islam, and their ensuring that these practices were performed in accordance with the 'true' Islam. They applied the distinction between 'religion' and 'cultural traditions' and perceived themselves to be detecting the 'true' message of Islam and discarding 'cultural misunderstandings'. As one possible strategy, their dismissal of certain *hadiths* (narrations about the exemplary sayings and conducts of Prophet Muhammed) as being 'false' and androcentric, could be mentioned. Also their highlighting of such *hadiths* that bring to the fore women's interests.

In fact, within the frame of their Islamic movement the young women received recognition as pious subjects, personally responsible before God. This means that they also were ascribed the right and duty to look for religious knowledge and support for strengthening their piety. In turn, this means that the young women found some space for themselves in the mosque and in other knowledge-producing arenas – spaces that are not always assured for women, either in Sweden or in Muslim societies.

Managing racism and sexism

To conclude this chapter, I discuss some empowering aspects that the women perceived by becoming 'practising Muslims' of the 'true' Islam. I begin by commenting on their dilemmas in connection with racialised power orders. When enrolling in Muslim youth associations, influenced by the Islamic revival, the young women were offered consolation by the notion of Islam as a religion that counteracts racism, both such racism that is ascribed to Muslims by 'outsiders' and the one operating 'inside' Muslim communities:

> Latifa: Islam gets rid of all that racism, skin colour, or that cultural stuff. All are
> equal before God.
>
> Pia: Aha. And that feels good?
>
> Latifa: Indeed it does! Every time I look at my friends I feel so happy. It's us,
> the coming generation, we, the Muslim youth in Sweden, raised in Sweden, sort
> of... We are the ones who are going to eliminate racist thinking, because we do
> not care about where people are coming from. We do not think like that.

Latifa and the other young women adopted the idea about Islam as an
anti-racist religion, and perceived themselves as embodying this progress as
'the new generation' Muslims. As such they were supposedly less biased and more
enlightened than the parental generation, thanks to their increased knowledge
about 'true' Islam and its message about unification in piety.

As to external racialisation, the women expressed feelings of alienation
from non-Muslim Swedes, who constantly positioned them as the Other, while
demanding answers about 'what Islam says' and 'what Muslims do'. The women's
Islamic community, nonetheless, offered them a positive understanding of this
representational burden. They were enlightened about the concept of *dawa*,
that is, a religious duty to inform about Islam, which would reward them with
dignity and religious merits. Furthermore, the women fostered a notion about
dawa as a possible means for preventing non-Muslims' racialising practices.
If only people could get information about the 'true' Islam and disregard 'cultural
misconceptions', Muslims would gain respect and recognition. As exemplified by
Latifa:

> In a way, I can understand the Swedes. I mean, they get these images from the
> mass media showing Islam as something horrible. In fact, I was thinking in the
> same way for a while: 'We Muslims are truly insane!' You know, I was so young
> when I came to Sweden and I got such a negative image of Islam when I watched
> TV. That men beat their wives. Abuse them. Islam, Islam, Islam. But this is, in
> fact, a matter of the so-called Muslims doing stupid things, and then the Swedes
> cannot understand that this is actually not Islam. But I think that the only thing
> one has to do is to change this negative image.

Latifa hopes to put an end to racism and Islamophobia through information.
The task of providing information is understood in terms of *dawa*, and based
on the distinction between 'true religion' and 'cultural misconceptions', 'real'
and 'so-called' Muslims. As indicated in the quotation, this distinction also has
extraordinary implications for gender relations and women's rights. In line with
Latifa's rejection of physical abuse, all women in my study firmly stated that
'honour killings' and 'female genital cutting' are inconsistent with Islam. Out of
the same rationale they took part in deciding the ways in which Islam should be

applied in their everyday life – here and now. Indeed, it would be appropriate for them to work outside the home, study at the university and drive a car. The women admitted to adhering to several religious leaders simultaneously and to taking independent decisions on whose teachings to rely on. This is, undeniably, a break with the tradition to hold on to one single Islamic law school given to any individual Muslim by birth into a certain family and nationality. And this, again, is a sign of religious revival: the sidestepping of traditional authorities (religious, parental) and the participation of 'laymen', women and youth in the reading of the sacred scriptures (Roy 2004).

In other words, the young women were recognised as religious subjects, allowed to enter mosques and to participate in pious activism and learning. They were reflecting on their religion and questioning their parents, but did not break with these crucial points of reference. While their parents could still be proud of their daughters growing up and maturing as Muslims, their religious transformation could also be read as a way of making independent selves, with an alternative 'Islamic' community outside families and ethnic networks.

This reading coincides with the young women's narratives, and makes up a basic argument in their counteracting of the stereotypical description of 'the Muslim woman' as a *passive* victim to multiple oppressions. Thus, I would suggest that the recognition of the women as religious subjects could lead to a general recognition of them as capable persons with voices of their own. And this in turn allows for an understanding of the Islamic revival and Muslim youth associations as a way *out* of sexist and racist oppression.

This kind of 'success story' is an important one to be told. I would, however, like to refer to a parallel story of the women's enrolment in the Islamic movement as a way *into* the reproduction of male dominance, honour ethics, exclusion and hindrance for women's agency. The complexity of the Islamic revival can only be partially represented in the parameters of this chapter, but is a crucial point in my overall analysis of the young women's everyday negotiations on gender and agency.

Acknowledgements

This article draws on the author's research funded by The Swedish Research Council, The Swedish Council for Working Life and Social Research, The Bank of Sweden Tercentenary Foundation and The Royal Swedish Academy of Letters, History and Antiquities.

Chapter 15
Engaging with Teenage Girls' Understandings of Religion and Gender

Jeannine Heynes

Introduction

In the debate over whether or not Britain is in an era of secularisation (i.e. that Britons no longer place religion as a high priority) (Davie 1994; Bruce 1995), many argue that religious education (RE) is becoming increasingly important in the 21st century as a means of understanding one's self and society and therefore has an important place in young people's education (Cush 2007c; Wright 2005). This belief is built into RE's national curriculum which *specifically* aims to 'develop pupils' awareness of themselves and others' (Qualifications and Curriculum Authority 2004, 9). But what are the implications of that awareness when thinking about how RE can shape girls' ideas about gender? This chapter discusses research done with girls between the ages of 14 and 18 and their perceptions of the representation of gender in RE material.

The girls were asked to talk about whether or not religious beliefs and practices were approached using the perspectives and experiences of women, and if, (and how) the gender of God was discussed in the RE classroom. The research project allows for a better understanding of the various ways that girls talk about issues of gender and religion and reveals how the discussion of gender can shed light on what is known about girls' perceptions of religion, as well as how religious discourse can influence girls' understandings of gender. This study is important because very little is known about how girls think and feel about issues related to religion and gender. For many years feminist theologians and philosophers of religion have argued that religious discourse is fundamentally masculine and sexist. By identifying the ways in which women have been ignored, marginalised and/or devalued through religious beliefs and practices, some feminists (Plaskow 1990; Fiorenza 1992; Gross 1993) argue that there needs to be more women included and celebrated in religion, while others argue that *any* teaching about religion reinforces gender stereotypes and gender roles (Basow 1992). While the focus of feminist theology has brought attention to the ways in which all major religions are based on male-dominated ways of knowing and teaching, the literature has focused primarily on the influence religion has had on adult women. Rarely has feminist theology listened to the experiences of girls who are RE students, and who are being asked to learn *about* religions and *from* religions in school

(Qualifications and Curriculum Authority 2004). Studies in gender and education have shown that what girls learn in school affects how they think about themselves and their positions and capabilities within society. Anita Harris (2004a) reminds us that schools are sites where girls interact with ideas and beliefs about gender, and where stereotypes about femininities can either be challenged, reinforced, or go unnoticed. Because RE is a school subject I argue that we need to know more about what students are learning in RE and the effects of this. Discovering how gender is represented in RE is important because it is linked with the way RE influences girls' thinking.

Methods

Two questions I engaged with in my research included:

1. What do girls learn and think about the representation of women and gender in their RE classes?
2. What are the implications for girls, if any, of talking about, and reflecting critically on, the representation of women and gender in their school-based Religious Education?

I chose to work with girls aged 14 to 18 years old, as RE students at this age are asked to 'develop their own values and attitudes in order to recognise their rights and responsibilities in light of their learning about religions' (Qualifications and Curriculum Authority 2004, 30). In other words, RE is *meant* to shape students' views at this level. I therefore made the decision to approach the topic of gender with female RE students whose level of education was already asking them to reflect, be critical, analyse and develop their own thoughts with regard to what they were learning about in RE.

In order to address my research questions I chose to listen to girls talk in focus groups and in individual interviews about their ideas and opinions of gender in RE. Listening to girls' dialogue is useful in understanding how girls understand society. In Elizabeth Frazer's (1988, 353) research with girls, she argues that the process of talking with girls 'tell us more about the concepts and vocabularies extant in the culture, and different groups' access to them'. In other words, the ways in which girls talk about things reveals what they 'know'.

I was able to conduct focus groups and individual interviews with 32 girls. The girls who participated in focus groups were the same girls who were independently interviewed. I spoke with 20 girls from an independent school (Ind) (a privately funded school) and 12 from a comprehensive (Comp) (a state school for children of all abilities). At the independent school I conducted 3 focus groups and 20 individual interviews, and at the comprehensive school I conducted 2 focus groups and 12 individual interviews (2 girls were absent for the interviews) (see Table16.1). Religious backgrounds (which varied in definition) were identified by the girls themselves and were used as a point of reference in the interviews. Since I did not know the names of the girls when I first met them in the focus groups I could not use their names during the transcription (due to lack of time to learn all the girls' names during the focus group meetings). Therefore I decided to concentrate on the flow of the conversation between the girls. At the beginning of each new conversation in the transcription I labelled the first speaker S1 (student number 1) and the responding girls' voices S2, S3 and so on. This allowed me to keep a record of the conversations between certain girls. I labelled myself as 'J' in the conversation.

Table 15.1   Ages and religious backgrounds of female participants in the study by year group

	Number of Girls	Age Range	Religious Backgrounds
Independent School			
- Year 10	8	14–15	4 Christian, 1 Hindu, 2 Atheist, 1 No Religion
- Year 11	8	15	3 Christian, 1 Muslim, 4 No Religion
Sixth Form	4	16–18	4 Christian
Comprehensive School			
- Year 10	8	14–15	3 Christian, 5 No Religion
- Year 11	6	15–16	1 Christian, 5 No Religion
- No Sixth Form	-	-	-

Findings

In the focus groups, the girls were asked questions about how women, and the topic of gender, featured in their RE lessons. What was made clear in all the groups I spoke with was that women and girls were *not* featured very often in their study of religion, and when asked to talk about it with me the girls verbalised how women were portrayed as marginalised characters, if they were mentioned at all. For example in a conversation with year 11 girls I asked: Are women mentioned in the stories you talk about in RE?

S1 – Nope.

S2 – If we do they're made to be weak characters, not necessarily the ones that are strong people.

J – Can you give me an example of that?

S2 – Say when Jesus was in the tomb when the woman went to him she didn't know what to do and she had to run to a man to know.

S3 – Like you know in Noah, it was like Noah made the ark and got all the animals and then he like brought his wife (laughter).

S4 – There's Mary isn't there? I guess that's it.

S1 – There's nothing about women in the textbook.

(Independent school, Yr 11, ages 15–16)

When asked to talk about *why* they thought women were not featured very often in their RE classes the girls began to reveal their impressions of religion and gender in general. Some of the girls' initial responses revealed that they saw gender inequalities primarily located within religions:

Nowadays women do have the same opportunities as men, but it's only really in religion where they're still being stopped to do things. A woman can be in the army but there still can't be like women priests and stuff with the traditions and obviously like in Islam some women are still forced to wear those big black veils. (Ind, A-level)

The girls at the Independent school seemed to distance themselves from religion as they talked about religion as "other". For example religion affected *other* people:

I would think that in different countries [the topic of women and gender] might bother *them* more, but I think now, it doesn't really bother *us* as much, but I'm sure it would to *other* people (Ind, yr 10, my emphasis)

Some girls made reference to religion as something that happened in another time and argued that gender inequalities would inevitably be a part of religion since religion took place in the past.

Maybe because in history it's always been like men being portrayed as bigger than women and religion's kind of like history. (Comprehensive, Yr 10)

The girls in the comprehensive school also distanced themselves from religion as they talked about religion as another formal institution (much like their own classroom and school) that represented authority which the girls felt was unfair, sexist and did not relate to their needs:

> S1 – I think it's unfair I do. Cos men think they have more power and authority over women all the time and they just don't.
>
> S2 – Who wrote the Bible?
>
> S3 – Different men probably.
>
> S2 – Is there any women who wrote the Bible?
>
> S4 – It's 'cos they don't trust women. They think they should just sit home and cook and clean and take care of the children whereas men take care of the world. (Comp, Yr 11)

When they spoke about women in religion the girls' comments revealed that they saw religion to be a negative thing for women:

> S1 – Women get put down. It's always the men that are the most powerful. Women come next.
>
> S2 – Only bad women are in the Bible, like prostitutes and Eve. Then women get punished because of Eve. (Comp, Yr 11)
>
> S1 – Whenever we talk about women our teacher always goes on about Eve and makes her out to be weak and that she didn't have a choice. And why did Eve have to eat the apple? Why couldn't Adam? It's just discrimination. (Comp, Yr 10)

If girls who are a part of RE classes only come in contact with negative impressions of women, or are denied an opportunity to discuss issues of gender in religion, then it is not surprising that these girls should distance themselves from religion, as the message being sent to girls is that religion rarely includes or appreciates people like them.

While many of the girls I spoke to perceived religion as something which was historical, affected other people, and did not relate to them, it was during our discussion about the gender of God where the girls began to reveal how religious discourse can influence and shape people's understandings about gender in the present day. In a discussion about God's gender, ambiguities in the girls' own discourse began to arise. Where they had previously argued that religion was historical and was not something that affected their own lives, it was in the discussion about God's gender where the girls began to realise how people's concepts of a gendered God might have an affect on them, as females, today. When asked whether or not the girls thought the gender of God made a difference to people one of the girls at the independent school made a connection between why God is male and what that says about gender relations in today's society:

> Well it fits into the men having the main role in ritual, where they're all powerful, so I guess a lot of men might find it hard to believe that a woman can be an all powerful God. In today's society, if you're a woman in a high power job, people will say she's a bitch and she's ruthless, but if it was a man they wouldn't say anything about if, if they wanted to be prime minister or some high up job. So I guess that they don't really want, like the idea of a powerful woman, or a Goddess, people see that as bad, they see the idea of a powerful woman as bad. (Ind, A level)

Some of the girls at the comprehensive school expressed the idea that if the gender of God changed then women's positions in today's society would change, revealing that they made a connection between religion and gender relations in today's society. Even though some of the girls thought there might not be a God, most of the girls assumed that things would be different for women today if God was thought of as a female:

> The world would be completely different I think if God was a 'she'. I think women would get respect. 'Cos if we're run by a female. God runs everything. So if God is female then a female controls the world and more respect for women. Women could do more things. (Comp, Yr 11)

The focus group method allowed for consciousness-raising among the girls about women's presence, or rather absence, in their study of religion, as the focus group was the first time these girls had ever been given the opportunity to talk about women and gender in relation to their Religious Education. When the girls were asked how they felt about women having such a low and negative representation in their RE classes the girls revealed how the very concept was new to them:

> I have never really thought about it until just now. (Comp, Yr 11)

> I guess if you think about it, now that you've like asked about it, we've just realised that we don't actually talk about women, but before now we never noticed. (Ind, Yr 10)

When given the opportunity to talk about women and gender in RE the girls enjoyed the process of talking and thinking things through together. It made them aware that there are other perspectives to be heard on the topic of religion, including their own:

> It was good 'cos we haven't done that before, like in school no one speaks about stuff like that (women in religion) but it's good when other people come in and we can talk about it. (Comp, Yr 10)

> It (the focus group) made me think about women and how they are seen. Over the next week I was looking at it and thinking, 'Yeah this is quite unfair. How is this working?' (Ind, Yr 11)

> It made me think how women don't play much of a part in the religious views and things. That made me think, I've never thought of it that way before, 'cos we kind of accept it, in our society, men in religion tend to play a bigger part and I don't think there are many religions that have women as either equal or more powerful, or play bigger parts in the stories and things. I kind of just accepted it because nobody's ever told me any different. (Ind, Yr 10)

Without the perspectives of females, students of RE are only exposed to a masculinised interpretation of religion, ethics and values. These masculinised perspectives shape girls' view of society and themselves. As one of the girls at the independent school explained:

> If you think about it, roughly half the world is women so if you don't look at it (religion) from both male and female points of view it's going to be really one sided and it's not always going to be right. You're not going to get both sides. (Ind, Yr 11)

The girls' negative perceptions, and often ambiguous ways of talking about women and religion, points to the need to emphasise the topic of gender even more so within the RE curriculum so that students are not denied an opportunity to think positively about women within religion and do not become confused or ignorant about gendered implications within religion and in wider society.

By asking girls to think about and respond to questions related to the representation of women and gender in RE I was able to hear how girls worked through their understandings and opinions of religion, women and gender. It must be noted, however, that there are limitations to the method of talk. By listening to girls talk about a certain issue, or answer particular questions, their responses do not necessarily reflect their entire way of thinking. Elizabeth Frazer (1988) recognises that girls' talk must be understood in context, as it will be influenced by group dynamics and/or by individual interviews with the researcher. Holland and Ramazanoglu (1994) also observe the limitations of talk in interviews, as respondents may be limited in their language when talking about new or sensitive issues related to sex, gender and the like. While 'talk' may not reveal the entirety of respondents' thinking, research which allows girls to talk about their thoughts and opinions in a particular context is still important. The method of talking can tease open girls' positions on things and engage them with a process of consciousness-raising allowing them to articulate what they know and how they understand things.

Conclusion

This study engaged with girls' knowledge, opinions and critical analysis of the ways in which religion is taught to them and understood by them. Girls in both schools recognised that women were mentioned less often than men when learning about religion. Pictures of women were not shown in the girls' textbooks or around their RE classroom, and none of the girls in either school appeared knowledgeable about women's roles, contributions or experiences within contemporary religious communities. When talking about religion, many of the girls distanced themselves from religious beliefs and ideas as religion appeared historical or irrelevant, particularly with regard to how religion portrayed women. When the girls were asked to think about the gender of God they expressed that the sole use of calling God 'he' was unfair and sexist. When the girls reflected on the gender of God they recognised how it influenced people's views of gender and the roles of men and women. If, as my research suggests, RE is one of the only places in Britain where girls come in contact with religion, the layers of gendered issues within religion must be reassessed with girls' sense of identity in mind, encouraging belonging and a healthier understanding of themselves and others.

Chapter 16

British Sikh Youth:
Identity, Hair and the Turban

Jasjit Singh

> There's nothing low-key about turban wearing. I had experiences of being chased
> by gangs and being beaten up. I was laughed at by doormen as they refused me
> entry into night clubs; the times they let me in it was the fellow clubbers who
> found me hilarious. I got accustomed to being made to feel not terribly welcome
> anywhere. I remember with horror watching my turban roll down Garnethill,
> having been dislodged by a rather cruel school 'friend'. (Kohli 2006)

This account by Hardeep Singh Kohli highlights some of the racism and ridicule
faced by many young British Sikhs in maintaining the Sikh identity. This chapter
uses the findings of qualitative research to examine these issues, and to understand
what identity meaning(s) uncut hair and the turban have for young British Sikhs in
twenty-first century Britain.

Sikhs are taught about the importance of the uncut hair and turban when
learning about the creation of the community of initiated Sikhs, the *Khalsa* by
the tenth Guru, Guru Gobind Singh. Tradition describes how on *Vaisakhi*
1699 Guru Gobind Singh, instructed the *Khalsa* to adopt the 'Five Ks', so called
because the Punjabi name for each item begins with the letter 'K' (Nesbitt 2005,
51):

- *Kesh* (uncut hair)
- *Kangha* (comb)
- *Kirpan* (sword)
- *Kachh* (cotton breeches)
- *Kara* (steel or iron bangle)

Of these five, it is the *Kesh* which, according to Singh, is the main symbol of
the Sikh faith (2000, 9). The situation with the turban, however, is slightly more
complex. As Singh and Tatla (2006, 127) note, although the turban is not one of
the five Ks, it is 'synonymous with Sikhs and .. has become the premier symbol
of communal identity and its honour, whereas an inability to wear it is a sign of
collective dishonour'.

The role of the uncut hair and turban as key aspects of the Sikh identity is
therefore clear. As studies of the Sikh identity have primarily focused on the

historical evolution of these symbols rather than their contemporary meaning (e.g. McLeod 2001), this chapter will focus on understanding what kinds of identities are provided to young British Sikhs by the hair and turban. The findings presented are the result of 25 semi-structured interviews held with young Sikhs between the ages of 18 and 32, sampled purposively based on the different ways in which Sikhs manage their hair and turbans.[1] As young people are notoriously difficult to get hold of as they tend to be very busy and mobile (Denton and Smith 2001) half of the respondents were interviewed at a Sikh youth camp, with the other half being gathered through snowball sampling.

Hair and identity

In her study of hair practices amongst black women, Banks describes hair as an 'important medium by which people define others and themselves ... [which] can reflect notions about perceptions, identity, and self-esteem' (2000, 26). In this regard, a male turban wearer with a full beard considered the keeping of uncut hair in its unshorn state as 'our *nishaani* [sign], it's what defines a Sikh'. Indeed for some, it appears to be the practices related to uncut hair and the turban above those of worship and belief which identify an individual as a Sikh. When asked why he did not regard himself as a Sikh, a male with a haircut felt that this was because 'I haven't got the Sikh identity yet.' A female with a haircut noted that she felt 'less of a Sikh – like whenever I go to *Gurdwara*, sometimes I feel like I really shouldn't have cut my hair'. From this brief assessment, it appears that most young Sikhs are aware of the importance attached to uncut hair within the Sikh community whether or not they adhere to these hair practices themselves.

The very fact that some Sikh youth are themselves making efforts to transmit the importance of uncut hair to their peers demonstrates that they regard the uncut hair as a significant part of their identity. At the 'International Keep Your Hair Day' organised by Sikh youth at a Leicester *Gurdwara* in July 2007, many of the reasons given for keeping the hair were scientific ('The Hair produces vitamin D') as well as religious ('Guru Gobind Singh Ji said that the uncut hair is his stamp'). It may be hypothesised that the exposure of these Sikh youth to their non-Sikh peers has given rise to the need to present scientific as well as religious reasons for the keeping of uncut hair.

The manner in which the hair is kept also provides a form of identity, as demonstrated by a non-turban-wearing Sikh female who was clearly aware of the identity meanings transmitted within the Sikh community by keeping or cutting the hair: 'I'm probably viewed by many as being religious especially because

---

[1]   In total, six categories of Sikh were developed: Male wearing the turban with full beard, Male wearing the turban with trimmed beard, Male with haircut, Female wearing the turban, Female not wearing the turban with uncut hair, Female not wearing the turban with haircut.

I don't cut my head hair and I attend the *Gurdwara* fairly regularly and in that sense I "look" and act religious.' This perception is further highlighted by the observation of a Sikh female whose friend 'has really long uncut hair but she smokes – that really annoys me that she doesn't cut her hair yet she smokes'. The view that Sikh women with uncut hair are somewhat more religious than those without concurs with Miller's observation that in Indian culture, long hair has generally symbolised tradition whereas short hair symbolises modernity and defiance (1998, 264).

Although the uncut hair is only kept as an external symbol by Sikh women, it is clear that Sikh males also need to consider the meanings conveyed by their most public piece of hair, the beard. This male with a haircut, growing his hair in order to eventually wear a turban, highlighted the importance of managing the growth of hair, to ensure that the correct hair meanings were being conveyed to his peers:

> I wanted to have my head covered before I started growing my beard – just because it looks very Islamic … When I was keeping my hair and when my beard was quite long … my closest mates [would ask] what are you doing at Sikh soc, you should be at Islamic society.

This supports Olivelle's assertion that the meanings conveyed by hair 'are derived always from its relationship or opposition to other ritual functions of hair existing within the same society' (1998, 38). In addition to the meanings conveyed to society in general, it is clear that hair practices convey special identity meanings within particular communities. One respondent, for example, highlighted that 'it's the uncut beard that differentiates between people … to decide whether someone is religious or not'. It appears therefore that for Sikh males, it is the combination of hair practices which convey a particular meaning, as this male with a turban and full beard describes:

> If you've trimmed, by that stage you've lost the respect for the *Baal* [hair] anyway, so the *Pag* [turban] really isn't anything of any meaning.

The method by which hair is managed clearly conveys a specific meaning, with religiosity being represented by uncut head hair on a Sikh female and the combination of the turban and full beard on a Sikh male. As we shall see, this distinction in hair practices is being challenged by some young Sikh women using one of the most distinctive symbols of the Sikhs, the turban.

The turban and identity

From her ethnographic study of the turban practices of Sikh women in North America, Mahmood concludes that the hair and turban are a public symbol of commitment, respect and power which indicate a Sikh's 'allegiance to the orders of the Guru and a commitment to remain very firmly in the world while seeking spiritual salvation' (Mahmood and Brady 1999, 52–3). Nevertheless, as with the keeping of the uncut hair, the wearing of the turban alone does not indicate an adherence to the ideals of the Sikh Gurus. For some, the wearing of the turban is 'now devoid of religious connotation [and] is simply a part of my attire' (Singh 1997, 31) whereas others only wear the turban due to familial pressures:

> There's this boy I know who wears a turban but he says straight out that he only
> wears it because his mum and dad don't want him to cut his hair.

As a container for the uncut hair, reasons for wearing the turban are linked to those for keeping the hair. Like the hair, the turban is regarded by many young Sikhs as a religious requirement as 'it's an order by Guru Gobind Singh that Sikhs have to be distinctive'. As well as this religious reason, the turban also clearly provides young Sikhs with a sense of belonging:

> It's the way Sikhs are supposed to pronounce your identity, announce your
> identity, your religion, your faith. If you're a Sikh you wear a turban, the two
> go hand in hand.

The idea that the turban is a requirement of being a Sikh is highlighted in the *Sikh Rehat Maryada*, the code of conduct for Sikhs published in Amritsar, in which, Chapter X, Article XVI, states that 'For a Sikh, there is no restriction or requirement as to dress except that he must wear Kachhehra ... and turban. A Sikh woman may or may not tie turban'.[2]

Despite this optional status of the turban for Sikh women, Sikh women belonging to Sikh groups which emphasise the wearing of turbans for both genders[3] are using the turban to emphasise the Sikh Gurus' teachings on equality. As Mahmood explains, even though 'it is difficult to find references to women being told how to keep their hair or wear their turban ... in the eyes of contemporary Sikh women,

---

[2]   Available at http://www.sgpc.net/rehat_maryada/section_four.html, accessed 23 July 2007.

[3]   The main groups in question are the Akhand Kirtani Jatha (AKJ) and the Damdami Taksal (DDT) and Sikhs belonging to the 3HO movement. As Nesbitt explains: 'Women members of the Akhand Kirtani Jatha are especially conspicuous as they wear a small under-turban beneath their *chunni* (scarf). The reason for this is that ... the Jatha lists among the Five Ks not *kesh* (hair) but *keski* (the headcovering in question). Their argument is that the Ks are all required of women as well as men, and that a part of the body itself cannot be one of the Five Ks' (Nesbitt 2005, 84). The DDT also assert that 'the Guru's command is for both men and women to wear turbans', although they disagree with the AKJ stance on the *keski* (see the *Damdami Taksal* Code of Conduct which states that '*Keski* is not a *kakkar* (one of the five K's)', http://www.ualberta.ca/~rvig/rehat.pdf, accessed 11 December 2007). Regarding the 3HO movement, Nesbitt explains that 'both male and female followers dress in white, including equally tall white turbans for both' (Nesbitt 2005, 101).

this absence suggests that all Sikhs, men or women, were included in the Guru's commandments' (1999, 53). Nevertheless, as this female with uncut hair observes, a Sikh female wearing the turban conveys a different meaning to a turban wearing male, and brings with it an extra responsibility:

> I don't want to have to live up to someone else's ideals … it's what I think other members of the community would assume my behaviour to be if I were wearing a *Dastaar* [turban] … [it] would be over and above a male contemporary wearing the *Pag* [turban].

This notion of the turban carrying a sense of responsibility was noted by respondents of both genders, especially with reference to living in British society:

> You're almost carrying the mantle for Sikhism in a way, 'cos you're such a minority … I think you've got a really, really big responsibility in this country. In India, a Sikh steals, fine – you've got another Sikh who's doing good. Here I'm the only Sikh in my area. I do one bad thing, then that reflects badly on all other Sikhs.

The fact that the turban carries a responsibility and represents religiosity and conformity may explain Kalsi's observation that the number of young British male Sikhs wearing the turban is diminishing. From his analysis of Sikh marriage advertisements in a Punjabi newspaper, Kalsi notes that in only 1 of 33 advertisements does the Sikh family state that their son wears a turban. However in contrast to Kalsi's suggestion of a 'growing preference among Sikh girls for clean-shaven boys' (1997) of the 11 females interviewed, 10 expressed a preference for marrying a turbaned Sikh. Indeed, 1 found the turban 'necessary and attractive' while another 'respect[ed] Sikh guys who keep their identity'. However, the fact that only 1 turbaned Sikh male wished to marry a turbaned Sikh female, indicates that the turban is still predominantly a symbol for male Sikhs. The difference in the turban meanings broadcast by males and females was also demonstrated by a male turban wearer who explained that he would choose not to marry a female turban wearer 'because a lot of female turban wearers may belong to a particular group which I am not a member of'.

Clearly therefore, the turban transmits multiple meanings depending who is wearing and who is viewing the turban. Although the style of 'Sikh' turban is distinctive from those worn by other minority ethnic groups, for example, Muslims (Schmid 2001), the fact that not all in wider society are aware of these differences has made the wearing of the turban problematic for many young British Sikhs. As one respondent explained 'anyone with a turban is assumed to be a Taliban or Islamic militant'. The widely publicised meaning of the turban as a symbol linked to terrorism appears to be a growing concern for young Sikhs wearing the turban in Britain, given the number of hate crimes committed against Sikhs worldwide since the attacks of 11 September 2001 (Sidhu and Gohil 2008).

Conclusion

As this chapter has demonstrated, although hair and turban practices vary among young British Sikhs, both of these symbols carry important meanings. As every single respondent was aware of the status of the hair and turban within the Sikh community, it is clear that the cultural and religious importance of these symbols is being successfully transmitted to young Sikhs either by parents, or increasingly by young Sikhs themselves. The fact that young British Sikhs are now also making efforts to transmit the importance of these symbols to their Sikh peers highlights the importance of identity in an increasingly pluralistic society, and demonstrates an increasing confidence among young British Sikhs in viewing themselves as both British and Sikh. The methods being used by these young Sikhs highlight the increasing role of new technologies in identity transmission, as young Sikhs around the world try to present the turban as fashionable and appealing (MacKinnon 2003) and in the case of the founder of the 'Rate My Turban' website, 'to showcase turbans as an art form' (Whitwell 2007).

As well as being markers of identity, the hair and turban practices of young British Sikhs appear to primarily convey identity meanings *within the Sikh community*, as opposed to wider society. As 'meaning is established only when the response elicited by some symbol is the "same" for the one who produces the symbol as for the one who receives it' (Mead 1930, 133–40), the turban will only make Sikhs distinctive if wider society is aware of the difference between Sikh turbans and those of other minority ethnic groups. Indeed, many of the hate crimes faced by Sikhs all over the world have resulted from the fact that both Sikhs and Osama Bin Laden wear turbans, and that the general public are not aware of any difference between the two.

The events of 9/11 clearly added to the pressure felt by those young British Sikhs who maintain a distinct identity, especially those who also maintain a full beard. Even so, whereas Sikhs all over the world have removed their turbans in order to disassociate themselves from the image of Osama Bin Laden (Grennan 2001), none of the British Sikh respondents said that they had done so, or would do so, even though some had experienced increased racism post 9/11. It can be hypothesised that young British Sikhs continue to wear the turban post 9/11 primarily because they have the confidence to do so being a well-established community and also because Sikhs have won the right to wear the turban in Britain (Singh 2005,161). The turban may also be being used by many young British Sikhs to distinguish themselves from British Muslims, given that the majority of the Muslim population in Britain do not wear turbans, in accordance with Olivelle's view that meanings of hair are derived in opposition to other ritual functions of hair existing within the same society (1998, 38).

Returning to the main theme of this volume, 'Religion and Youth', the fact that a number of the respondents had cut their hair and removed their turbans just before or during their teenage years highlights the impact of biological factors on identity practices, as changes caused during adolescence lead to an increase in self awareness and to the growing importance of body image (Simon 1995, 46). Rather than generalising on reasons why some young Sikhs discard the hair and turban whilst others take these symbols on, further research is required to understand which factors impact most on this process. Nevertheless, from the strong justifications given by those respondents who keep their hair and turban, it is clear that these symbols carry an important meaning. Whilst for some the maintenance of these symbols is simply a matter of distinctiveness and for demonstrating group membership, for others it is these symbols which act a daily reminder of their commitment to Sikhism. Although contemporary Sikh practice demonstrates differing hair and turban rules for males and females, young British Sikhs appear to be comfortably managing the differing identity meanings presented by these articles of faith depending on the particular context in which they find themselves. As symbols of ethnic identity, it is clear that the uncut hair and turban will continue to be an important if not the most important component of the identity of young British Sikhs.

Chapter 17

'A Place to Grow Spiritually and Socially': The Experiences of Young Pilgrims to Lourdes

Alana Harris

In seeking to account for the revival of pilgrimage in our contemporary culture, the Oxford Dominican Timothy Radcliffe has characterized this form of spiritual seeking as particularly attractive to young people as it may be 'expressive of deep conviction, but also give space for the unsure, those who travel hoping to find something on the way or [even] at the end' (2005, 10). This form of contemporary spiritual journeying and communal gathering can take a variety of guises across Christian religious traditions – from the unprecedented numbers of young people attending events like Spring Harvest or World Youth Day, through to the revival of more 'traditional' pilgrimage paths traversing Europe and popularized within literary and youth culture such as Częstochowa and Santiago de Compostela, (Galbraith 2000; Coleman and Elsner, 1995; Coleman and Eade, 2004; Badone and Roseman, 2004). This chapter will examine one specific example of this growing global phenomenon, namely the increasing numbers of British youth travelling to the Marian shrine at Lourdes in France to assist sick or elderly pilgrims and to explore their own spirituality (see Lamb and Siedlecka 2006; Lambert, 2004; Vayne et al., 2007, 44–5). Stemming from a larger study of motives for and experiences of pilgrimage across Christian and New Age/Pagan sites, this chapter draws upon extensive fieldwork, detailed questionnaire data and in-depth interviews with youth travelling with the (Arch)Dioceses of Westminster and Salford and as an independent group from Limerick. It contends that through prayer and ritual, socializing and the establishment of interpersonal relationships, as well as through acts of self-abnegation and service, twenty-first century pilgrims to this nineteenth-century shrine in the Pyrenees are offered, as one young Mancunian expressed it, a space 'to develop my faith and to grow spiritually and socially' [Pilgrim #12, 2007]. This chapter will explore the implications of these dimensions of pilgrimage for understandings of the ways in which some young people are choosing to interrogate their spirituality within a traditional, but also profoundly modern, transformed and customized context.

Background to the research: The 'Pilgrimage Project' and research methodologies

The material used in this chapter derives from written responses gathered from 27 young pilgrims from Burnley in 2006, and the main phases of the Lourdes fieldwork completed for the Pilgrimage Project (conducted out of the Ian Ramsey Centre, Oxford and funded by a Fundação Bial Bursary) in July 2007 and July–August 2008. Participant-observation and data collection took the form of a detailed, interview-format questionnaire, comprised in the first section of validated psychological scales related to magical ideation, religious belief, health psychology and personality. The second section of the survey encompassed socio-demographic and qualitative questions designed to elicit the motivational, behavioural and cognitive aspects of the pilgrimage experience. The completed sample for the Lourdes site totalled 117 questionnaires from pilgrims from the north and south of England and the Republic of Ireland, 50 of which were collected from young people aged 18–30. From this subset, 32 respondents were female and 18 respondents male – a distribution which is broadly in line with the gender breakdown amongst young people across the pilgrimage group as a whole. Moreover, from within this sample, 77.6 per cent of questionnaire respondents had been on pilgrimage to Lourdes before – a finding which is broadly comparable to a study of Dutch Catholics to Lourdes (and other pilgrimage sites) conducted by Post et al. (1998). As this earlier research found, for many of these travellers a pilgrimage was a 'rite of confirmation' rather than a 'rite of passage' (Van Gennep 1960; Turner and Turner 1978). Nevertheless, as this chapter also seeks to illustrate, for a substantial minority of young people visiting the shrine for the first time, this site and the 'sacred space' constructed by the pilgrimage process might also provide an initiatory opportunity for spiritual exploration, encounter and transformation. As the remainder of this discussion will tease out, a pilgrimage to Lourdes allowed these young people a context in which to explore and deepen their understandings of themselves and their spirituality, to establish and strengthen friendships and inter-generational contacts, and to situate themselves within a religious tradition and history, whilst also negotiating their relationships to church hierarchy and doctrinal authority.

Sacred sites and self-exploration: identity, affectivity and contemporary spirituality

In many ways, the continuing popularity of pilgrimage to Lourdes with young people offers an interesting context in which to explore the nature and purpose of contemporary 'spiritual seeking' (Bellah et al. 1985; Giddens 1991; Wuthnow 1998; Garnett et al. 2006) – for this form of exploration may offer an authentic, experiential and flexible vehicle for self-construction and expression which does not fit neatly into existing models arguing for a 'detraditionalization' of authority

(Heelas 1996) or a 'spiritual revolution' confined to New Age and holistic practices outside the mainstream churches (Heelas and Woodhead, 2005). Indeed, as Flory and Miller have argued in a North American context, 'this individual questing, searching, and seeking for spirituality and spiritual fulfillment does not necessarily connote a complete break with all commitments to religious communities of the past' (2008, 157). In written responses collected from Lancastrian youth aged 16–25 on a 2006 diocesan-based pilgrimage, virtually all the respondents identified the pilgrimage as a time of 'personal journey', to explore 'many questions about their faith', 'grow closer to God' and as a flexible and adaptive forum for reflection, exploration and thinking about life direction. Similar qualitative reflections about the pilgrimage as a liminal forum for exploration and experiential growth also emerged strongly from the 2007 and 2008 fieldwork in this study, with one 35-year-old male describing his pilgrimage as 'a re-focusing of my life, peace, healing and I turned 30 here, so consider it important to be in such a place at such crossroads in life' [Pilgrim #6, 2008]. A female in her late twenties also articulated a sense of Lourdes as a space 'away from "the world" to reassess priorities … (especially) as I am about to start a new job, so I am glad of the opportunity to reflect on changes in my life' [#18, 2008]. Less reflexive and more open-ended searching was present in the responses of two 18-year-old females from London, who explained their reasons for coming to Lourdes as 'curiosity and for the experience' [#10, 2008], as well as 'to answer some questions' [#14, 2008]. Given the high number of 'repeat' pilgrimages, many of the explanations for coming (back) to Lourdes centred on 'spiritual recharging', or the opportunity to 'deepen my understanding of the meaning and purpose of religious practices and … concentrated time to focus on my faith' [#4, 2008]. Nevertheless, this was also frequently accompanied by an articulation of the differences between each pilgrimage, for example, in the reflections of a 27-year-old Mancunian solicitor who wrote of her fifth journey to Lourdes in 2007:

> I have felt a real sense of community and direction. I feel happy. I have felt physical and emotional feelings which I have never before. I have relaxed and become more open. [#29, 2007]

Within a significant number of the responses there were also narratives premised around themes of questing, questioning and spiritual curiosity, exemplified by the 30-year-old 'Buddhist student' who accompanied the Westminster pilgrimage to 'appreciate the challenges facing others, (to experience) a greater sense of belonging in the community (and to develop) a greater understanding of my own spirituality' [#27, 2008]. Her account was not dissimilar to that of a 27 year-old male IT worker from the north of the country, who reflected:

> I have looked at many religions [and] it appears that religion is designed to build hope. It does this very well. Religion works as long as people believe in it.

However, experimentation is essential. I have witnessed apparent miracles and
religious experiences but this can be explained through hope. [#19, 2007]

Writing on the spirituality of those known as Generations X and Y, Lynch has
identified the desire of young people to 'seek meaning that feels personally
authentic to them rather than being prepared to accept "pre-packed" truths provided
by religious, political or corporate organizations' (Lynch 2002, ix). Nevertheless,
for some young people, as for these Catholic pilgrims (Figure 17.1), an interrogation
of faith and a search for the spiritual did not necessarily lead to a rejection of
traditional religious forms for, as Charles Taylor contemplates, religious questioning
can also take place within 'extremely powerful religious communities, because
that's where many people's sense of the spiritual will lead them' (2002, 112).

Figure 17.1   Salford Youth at the Torchlight procession, July 2007. Reproduced
              with kind permission of Salford Diocese

Another dimension of contemporary spirituality highlighted within the broader
research focusing on young people and spirituality is an emphasis placed upon
affective and bodily religious experiences and the prevalence of therapeutic
preoccupations. These dimensions are also present in the Lourdes fieldwork,
unsurprisingly given the reputation of the shrine over its 150-year-long history
for miracles, healing and conversion [see Harris 1999; Kaufman 2005]. A typical
response was that of 16-year-old Londoner writing of the benefits deriving from
his pilgrimage as 'spiritual energy and physical energy which I often seem to lack'
[#2, 2008]. The language of 'well-being' was also common throughout many
reflections [see #4, 2008], with an 18-year-old Mancunian elaborating:

> I feel that Lourdes gives me personally a sense of well-being … It enables me to focus on my faith and allows for growth. Praying in Lourdes is a different experience. I feel there was a connection with those I have lost of late and it was a very unique experience. [#59, 2007]

For some young people, such as a 15-year-old girl from Burnley, the pilgrimage enabled her to 'feel happier spiritually and more comfortable with my personality and my life in general' [#36, 2007], whereas others were explicit about their desire for physical (or spiritual) regeneration:

> I came for healing and to be close to God and his Mother. One [request for] healing is for me but more importantly for others in my life … I have enjoyed being able to help and believe that by helping others, I help myself. [#6, 2008]

In a section of the questionnaire which asked respondents voluntarily to write about any 'physical, emotional or personal problems' from which they currently suffer, around one-fifth mentioned work/family problems or mental health issues, with a smaller number also highlighting physiological concerns. A deeper engagement with these difficulties, and the hope of an amelioration of distress suffered from them, were anticipated outcomes of the pilgrimage for this sub-category of respondents. In oral reflections, this was described as the desire for 'healing', which might encompass understanding and acceptance of an illness, rather than the search for a 'cure'. These aspirations were also present, although more fulsomely articulated, in the descriptions of older pilgrims, who described their pilgrimage as a way of dealing with 'brokenness and grief' [#13, IR2008] and as providing a 'sense of peace', having come 'to Lourdes very troubled' and 'crying over things' whilst there [#18, IR2008].

Collective spirituality, cross-generational contacts and re-engagement with church tradition

In his recent study of the religious identity of British youth influenced by or raised as Roman Catholics, Fulton has examined the premium placed on an experience of intimacy with God by those who remained in the institutional church, and also the strongly communal emphasis within the spirituality of many of these young adults (2000, 137–59; 1999, 166–8). Similarly, within a study of a variety of religious communities appealing to American young people, Flory and Miller discuss the emergence of a form of spirituality which they call 'expressive communalism' – a spirituality which places 'a new, or perhaps renewed, emphasis on an embodied worship and service, and a desire for seeking, creating, and committing to a particular faith community' (2008, 185–93). Such communal and social aspirations, supplementing the expressive, experiential and embodied spirituality already described, also emerge within this study of young people's expectations and enjoyment of the pilgrimage experience in Lourdes.

Structured communal services and devotional rituals inevitably formed a large part of the daily activities in Lourdes and the level of reported participation by young people in daily mass, the torchlight processions and communal prayer events (such as the rosary) over the course of the pilgrimage was therefore quite high. This was, however, in sharp contrast to the level of institutional involvement of many of these young people when at home in Britain, with 14 per cent of those responding to a question on mass attendance at home indicating they 'rarely or never' attend mass, a further 14 per cent reporting attendance of church services 'monthly', and a further 12 respondents (25 per cent) declining to answer the question. Interestingly, these overtly religious and ritually-structured components of the pilgrimage were identified by some as the most important and transformative aspects of their time in Lourdes, providing for one 20 year-old an 'emotional sense of unity' because 'group prayer sometimes feels stronger than praying alone' [#17, 2008]. Within the 2006 sample, the Burnley youth wrote also about the weight of history evoked by the torchlight processions, the sense of the 'sacred' within the Grotto, the use of statues and candles to aid prayer, and the opportunity to view the liturgy in a deeper way. For example, one 16 year-old wrote about learning 'to pray properly, instead of praying alongside the monotonous drone of the mass' and another young man of 20 spoke of his 'greater appreciation of liturgy and public and formal prayer' which aided his 'feelings of groundedness, centredness and orientation' [#28, 2008]. For some this was explicitly tied to a re-appreciation of the history and traditions of the shrine, such these striking reflections from a 22 year-old female:

> Lourdes is a humbling place. Mary appeared to Bernadette who was impoverished and uneducated. It has reminded me of the importance and beauty of simplicity. It has also shown me powerfully the love and faith of others and through them, God's love. [#16, 2008]

Whilst others also wrote about the experience of 'closeness to God and Mary' [e.g. #19 and #25, 2008], for the vast majority of young people surveyed, compared with the older cohort, Marian devotions were not an important aspect of their faith and there were certainly others who were not impressed by such structured prayers and rituals, candidly responding: 'I don't really like them' [#10, 2008]. For an overwhelming proportion of the young pilgrims, an important aspect of these communal activities was the sense it gave of solidarity and a collective identity – such as this reflection from a woman in her late twenties:

> The religious and spiritual experiences are not usually appreciated until you get back to 'real life' and get over the post-pilgrimage exhaustion. However, this year I experienced huge relief – I am not the only Christian in the world after all! It is a fantastic opportunity to be with other Christians and experience the true universality of the Church. [#18, 2008]

This sense of a safe place to explore one's spirituality and to express one's Christianity was expressed in liminal terms, of being outside 'real life' when on pilgrimage. Nevertheless, at the same time the pilgrimage also created an appreciation of what could be deemed really important, improving 'my sense of purpose … awareness of "real life" and the misfortunes others have to bear' [#12, 2008]. Pilgrimage to Lourdes operated for some as an inversion or respite from the structures and pressures of the ordinary, whilst for others it simultaneously offered a critique and challenge to perceptions of an individualized, secularized and sanitized 'ordinary' lifestyle.

Contact with and assistance of the elderly and sick pilgrims was the most reported activity undertaken by young people in Lourdes, facilitated by the structured arrangements made for this assistance in the hospitals and at the shrine (Figure 17.2). Common to the responses was the sense of purpose, fulfilment and self-worth that this involvement provided. Many explicitly reflected on the ways in which this social ethic and opportunity to serve counteracted their initial repulsion at the overt commercialism of the Pyrenean town, transforming this from a 'holiday' to something 'fun and social' but also meaningful through 'the building of relationship, a sense of being needed, and [the creation of] a whole new view of the way [we] look at things' (Field notes, 2006).

Figure 17.2   Some of the 350 young people who were part of the 2007 pilgrimage. Reproduced with kind permission of Salford Diocese

Similar sentiments were expressed by an 18-year-old schoolgirl who highlighted the 'sense of community' forged by 'giving up my time to help people' and the way in which she now feels 'more accepting that people are not necessarily like me' [#31, 2007]. Another 17-year-old American student travelling with the Salford group spoke of 'the shock that comes with working with those who are completely helpless', with the result that 'I have learned to be proud of myself and ... grateful for all that I have' [#33, 2007]. This was echoed by a London university student who reported: 'The sick evoke an emotional response, as does the atmosphere. [A] sense of duty and being called. Being with the sick changes my mind/outlook more than any other activity' [#17, 2008]. As a Mancunian female in her twenties surmised, this 'care for the sick and learn[ing] from their experiences and what they can teach me' was part of her motivation for coming to Lourdes, but this was also supplemented by a desire to 'make companions and spend time with other Catholics, allowing time for discussion about major issues of faith I may struggle with' [#13, 2007]. Whilst working with the sick provided the primary focus for these experiences of belonging and feeling needed, this was supplemented for some by the friendship and support also experienced from other older Catholic pilgrims and clergy, forging 'a real sense of caring and community, selflessness and understanding' [#52, 2007].

Figure 17.3   A night out at *Miam Miam's*, 2007. Reproduced with kind permission
               of Salford Diocese

This sense of shared community and common identity was reinforced by the overtly social dimensions of young people's experiences in Lourdes, particularly the sense of sociability and community forged by the after-shift activities and nightlife. Whilst certain sensationalized newspaper reports juxtapose such 'secular' activities with 'pious' notions of pilgrimage, such as a full-page *Sunday Telegraph* spread condemning 'shameful binge drinking' in Lourdes (Allen, 2006) such usually-measured activities may also be seen as building '*communitas*' or creating a Durkheimian sense of 'intimacy' – for example, the Salford group has their own regular drinking haunt, *Miam Miams*, where priests, youth and older pilgrims share a pint and exchange tales of the day (Figure 17.3). The importance of this element of the pilgrimage for the young is reflected in a representative reflection from a 23 year-old: 'I was expecting hard work, hard play/socializing and gaining spiritual strength from this pilgrimage. I also expected to gain new friends from this pilgrimage … and catch up with old ones' (#26, 2007). Another male university student, describing his third return turn trip to Lourdes, enthused: 'I love it, I love the idea of working your pants off all day and having a great drink afterwards. There's a sense of community, of family, here that I've never found anywhere else' [Field notes, 2006]. The earlier-mentioned Buddhist accompanying the Westminster pilgrimage seemed to sum up this sense of collective identity and cross-generational community in her reflections on the experience of the pilgrimage: 'I had an acute sense of being connected to others and as though there was a force of unconditional love and understanding uniting us all' [#27, 2008]. Within all these accounts, there may be discerned an estimation of the pilgrimage as a form of spiritual quest, but also as the American sociologist of religion Wade Clark Roof contends, an example of the ways in which contemporary spirituality is most effective when it engages the 'emotions and impulses, involving not just heads and hearts but bodies' (1999, 46).

Conclusion

This chapter has briefly teased out some of the implications of a study of pilgrimage for our understandings of contemporary religiosity and spiritual searching, and has sought to illustrate ways in which some young people are using institutionalized religion and traditional rituals in the modern search for meaning, personal well-being, identity formation and collective belonging. It has sought to sketch some of the varied experiences and diverse motivations behind this embodied form of spiritual journeying – implicitly endorsing a methodology for examining contemporary spirituality which takes seriously 'lived' religious practices and the various ways in which 'belief' may be defined and explored beyond statistics or single measures of religiosity. For this reason I will conclude with the written reflections of an 18-year-old girl in the final year of school which seem to encapsulate the varied issues this chapter has explored:

> [I came to Lourdes] to meet new people and make new friends. To feel closer to
> God. To feel peace of mind afterwards and spiritually stronger … [I feel] proud
> that I have done something good this week by helping others. [#64, 2007]

For this young woman, as for many of her contemporaries, a pilgrimage to Lourdes allowed the exploration of a personal, embodied spirituality, exposure to collective religious experiences and the formation of an intense relationship with God and with fellow believers. To this could be added the expression of altruistic impulses and the enjoyment of travelling and leisure time. For this young woman, as many others surveyed within this research, Lourdes provides a place to grow spiritually and socially.

Chapter 18

Religious Socialisation and a Reflexive Habitus: Christian Youth Groups as Sites for Identity Work

Nicholas M. Shepherd

In this chapter I argue that young people are involved in a process of identity work around being 'Christians' and advocate that an understanding of this process is one rooted in their development of a reflexive faith habitus. I will begin with a brief account of how socialisation within Christian communities is largely failing as a mechanism for faith transmission and suggest one reason for this as being that young people have a 'choice' whether to continue to believe or not. From this I build on work which looks at how young people negotiate choices over identity and apply this to analyse data from an empirical study on young people's participation in Christian youth groups.

Faith in a changing world – religious socialisation and choice

A steady stream of research (Kay and Francis 1996; Voas and Crockett 2005) suggests that growing up in a family that espouses and participates in a particular faith tradition does not mean that a young person will automatically adopt their parents' faith. Voas and Crockett propose that at best such young people have a 50/50 chance of 'believing and belonging' into adulthood. Such disaffiliation marks a 'failure in religious socialisation [resulting] in whole generations being less active *and* believing less than the ones that came before' (2005, 20). Voas and Crocket argue that intergenerational transmission of faith is the fault line where secularisation is felt within the faith community. Attributing more specific causality is difficult and an ongoing source of enquiry. However, a strong candidate for consideration is perhaps 'choice'.

In surveying the influence and relationship between modernity and religion, MacLaren (2004) proposes that the notion of having choice is crucial to understanding faith and identity in late-modern culture. Traditionally, in pre-Reformation Europe, the ability to choose to believe was not an option, being Christian provided for a 'general need for identity within a sacred society' (MacLaren 2004, 101). However, in a de-traditionalising society such a choice is available and viable and MacLaren suggests that it is at the juncture of young adulthood such choice is 'forced upon young people' (MacLaren 2004, 101). The conditions that influence and affect this choice are necessarily complex, which is why Schweitzer (2000, 2004) argues that rather than looking for explanations for trends in affiliation and disaffiliation in 'grand theories', such as secularisation or lifecycle theory, greater attention should be focused on biography and emerging theory from such research. Biographical studies attest to the collision of influences and events that affect faith and identity which become apparent from qualitative investigation of young people's life courses and lived experiences of faith (Schweitzer 2000, 94). Such perspectives have long been the forte of empirically driven studies of youth identity within the sociological and cultural study of youth. Unfortunately, very little research within this field is conducted with an eye to the relationship of religion and identity (Spalek and Imtoual 2008).

Choice in a changing world – the dynamics of identity

The necessity to make choices around identity is helpfully given the shorthand of 'identity work' (Johnson et al. 2004, 265). Identity is not 'found' but discovered through effort or as the result of something worked towards (Bauman 2004, 15–16). Such work can be understood as a requirement to appreciate and integrate one's understanding of self in relation to the shared histories and practices that we participate in (Hall 1996, 13). A key tension in assessing identity from an empirical perspective is whether to favour the agency of the individual in navigating and assimilating their identity or whether identity is a function of the groups to which individuals belong; this is a moot point within the cultural study of youth (Blackman 2005, 14–15). Some favour a modified retention of collective 'social identities' such as those formed through place, class and employment (Furlong and Cartmel 1997, 113). Others suggest sub-cultures or scenes to be the sites where young people engage in pivotal identity work (Hebdige 1979; Thornton 1995; Maira and Soep 2005) or stress the importance of identity work though engagement with popular culture and associated lifestyles (Willis 1990; Bennett 2000; Miles 2000). Miles suggests that preference towards favouring agency or social context is belied by the use of two key theorists: Anthony Giddens (reflexivity) or Pierre Bourdieu (habitus) (Miles 2000: 19ff.).

Giddens offers a high view of agency in forming identity. In common with Beck (1992), Giddens sees there being an inherent *risk* to understanding of self within late modern life. In response, 'self-identity becomes a *reflexively* organised endeavour' where individuals engage in 'life planning' – weighing risks in the light of knowledge they gather or seek out from those with expertise to assist their choices (Giddens 1991, 5). Giddens does not deny that social conditions affect life choices; agency is both inhibited and augmented by socio-economic factors (Giddens 1984, 15–16). However, use of his theory tends to emphasise the ability of the individual to make choices and make sense (coherence narratives) of their life decisions (cf. Devadason 2007). In contrast, use of Bourdieu tends to emphasise an identity determined by social context, especially through early childhood socialisation (Jenkins 1992, 178–97). Bourdieu is associated with the notion of 'habitus' (Bourdieu 1977a). Habitus is a theoretical construct to explain how a person adopts views and practices within specific 'cultural fields' within which they are embedded (Webb et al. 2002). Habitus informs identity because it is the way we know about our position in social structures and appreciate our cultural tastes (Miles 2000, 25). The principal of *capital* is the way in which the capacity for a person to operate successfully within a particular group is explained. Habitus and capital have been an influential theoretical basis within sub-cultural studies, explaining participation through acquiring cultural capital (cf. Northcote 2006) or suggesting that the power of the group identity generated counters a marginalisation felt in society (cf. Hundeide 2004).

Reflexivity or habitus offer scope for understanding how young people might negotiate the identity work necessary to hold to their faith in contemporary life. However, Adams argues that whilst Giddens does not directly engage the work of Bourdieu a hybridisation of their approaches is possible (2006, 513). As I will outline shortly, data from my research shows that those who grow up in a community of faith being 'a Christian' is both a collective social identity, a personal choice and a 'youth' lifestyle, thus a hybrid view of reflexivity and habitus is theoretically helpful.

Adams draws on the work of Sweetman (2003) who considers the late-modern habitus, the way in which society lays down our perceptions of self, as inherently reflexive. The logic behind this position is that since reflexivity has become a necessary facet of modern life we unknowingly adopt this way of being into our habitus. Thus, persons who are able to be more reflexive (in particular areas of life) demonstrate a higher capital (in that particular area) and are seen to be able to exercise choice. Further, since habitus is formed within particular cultural fields, it is possible to see that as people traverse different fields they may experience some conflict in their understanding of self. Here, Adams uses the work of McNay (1999) to argue for a limitation to the reflexive authoring of identity. MacNay argues that in late-modern society women move between unequally aligned fields of practice with differing expectations and obligations associated with gender. Women's experiences between one field and another, for instance the work-place to the home, become transposed or confused and in some cases there might be a 'lack of fit' which results in a crisis, a form of reflexivity which necessitates a re-orientation of the habitus (Adams 2006, 517). It is this type of appreciation of habitus as 'a notion of habitus tempered by an ambiguous, complex, contradictory reflexivity' (Adams 2006, 521) that I have adopted in my enquiry into young people's faith and identity.

Faith through participation – the youth group as site for identity work

Between 2003 and 2007 I engaged in a piece of extended fieldwork with two groups of Christian young people (aged 14–17). Here I outline some brief reflections on the data gathered with one of these groups. All bar three of the young people (n=46) in this group grew up in what they described as Christian homes and went to church from an early age. Through group and one-to-one interviews, I explored young people's experiences of being Christian and the role that the group plays in their faith. Three facets of the data support the notion that faith requires a reflexive habitus and that the group is the place where such a habitus is generated. First the assertion by young people 'brought up to believe' that continuing to do so is 'their choice'; second that faith in God and belonging to the group provide an interconnected source of identity and third that ongoing participation in the group is seen by young people as significant in managing challenges to faith and identity.

Brought up to believe – my choice my faith

The first tension evident in the accounts was that whilst these young people had a deep seated sense that they had been brought up to believe, they held a comparatively strong view that continuing to believe is their choice. It is unsurprising that young people raised in Christian families and involved in church from an early age develop a habitus of faith through such socialisation. One young man describes his sense of faith as if 'the values of Christianity are ingrained in my person'. Another that '[my life] just wouldn't exist … I wouldn't have my closest friends, my family, everything would just fall to pieces, I think. It's what holds together my life.' These comments illustrate the depth to which being Christian is felt, offering support that it is engrained in their habitus. However, for some there is also a 'nagging doubt' that they only feel this way because they have been raised in these families, a sense exacerbated as they begin to experience challenges to the assumptions they hold about their beliefs and come into increasing contact with alternative positions and lifestyles. It is into this context that personal choice becomes an increasingly important aspect of their sense of being Christian and the youth group plays a pivotal role in the turn to such a personal faith.

A key aspect of participation in a Christian youth group is the way in which this group, and the associated camps and conferences, facilitates a process of personal choosing. Whether this is encouragement to become baptised or confirmed; respond to appeals to make choices to believe at worship events, or engage weekly in singing songs such as 'my Jesus, my Saviour' – personal faith is a key characteristic of the evangelicalism that this group is steeped in. In addition, practices such as writing and telling a testimony (one's personal story of developing personal faith) helps a young person to articulate and appropriate the way in which choice is central to their faith. The need to choose comes from both within the community, in the need to take their own place within it (Westerhoff 2000) and from their experience of faith being marginal to other areas of life. Despite the deep-seated sense of faith as something they were brought up to believe, these practices provide ways for young people to make faith 'their choice' and 'their decision'. Here then the idea of a 'reflexively endowed' faith habitus is helpful. Such a view affirms that choice is an aspect of their faith, but also that this is appropriated from participation in the group – not an indicator of unfettered reflexivity. Such a reflexive habitus helps to integrate 'choice' as important and a normal part of being Christian. As I discuss next, negotiating choice is also seen in the day-to-day operation of faith.

A God to rely on, a group to fall back on

Hunt suggests that religion can be a strong source of identity for people in a late-modern world; providing ethical and personal narratives (2005, 35). The young people in my study show signs of drawing on these facets, but a stronger motif emerges from the way in which they express faith; God is personally there for them! One comment is particularly illuminative from the point of reflexivity; God is 'someone to be there in all your decision making'. In other conversations young people would talk about the place of prayer in their lives as being a place to go when 'I find things are hard in life generally' or, 'it helps me sort out all the thoughts in my head and helps me keep calm'. Here, a tangible aspect of faith, as a relationship with God, is the reflexive management of self. Indeed acts such as prayer can be read as providing a form of capital to be reflexive and manage the struggles and issues faced.

This facet of young people's spirituality has been recognised by others, notably Elkind who postulated that a God to talk to is an especially helpful relationship for young people (1998, 52). However, habitus helps connect such a personal reflexivity to the context within which faith is formed and sustained – in this case I am arguing as being the youth group. The supporting structures for this are seen again within the lyrical and emotional content of forms of worship and the ways in which pastoral support and group discussion are often orientated around the very transitions and decisions that cause the stresses mentioned. This is not the totality of the way in which these young people view their faith, but it is a strong aspect within it. In both written accounts and interviews, the group is talked about as a place of security and support – a place to share your 'worries, hopes and experiences'. Without misrepresenting the depth to which an existential belief in God provides ontological security, it is important to see that reflexivity and faith are structured by the way in which participation in the group provides a rich set of religious practices and language for young people to use in reflection and discussion about struggles and choices. This illustrates how reflexivity is embedded in the practices of faith and adopted within a reflexive habitus of faith that offers strong foundations for identity in a context where choice is valued. Choice then is negotiated by being adopted as part of a reflexive habitus of faith.

However, in the last segment of data, I will discuss how crisis is also an important influence of faith and identity as young people traverse different social fields and are required to engage in further identity work in order to hold faith as a source of self-understanding.

Faith out there; faith in here

School is the environment these young people cite as being the primary negative experience of being Christian. One young person put it like this:

> You're completely different around school friends … [at] weekends, there are other people around me who are Christians and I don't have that safety 'on', anymore. Because, at school, I kind of put on like a safety catch … a mode where you are on guard.

It is identity here that is under a safety catch – the need to be active and self-conscious in the way in which being a Christian is represented in the school context. The contrast between the freedom to express Christian identity in the group and a caution at school is evident in this quotation. Other young people respond differently to this tension. One boy says:

> Actually, in a weird way, I find it helps, like, because when people criticise me and stuff … I have to sort of defend myself, but I find that if I do that successfully, or even unsuccessfully … I can know that what I'm believing is something that I understand, I haven't been, like, spoon-fed.

Both these young people though experience a 'crisis' similar to that which MacNay discusses around gender roles – here it is the way in which faith and identity relate. The two young people respond differently, but are required to manage the experience of field crossing by in some way seeking to reshape their faith habitus. In the first case it is a protective strategy, with the group being used to bring a sense of relief at being 'oneself' again. In the second instance it is a proactive strategy of drawing strength from faith being tested. However, even in this approach participation in the group is significant, since the role of teaching and peer support is highlighted by the young people as being vital in addressing the challenges to belief they encounter in school. It is this connection that again underscores the importance of viewing the relationship between faith and identity as a process of identity work around the formation and maintenance of a reflexive faith habitus.

Religious socialisation and a reflexive habitus

I suggest then that the youth group is both a site for personal identity work and a structure for addressing the challenge of holding a faith identity within a larger societal context that treats such positions with suspicion or indifference. By seeking to examine young people's actual experience of faith, situating this in a biographical context, issues of faith and identity can be examined in nuanced and novel ways. Theory and methods from the field of youth cultural studies can be helpful in engaging in such work, not by assuming faith to be a facet of a particular cultural or ethnic identity, but by seeking to make associations between what young people do and say about faith and theoretical perspectives on identity work within late-modern society. Indeed, as such studies grow perhaps these types of empirical studies might be able to contribute to understanding on the way young people form identity, not just with respect to faith.

PART V
Transmission

As the introduction and Parts I and II of this volume highlight, sociologists of religion and youth have been particularly concerned with the declining numbers of participants in organised religion. One area of research has been in cohort studies (see Part I) and a key aspect of this has been in looking at routes of faith transmission between cohorts and between religions and their converts. Daniele Hervieu-Leger's 'chain of memory' has been a particularly influential theory, exploring the way in which popular culture and family transmission relies on memory and its mutation. The four chapters in this section address these issues directly looking at both the role of institutions and families in religious transmission (Warner and Williams), exploring specific cases of mixed-faith parents (Arweck and Nesbitt) and clergy families (Guest), and finally, as part of a Europe-wide study, the role of confirmation on religiosity (Christensen et al.).

Chapter 19

The Role of Families and Religious Institutions in Transmitting Faith among Christians, Muslims, and Hindus in the USA

R. Stephen Warner and Rhys H. Williams

In this chapter we examine the 'lived reality of faith transmission' from parents to children in the context of religious institutions. While we acknowledge that our findings are based on a small and unsystematic sample of families and religious institutions in one American metropolitan area, we are convinced that our findings have potential for application to many settings. It is true that there are some particularities about religion in the USA, such as the fact that religious education is done by religious institutions within civil society, not by state schools or an established church. Nonetheless, our sample includes Christian, Muslim, and Hindu families and institutions, and varies by race and ethnicity, by social class, and by time in this country. Thus, we have confidence that we have found some significant commonalities and processes.

In the Youth and Religion Project, funded by grants from the Lilly Endowment to the University of Illinois at Chicago, we studied the religious experiences of youth and the religious institutions that serve them in the Chicago metropolitan area (hereafter 'Chicago') in three phases. First, we conducted focus groups and individual interviews with college students living in or originating from Chicago. Second, we canvassed scores of local religious institutions to get a first-hand look at the range of programs for youth they offered. (In this phase of the project we defined 'youth' very broadly to include single adults into their late twenties.) These institutions were primarily Christian, but we also did significant participant observation research with several Muslim and Hindu institutions and organizations.

Third, choosing six of these institutions, four Christian and one each Muslim and Hindu, we then asked their leaders to identify 'exemplary families' among their constituents, families that in the eyes of these leaders were doing a good job of passing on the respective faith to their minor children still living at home. We recruited twelve families from these lists, two from each institution, and conducted on-site observational research on the ways that religion was expressed in each family: we (a team of researchers under our direction and including us) went to the church (mosque or temple) with the family, went with them to other events and places that were part of their religious life as they understood it, and were present for, occasionally participating in, home religious observances. The twelve families were diverse not only in terms of religion but also social class, ethnicity, native versus foreign born, and family form, ranging from single-parent working class African-American families through lower-middle-class two-parent families (African-American and Hispanic) to middle-class families (white and South Asian), to upper-middle-class South Asian, Middle Eastern and white families. Several were recent immigrants. From these sources – individual and group interviews, observations within religious institutions, and observations in private homes – we amassed a rich store of triangulated data. Based on these data, we stress five points about faith transmission.

Working hard at religion

Perhaps the single most important finding of our research is that our exemplary families and the institutions they affiliate with *work very hard at religion*. In the past, perhaps entwined with the European roots of our white Christian families, the southern roots of our African-American families, or the South Asian roots of our two Hindu and one of the Muslim families, religious identity and practice were taken for granted, with children breathing in the same religious atmosphere their parents and grandparents had for generations. But in the highly mobile, American metropolitan context, religion is not, and cannot be, taken for granted if it is to be passed successfully to youth. The particularities of religion in America, combined with changes in the US economy and population, have in some ways turned everyone into a member of a 'minority' faith.

It has always been true that religion had to change with the times in order to survive, and most of our families had experienced within living memory major social transformations that required rethinking how religion was done. Migration, whether across oceans or within the nation, is one such change. But economic changes demand adaptive responses from all those who wish to pass on their cultural heritage to offspring. Children will lead very different lives than their parents, doing different jobs that require different kinds of education and training. And young women increasingly spend time in the paid labor force. Even when staying right at home, a family in effect moves into a new society when the economy is restructured (see Warner 1993).

American churches accommodated successfully to one such change in the past, the move from a rural farming and craft economy to an urban industrial and commercial economy. As men spent most of their waking hours away from the home at work it fell to their wives to become the in-home *de facto* providers of religious and early secular education; the male-breadwinner nuclear family pattern became dominant (Ryan 1981). Churches, overseen by an increasingly professionalized male clergy, came to rely on the unpaid work of women in such volunteer roles as Sunday school teachers and fundraisers.

Since the 1970s, the male-breadwinner nuclear family pattern is increasingly precarious. Many churches are organizationally stuck in its heyday of the 1950s (Marler 1995), but the most innovative churches today are working hard to overcome the reliance on unpaid female labor, involving more women in professional clergy roles and more men as volunteers (Edgell 2006). Among families in our study, many of the husbands were as active in the affairs of the religious community as were their wives. If it was the case for several American generations that religion was women's work, that is not the case today. We are not claiming that 'economics determines faith'; rather, socio-economic changes have put almost all families into a situation where they must directly engage the task of passing along their faith.

Extending the family

Whether they think of it this way, many of our families were responding to the relative decline of the nuclear family pattern by *re-extending the family*. There was nostalgia evinced by our white families for the ways of the past, and there was often a temporary nuclearizing effect of international migration among the Hindu and Muslim families who had to leave extended kin behind. But our South Asian families in effect tried to hold onto the extended family norms of their countries of origin. The most affluent of them worked to maintain their children's relationships with their extended kin in India through expensive international travel and sponsorship of relatives for their own immigration. Others encouraged the younger generation to regard unrelated adults of the co-ethnic and co-religious community as fictive kin, 'aunties and uncles'. Our African-American families can be seen as forward-looking pioneers in extending the family (Stack 1974). The long-standing economic marginality of African-American men and consequent instability of marriage among the African-American poor has long meant that black mothers had to rely on their female kin and neighbors for childcare and household support. Our families found some of this support through their churches. Some of our families – from all corners of the economic and ethnic differentiation they spanned – enjoyed what we call *religious magnetism*, by which outsiders gravitated toward them. Some of these outsiders were youngsters from other families; some were relatively unattached adults; other outsiders were families themselves. Some outsiders seem to have been informally adopted by the family.

We perceived two positive functions of this 're-extension' of the family depending on whether the extension was 'vertical' or 'horizontal'. Vertical extension to blood relatives or fictive kin gave greater weight to the religious authority exercised by parents, who in the culturally diverse (for middle-class immigrants) or socially threatening (for inner-city racial minority youth) world they inhabit often find it hard to project their voices effectively to their children. Sociologists have heard this kind of account from Hindu immigrants (Kurien 1998, 2007). In one of our Hindu families, the parents were acutely conscious of their incapacity to articulate the grounds of their religion practice beyond the simple 'that's how my parents did it'. They sought out other Hindu adults whom they regarded as more religiously qualified than they to help them present religion to their teenagers. One of our African-American single mothers encouraged her daughters to look up to their pastor as a surrogate father, and he responded with a combination of chaste affection and stern admonitions. Otherwise beleaguered parents can thus point to other adults to say, in effect, that the standards being enunciated at home were not arbitrary idiosyncrasies. They are the way it normatively is.

Horizontal extension to neighbors and other visitors seems to increase the religious magnetism that in part occasioned it. Bringing additional youth into the home can contribute to critical masses needed for some religious observances. Outside youth, in the context of the religiously devoted home, can serve as surrogate siblings for only children or those whose siblings are too much older or younger to participate in favored activities. Adding to the numbers around the room can enhance the perceived objective reality of what transpires there. The apartment complex of one of our Muslim families became a religious neighborhood where Qur'an study and evening prayers were enhanced by the numbers of youthful participants in gender-segregated weekly gatherings. The religious significance of mealtimes in one of our Puerto Rican Pentecostal families was enhanced by the presence of non-related youth whose visits with the family were occasioned by attendance at church. Our findings add cross-cultural and inter-religious resonance to a theme we have heard discussed among mainline and some evangelical Protestant youth ministers, namely that youth ministry must be family ministry (see Dean 2004; DeVries 1994; Garland 1999).

Expressing religion inside the home

The mention of 'religious observances' in the context of the home brings to light another of our findings, one that would be no surprise to Jews or to traditional Hindus, namely that the *home at least as much as the temple is the center of religious observance*. Table grace and bedtime prayers are home-based religious observances with which American Christians are familiar, and we certainly observed these rituals among our Christian families. Hindu interviewees and focus group participants told us how great an impression was made on them by their parents' otherwise mysterious daily rituals at home altars, and during the family phase of the project we were shown the spaces reserved for the gods in our two Hindu homes, respectively an alcove and a spare bedroom. We knew that Muslim adults teach their youth how to recite the Qur'an in Arabic and model for them the motions of the five-times-daily *salat* prayer. We discovered that these teachings were not confined to the mosque but often undertaken at home. Indeed, one family told us that they prefer their children (all boys) pray with their father at home, except for the obligatory Friday congregational prayer at the mosque.

We found other home-based observances as well. We were present when one of the Hindu families hosted a religious singing ritual called a *bhajan* for a co-ethnic group drawn from those Chicago-area Hindus who speak the same south Indian language. We were present when one of our Muslim mothers conducted a home Qur'an study with her three daughters. We were also present for a fun-filled weekly ritual of one the African-American families, a single mother and her two daughters who spend one night a week doing Bible study and playing competitive Bible games. Each of the girls tried to be the one who could most quickly and accurately recite the books of the Bible in order, and then, to our amazement and one daughter's consternation, in reverse order. Another Muslim family discussed the moral implications of bedtime stories the children had been told in their pre-teen years.

These home observances serve to inculcate the lesson that religion isn't just something that belongs in the confines of the 'church'. When the family is invited to another family's home for such an observance it reinforces the point that the rituals in question are also not idiosyncratic but normal.

Enacting religion intergenerationally

When we began to share ideas about our research plans, we began to encounter a warning that was just then (at the end of the 1990s) being articulated among mainline Protestant youth ministry specialists. The warning was that it is a grave mistake for religious educators to isolate youth in the church in their own groups, meetings, and worship services. Such isolation was an extreme expression of the otherwise healthy principle that successful transmission of religion requires youth to become agents of their own religion, not merely followers of their family's traditions. In a mobile society, parental authority needs eventually to be supplanted by the autonomy of the emerging generation, and this principle was greatly underscored by the baby boomer experience of the 1960s and 1970s. But intergenerational isolation has its costs.

At first we looked for autonomous youth groups in all the religious institutions we visited, but we soon encountered another instance of the prophetic value of the African-American experience. We couldn't find autonomous youth groups in the congregations of the black church tradition that we surveyed. When we finally heard of what appeared to be such a youth event in one of the black churches, we attended and found that it was profoundly intergenerational, with adults in effect keeping an eye on the youngsters but also proving an appreciative audience for the youth's competent and inspired reproduction of the religious culture they were inheriting.

We then began to see other applications of the principle that intergenerational transmission of religion depends in part on *intergenerational experience*. So in several conservative Protestant churches (predominantly white as well as multiracial and black), we saw that Sunday school is offered to all ages, with each age- and sex-based class studying the same Bible text but at different levels of intensity and intellectual sophistication. This common experience could lead to religious conversation over the family dining table later in the day.

Perhaps the most striking scene of intergenerational religious observance is the line-up of young children next to their parents in Muslim congregational prayer. It is an Islamic norm that regular prayer expresses the equality of all believers before Allah regardless of station in life. If the king arrives early, he can be in front. If he arrives late, he is in back. So a boy just beginning school stands beside his father (shoulder-to-shoulder becoming shoulder to thigh) in a row of other men and boys on Friday at the mosque.

Involving youth as leaders

Finally, we found that some of the most enthusiastic embrace of the family's religious tradition and institution was expressed by those *youth who took leadership roles*. Yet the leadership roles they can play are highly varied. Among many Hindu youth, where leadership in the temple would be proscribed by the traditional prerogative of priests, such leadership is most easily found in autonomous youth groups when the child is away from home, that is, in university. Thus, we spoke with enthusiastic leaders of the Hindu Students Council on the UIC campus. Away from parental supervision, they were learning and articulating their religion in terms that they felt their peers could appreciate and that they themselves could understand. But they did not see themselves as altering the religion of their parents.

As a generalization, however, the most effective transmission of religious involvement seemed to come for those youth who took public and honored roles in the main (that is to say, adult-dominated) religious institutions while they were themselves still dependent minors. Some of the most active youth groups, which we found in multiracial Pentecostal and fundamentalist churches, spent a good deal of their (adult-supervised) time preparing to enact dramatic skits and musical performances for the main Sunday worship service, where their talents and their passion were greatly appreciated by their seniors. In effect, they were artistic leaders for that particular Sunday. In the black church well-coached youth provided most of the music and enacted most of the devotions, including prayers (but not the sermon) on youth day once a month. Young men, in their role as junior deacons, took their place as ushers during Men's Month. In one of our Muslim families, one of the sons took the role as *muezzin* each evening, calling the family to prayer, and another acted as *imam*, leading the prayer itself. As their parents saw it, these roles were not beyond the capacity of their teenagers. Adults were on hand to serve as models, coaches, and an appreciative audience for what the youth were learning and enacting.

One index of what we perceived to be the long-term effect of such adolescent leadership activity within their parental religious institutions is the enthusiasm and vibrancy of autonomous evangelical and Muslim student organizations among youth on the campus of one university where we did research. We suspect that the student leaders of these organizations had been set firmly on their religious course by the relatively confident modeling of religious identity and activity on the part of the parents and other adults in the religious institutions in which they grew up. They had been readied to take charge of a religious inheritance that they had been taught to regard as right and true.

An overall lesson to be drawn from these instances of working hard at religion, extending the family, expressing religion inside the home, enacting religion intergenerationally, and involving youth as leaders of the grown-up church is that the adaptations and changes that are needed for successful religious transmission to a new generation do not necessarily take the form of looking 'new' or 'modern'. They may be re-appropriations of older patterns. But they very often involve one generation's doing things differently than what they experienced in their own youth. In that sense, we return to the opening theme – that religion in the USA cannot survive if it is simply taken for granted.

Chapter 20

Growing Up in a Mixed-Faith Family: Intact or Fractured Chain of Memory?[1]

Elisabeth Arweck and Eleanor Nesbitt

Introduction

A recent UK-based study of families in which mothers' and fathers' faith backgrounds (Christian, Hindu, Muslim, Sikh) differ provides the context for this examination of transmission. Underlying the project was the question: how do young people, of dual religious inheritance, construct religious identities and understanding of religion? As their families often also combined different ethnic and cultural backgrounds, this chapter indicates the relationship between these components. The role of grandparents emerged as important, so our reporting spans three, in some cases four generations.

Faith transmission and socialisation

Sociologists know little about how faith or its related values are transmitted (values being understood as 'principled dispositions' or 'preferences conducive to the promotion of defensible goals of individual and social flourishing', see Carr and Landon 1999, 24). Religious transmission means the ways in which parents pass on religious attitudes and behaviours to their children. The relationship between the religious attitudes and behaviours of parents and children is the object of studies of religious transmission, which often use 'religiosity' measures (i.e. the ways in which we can identify people being religious, e.g. beliefs, church attendance, importance of religion in their lives, opinions about God, prayer). Faith transmission is inseparable from 'socialisation', a lifelong process of acquiring the core beliefs and practices of a social/religious community, which develops individuals' sense of self and identity. Sherkat defines religious socialisation as 'an interactive process through which social agents influence individuals' religious beliefs and understandings' (2003, 151). Beliefs and understandings constitute religious preferences – favoured supernatural explanations about the meaning,

[1] For funding 'Investigating the Religious Identity Formation of Young People in Mixed-faith Families' we gratefully acknowledge the Arts and Humanities Research Council (AHRC). Thanks too to the families who participated.

purpose and origins of life – which in turn inform commitments to religious organisations or choices of religious affiliation. Preference change is generated respectively by individuals (through their agency in making choices) and through social influences. Sherkat argues that the family is the primary agent of influence on religious beliefs and understandings 'throughout the life course' as well as being the primary context for religious choices (2003, 151–8).

The importance of the family relates the notion of transmission to that of generation, the passing on of religion, customs, culture and so on over time. The passing of generations marked the transmission of religion, as newer generations inherited religion primarily from older generations. However, accelerating change during the twentieth century disrupted this process. Students of religion have to consider how research can address generational issues and rethink the meaning of 'generation' and the responses of religions to forces – political, economic and cultural – that precipitate the construction and self-construction of new generations (see e.g. Cavalli 2004).

Some scholars have examined generational effects on religion in wider geo-political contexts, such as conflicts in Africa and the impact of colonialism and post-colonialism in South Asia. Others have investigated how different generations in Europe have responded to their Christian heritage or to the 'official' atheism of twentieth-century Central and Eastern Europe. (see *Social Compass* 2004) However, because of data constraints, little is known about how faith/religion is transmitted in the nuclear family – arguably a microcosm of wider society – and still less about the influence of the extended family (Sherkat 2003, 157–8).

While the family remains the primary influence on religious preferences and choices, knowledge of family dynamics in relation to these is scant. Areas awaiting investigation are: how far parents rely on implicit transmission of religion rather than making planned efforts to pass on their beliefs and the effect of gender in these processes.

Transmission and nurture

Distinguishing between 'passive' and 'proactive' transmission means distinguishing between the reproduction of aspects of parents' culture and faith tradition by their children as they copy and internalise parental behaviour and attitudes and parents' and others' often planned efforts to pass on aspects of culture or faith. The term 'nurture' has been used for 'socialisation' or 'transmission' by some religious educators. John Hull (1984) adopted the term from Horace Bushnell (1967) to mean 'the processes by which children born into a particular faith community acquire its characteristic practices and beliefs or some adaptation of them' (cited in Jackson and Nesbitt 1993, 15). Jackson and Nesbitt's distinction between 'informal' and 'formal' nurture reflects the two understandings of 'transmission' above. Thus, 'formal nurture' includes supplementary classes, run by minority ethnic and religious organisations, to teach mother tongue, devotional languages and music, whereas 'informal nurture' refers to ways in which children absorb their families' culture, values and beliefs at home, in community gatherings and on visits to relatives abroad (Jackson and Nesbitt 1993; Nesbitt 2000a, 2001).

Transmission in the sense of almost unconscious reproduction is observable whether or not parents identify goals, articulate the values or practices that they aspire to for their children or send them to supplementary classes and activity groups. Transmission occurs by 'osmosis' whereby the tradition filters into young people's personas. (Some parents in our study expressed the hope that their children would experience this.) Transmission in the second sense, as intentional induction, involves conscious motives to introduce young people to a religious tradition by engaging them in specifically religious social structures and contexts. Transmission of this kind connects families more strongly with the extended family and the respective faith community.

Both formal and informal nurture are illuminated by the dual meaning of the Sanskrit term *samskara* (literally, 'refining', 'polishing'). The first meaning is 'processing' by rites of passage – for example, the Hindu naming ceremony (*namakarana*). The second meaning is conditioning by the attitudes and expectations of one's family. Hindus do not remember the rites performed for them as young children, but become part of the chain of remembrance by participating in the *samskaras* of family members, such as weddings. Such nurture or transmission is reinforced through festivals and daily worship (see Nesbitt 2008, 677).

Transmission (or socialisation) involves a range of analytically separable, but practically inseparable, elements: culture, religion, ethnicity and language, as the next section discusses.

The linkage between culture, ethnicity and religion

For those with a religious outlook, having a faith is a way of life, not just a set of practices or observances. For Jews, Hindus and other faith communities, culture and faith are unquestionably intertwined. Even in Protestant Christianity, although the link is less obvious, transmitting one means transmitting both.

Parekh defines culture as 'a historically created system of meanings and significance' (2000, 143), which finds expression in language, myths, rituals, symbols, collective memories, customs, traditions, the arts, moral life, ideal of excellence, and in rules and norms. Although religion's role in different cultures varies, they influence each other profoundly. However, practices can be stripped of their religious basis and followed for cultural or social reasons (Parekh 2000, 148).

Parekh distinguishes three ways in which individuals respond to their culture. Some embrace it, striving to live up to its ideals and remaining fully within its confines. Some are innovative, borrowing judiciously from other cultures, thus enriching their own. Some are 'culturally footloose' and create an eclectic way of life (Parekh 2000, 149–50). Most families in our sample fell into Parekh's second category. However, the way in which they selected what they preserved or discarded was particular to each individual or family.

Ethnicity is linked to the communal aspect of culture, as culture is linked to a particular group of people (although the two can dis-aggregate, for example, when an ethnic community loses or abandons its culture). To be born into and raised in a cultural community means being influenced by its cultural content and communal basis. It also means building common bonds, undergirded by shared beliefs and memories. Being part of a community shapes one's personality, while embedding one in that social context and fostering identification with the community (Parekh 2000, 154–6).

Meanwhile, a culture's rules and norms simultaneously facilitate and discipline choices. While creating the conditions of choice, culture demands conformity, but is not deterministic. Adults interviewed in our study illustrated critical engagement of individuals with culture, including those who had experienced norms regarding dress and expectations linked to gender and status as restrictive.

Memory and religion

Parekh's references to memories which form part of culture and to the way individuals relate to culture resonate with Hervieu-Léger's metaphor of religion as 'a chain of memory' (2000). As our data arose from families, with several generations present (either physically or in individuals' awareness), images of forging and fracturing a chain can usefully be applied to the question of how parents, whose faith backgrounds differ, transmit religious tradition to their children. Moreover, consideration of the families' geographical settings (e.g. relative distance from relatives or a place of worship) suggests how chains of memory might be forged or fractured. For example, some families had places of worship nearby, but no connection other than through grandparents. One Hindu–Christian family, Mr and Mrs Pande and their daughters Rohini (aged 14) and Sonal (11), presented a constellation of connections.[2] They had tenuous links with three Hindu temples (about half an hour away by car): firstly, the temple or *mandir* in which Mr Pande's late father had publicly read the scriptures. (Subsequently, Mr Pande, who attended Hindu functions such as weddings, but played no part in the temple, had been invited to take an active role, but had not decided his response.) The second temple was associated with Mr Pande's mother helping in organising Gujarati classes to meet local Hindus' aspiration for young people to learn the language. (Jackson and Nesbitt 1993 found that parents regarded the Gujarati language as a top priority in passing on 'religion'.) Her grandmother's death prompted Rohini to attend the public classes in Hinduism at this supplementary

---

[2]   In order to maintain confidentially, pseudonyms have been assigned to all the participants in this study. The ages of the young people refer to their ages when contact with the respective family began.

school. The celebration of her examination results brought the family to the temple and Rohini was invited to help with teaching. The third temple, a complex built in South Indian style, attracts the family for Divali. More consistently with Hindu tradition than with more 'congregational' religions such as Christianity, Mr Pande did not think that young people needed a link with a *mandir* – they needed a safe, organised environment which religion might or might not provide.

The unyielding, imprisoning character of a chain connects (in terms of Parekh's analysis) to culturally bounded expectations which are communicated within families, by grandparents for instance. The Pande family's case illustrates (a) the interactive aspect of culture: individuals and institutions communicate with one another and negotiate their respective positions and roles; (b) how association with a temple was more important for first generation Hindu migrants, as a means to assert identity (Smith 1978, cited in Botros 2006), than for subsequent generations, who felt more at home in the UK; (c) a tendency in South Asian communities, in the first generation anyway, to consider family succession over suitability for a role on other grounds and (d) a continuing Hindu commitment to having Brahmins read the scriptures.

Mixed-faith families: intact or fractured chains of memory?

Most parents in our sample (28 families) had grown up in the UK and been socialised by school and other institutions. Those of immigrant background had simultaneously experienced (some of) their parents' heritage. Settling in a Western country fractured the chain. Some grandparents in our study had attenuated their practice, mainly to 'fit in'. For some, there had been no accessible places of worship, but decades later some had revived their religious practice and were keen to pass this on. The grandparental generation linked the grandchildren to explicitly religious aspects of tradition. This accords with Hindu tradition in which religious activity develops strongly in the last period of life, when the responsibilities of the householder – earning a living, rearing children and seeing them married and 'settled' – are discharged. Although Sikh teachings emphasise the importance of combining family responsibilities and devotion, regardless of stage of life, many Sikhs also follow this trajectory.

In our study, the grandparents' presence strengthened awareness of cultural and religious traditions and led, in some cases, to their continuation. Bobby, a Sikh father, was about seven when his paternal grandparents arrived in the UK. Family life changed: whereas Bobby's father had believed it important to adapt to Britain, Bobby's grandparents, especially his grandmother, sought to replicate Punjabi conventions. Religion took a more prominent role, partly because of her increasing involvement in the Sikh community. Bobby experienced this new regime as an imposition and his teenage response was to reject religion. His experience illustrates the tensions between generations, the demands and restrictiveness of tradition as well as individuals' responses. Bobby was 'proud to be a Sikh ... but

I do not subscribe to the religious element of it'. He had slowly removed himself from the expectations which, he felt, threatened to imprison him. A major step was his decision against having an arranged marriage.

Choice of spouse and religious preferences are strongly connected. Research shows that people with strong commitment to particular religious principles are unlikely to marry someone without these (Sherkat 2003, 157). When individuals override their elders' commitment to endogamous marriage, there is rupture. Bobby's also case illustrates the chain fracturing in other ways: as his parents had died, the link for his daughter Margarita (aged 9) was through his other relatives, but they lived about 30 miles away. Moreover, although Bobby and his family attended the *gurdwara* when visiting relatives, they did not go to their local *gurdwara*. Nor did they attend a nearby church that would have related to his wife Stella's Christian background. Her personal history also showed fractures in the chain. Although her mother attended church (her father was no longer alive), no overtly religious links in this Christian chain were being forged, as none of Margarita's activities with her grandmother had religious content.

Margarita's parents made no deliberate effort to place her within either parent's lineage (Sikhism or Christianity). However, in terms of culture and ethnicity, the chains are continued through the extended family and Sikh or Christian celebrations (e.g. weddings, major festivals). Here we see the separation of culture and religion in thought and practice, as Parekh suggests. Like her peers in many 'non-mixed' Sikh families, Margarita was ignorant of the Punjabi language in use at Sikh events, which were opportunities to dress in Indian clothes, see her Indian cousins and enjoy Indian food. She lacked the vocabulary (in English or Punjabi) to describe the scene or what happened at either *gurdwara* or church. Although Margarita's (non-denominational) school had a Christian character and had introduced her to some festivals and Bible stories, she showed no particular interest in Christianity or indeed religious issues in general. Her sense of family and her place in it were not matched by curiosity about religious aspects of her dual heritage.

While this family represents a case of chains with several fractures, the next suggests both fracture and continued lineage of belief. Mother (Sunita), a Christian, and father (Pappu), a Sikh, were Punjabi caste-fellows. Sunita had been born and raised in the UK, while Pappu had lived in India until marriage. Sunita's family (parents and siblings) lived nearby, providing strong mutual support. Pappu's family all lived overseas, but some contact was maintained through telephoning and occasional visits. Sunita and Pappu lived within walking distance of a *gurdwara*, but a 15-minute car ride away from Sunita's Mormon church. Sunday church attendance happened almost weekly, while visits to the *gurdwara* were only for Divali and Vaisakhi. However, during term time, the children attended the *gurdwara*'s weekly Punjabi classes, which included references to Sikhism. Punjabi was the language predominantly spoken at home and with grandparents. Divali was usually marked by a special meal or fireworks.

Were it not for its Christian element, this family might present a case of an unbroken chain of Punjabi culture. However, when Sunita was about six, the chain had broken as her father converted to Christianity, taking the whole family with him and re-orienting their lives to church teachings and causing friction with the extended family on the maternal side. The discipline of church life in Sunita's upbringing continued in her children's upbringing. Regular church attendance resulted partly from Sunita's parents' attention and practical support (for example, by calling for the family at the appointed time on Sundays). The grandparents' day-to-day involvement in the family's life further ensured the transmission of the (cultural and religious) values, which they (up)held, to the grandchildren. The children in this family received strong, consistent messages from both home (parents, grandparents, some extended family) and church.

The children's local Church of England school however introduced some discontinuity, as the Christianity they encountered in religious education and school assemblies differed from their church's Christianity. This was offset by Sunita seeing herself as the primary socialising influence in her children's upbringing, a role which is emphasised and reinforced by the church teachings. However, she supported the children visiting the *gurdwara* and being taught elements of Sikhism in their Punjabi classes. Some Punjabi values coalesced with the church's teachings, and where values diverged (e.g. about dating), Punjabi tradition prevailed. Meanwhile, Sunita's siblings had fractured the chain of tradition in different ways, as one no longer attended church and another remained unmarried.

Sunita's children identified strongly as 'Christian', were knowledgeable about their faith and looked forward to progressing from stage to stage of church membership. Their knowledge of Sikhism was scantier. They understood their respective age-related roles and responsibilities, while recognising the need to negotiate some boundaries between family life, church life and school life. Sunita's formative influence accords with studies that found mothers' significance in children's religious preferences and choices (Pearce and Axinn 1998; Yuri 2005). She was actively forging and strengthening links in the chain of religious and cultural tradition.

Conclusion

This chapter has related faith transmission to religious socialisation and nurture by examining what is transmitted and by what processes. Faith transmission connects with generation and ethnicity and is pertinent to the social and cultural changes of the second half of the twentieth century and the resulting fault-lines in the structures of traditional societies. Mixed-faith families are of particular relevance for examining the (dis)continuity of religious tradition, because they offer more possibilities in terms of continuing or creating chains of memory. The (extended) family appears as the prime agent of influence, but there is no evident pattern in the way parents and grandparents transmit religious and cultural values, not least because individuals' values mature and change. Further, families' internal issues, such as death and mobility, affect physical and emotional closeness. Families have memories and one adult in a family tended to be the custodian of family memories and was consulted when individuals' recollection of dates or events failed. Mr Pande had begun mapping the network of his family's connections to preserve such knowledge, now that his parents – previously the keepers of these memories – had died. Family dynamic is also influenced by the geographical and social context, which is often connected with migration. As Mr Pande indicated, 'we have to invent how to do things, as we go along'. The breaks in the chain relate to circumstances and aspirations, influenced by the cultural and religious landscape.

While strongly religious parents want to pass on their religion, some parents who feel less strongly wish their children to be introduced to one or more religions. Our interviewees wanted their children to have the option of becoming part of a religion tradition, whether their own or a different one, so forging new links or none.

Chapter 21

Socialisation and Spiritual Capital: What Difference do Clergy Families Make?

Mathew Guest

Introduction

Ever since Gordon Brown became Prime Minister of Great Britain in 2007, there has been renewed interest in the experience of those raised as children of the clergy. In the early months of his premiership, Brown made repeated reference to his father's status as a Church of Scotland minister and to how it was his upbringing as a 'child of the manse' that furnished him with the 'moral compass' that continues to inform his politics and social values. Brown is not alone among public figures in being the child of an ordained Christian minister: journalist and TV presenter Jon Snow is the son of an Anglican bishop, as are comedian Hugh Dennis and radio DJ Tim Westwood; the father of well-known TV personality David Frost was a minister in the Methodist Church; actor Denzel Washington's father was a Pentecostal minister; and former US Secretary of State Condoleezza Rice is the daughter of John Wesley Rice, a minister in the Presbyterian Church, whose experience of racial discrimination in Alabama shaped his daughter's emerging political stance. Such observations invite reflection on the significance that being a clergy child might have for one's values, particularly in relation to ideals of public service. The cultural stereotype of the clergy child – as either saint or sinner – is implicitly called into question and, as I demonstrate in this chapter, the evidence demands a more complex understanding.

So how might we make sense of this relationship between a particular kind of upbringing and the development of values within adulthood? In sociological terms, how can we measure the long-term consequences of particular patterns of socialisation? This is an important question for the sociology of religion because it probes the heart of the secularisation thesis – that is, how religious values are transmitted over time, and with what success? – *and* raises the possibility of a channel for religious influence within contexts in which Christianity is often presumed to have at best a highly diminished public profile. Despite this wider theoretical resonance, we struggle to find a large body of empirical research into these pressing questions, certainly within the UK, and indeed, further afield as well. Part of this problem is financial: studies of inter-generational value transmission are necessarily expensive as they demand a large number of interviews among different generational cohorts in order to have a sufficient evidence base for claims that apply across a particular society. Some North-American-based studies have successfully met this need, and the work of Wade Clark Roof (1999) and Christian Smith (2005), in particular, is noteworthy for charting trends in value change that apply across large geographical areas, and which therefore reveal important patterns in the changing character of US culture generally.

While these projects draw from survey and interview data, historian Callum Brown has offered a more nuanced picture of generational change in modern Britain by using oral history, piecing together the shifting ways in which Christianity has been maintained, from its status as part of the cultural fabric to an optional lifestyle choice, in his influential book *The Death of Christian Britain* (2001). Brown emphasises the family – particularly the role of women – as a key factor in shaping the status of Christianity as a social force, and in so doing offers a set of useful reference points for addressing the significance of clergy families in contemporary Britain. In response to a sociological drift towards emphasising the sovereign individual actor (e.g. Giddens 1991), other research has affirmed the importance of the family as an enduring influence over the values individuals profess in adulthood (Bengtson et al. 2002). According to this argument, contrary to some theories associated with post- or late-modernity, we do not exist as isolated individuals, but within persistent networks – of family, friends and colleagues – that continue to shape our identities as we develop throughout our lives. It is against the background of these insights that Douglas Davies and myself attempted an analysis of the significance of values learnt within clerical families, focusing on the family as a site in which values are learnt in a variety of complex ways (Davies and Guest 2007). In a three-year empirical study of the families of Church of England bishops across two generations, we asked whether there are patterns in the acceptance, rejection and development of what we refer to as 'spiritual capital'.

Spiritual capital and the transmission of values

While there is now less dispute over whether family remains an important site for the formation of religious identity, sociologists differ in their attempts to theorise the process of socialisation. One approach would draw insights from a resource mobilisation perspective, focusing on what it is that is acquired, learnt or developed via the socialisation process. Theories of resource mobilisation have been used to good effect in the study of social movements (Zald and McCarthy 1987) as they foreground the processes whereby groups are empowered to emerge and thrive within particular social contexts. The French sociologist Pierre Bourdieu has used a related model to explore inequalities in education systems (1977b) and the power imbalance found within some churches (1991). Bourdieu's theoretical framework is distinguished by his use of the term 'capital' to refer to valued resources operative in a given 'social field'. Such resources may take a variety of forms, including economic capital (money and finance) or social capital (significant relations between individuals), for example. In his work on religion, Bourdieu develops the concept of 'religious capital' as the power invested in religious authorities – most notably the priesthood. This 'religious capital' is embodied in things like specialist theological knowledge and sacramental oversight, both available to the priesthood but not the laity, and is expressed and sustained through the power of religious authorities to define the nature of salvation. While illuminating to a degree, Bourdieu's approach has its limitations. In a useful application and critique, American sociologist Bradford Verter (2003) has argued that a more subtle concept is needed if capital theory is to take proper account of the peculiarities of religion in contemporary Western cultures. According to Verter, Bourdieu's model 'treats religion as an institution but not as a disposition, as an intricate system of coercion but not as a liquid species of capital. In short, it employs categories that are too rigid to account for the fluidities of today's spiritual marketplace' (Verter 2003, 151).

Verter's critique of Bourdieu is helpful for a number of reasons. Not least, it demonstrates the importance of allowing changes in the social and religious landscape to modify the theoretical models we use to explain them. The utility of sociological theory is to be judged not just on its explanatory power but on its capacity to shed light on social phenomena without being ethnocentric or anachronistic. Verter's more developed understanding of religious resources, which he calls 'spiritual capital', presents a much more fluid, open-ended phenomenon than Bourdieu's 'religious capital', which is restricted by its indebtedness to a strict distinction between priesthood and laity. Rather, 'spiritual capital' is conceived as 'a more widely diffused commodity, governed by more complex patterns of production, distribution, exchange, and consumption' (Verter 2003, 158). Verter's model takes into account the characteristics of the contemporary religious landscape and, by retaining Bourdieu's emphasis on power relations, captures the ways in which capital may be converted into different forms. For example, spiritual capital may be vested in a position of institutional advantage – that of a senior cleric or religious official, perhaps – which is then used by its incumbent to acquire symbolic capital or prestige. Or spiritual capital may refer to religious knowledge, perhaps acquired through pre-ordination training, which is later used as cultural capital (knowledge that is accorded status in the broader cultural context). It is important to note that a capital-based approach to understanding religious values is not unproblematic. Some critics would take issue with the use of economic language to explain religious phenomena, arguing that the distinguishing qualities of religion are not done justice by a set of metaphors based on material acquisition and exchange. A further criticism may consider 'spiritual capital' to be so all-encompassing that it fails to command any explanatory power; if spiritual capital is so flexible and can be so easily converted into other forms of capital, then how can it be possible to say for sure whether a particular phenomenon should be properly categorised as 'spiritual capital' or not? These are important questions, questions that are thrown into relief when ideas of capital are applied within an analysis of the transmission of religious values.

Clergy families and spiritual capital

Between 2001 until 2004, Douglas Davies and myself conducted the 'Clergy and British Society' project, tracing the lives and influence of senior Anglican clergy from 1940 to 2000 (Davies and Guest 2007). A major part of this project concerned the adult sons and daughters of these (now retired) Church of England bishops, focusing upon the extent to which they have taken on the values affirmed within the clergy family of their childhood. We employed two research techniques, developed with specific aims and objectives in mind. The need to gather demographic background – particularly the individual religious and career histories of respondents – meant that a questionnaire was necessary, and we received detailed responses from 225 individuals, including retired Anglican bishops, their wives and their adult sons and daughters. The further need for an exploration into how bishops, their wives and children make sense of their identities in relation to spiritual capital required extended interviews, and we conducted 51 recorded, semi-structured conversations with a sample from among our survey respondents. These allowed us to examine how these individuals reflect on their experiences as members of a clergy family, on family life, its peculiarities, benefits and problems, and how these relate to the development of outlooks and values which have subsequently emerged. While we were enquiring about specific events and experiences, we were asking individuals to recount them often many years after these events took place, and therefore through the inevitable filters of time and subsequent life experience. As such, we were not seeking to uncover causal historical relationships or determinative trends in generational value transmission. While our questionnaire data allowed us to place our findings within a solid historical, ecclesiastical and cultural context, our interest was primarily in how individuals construct and negotiate acquired spiritual capital through the accounts they offer of their lives.

With respect to the clergy children, our thematic foci were careers and religious identity; we wanted to explore how the spiritual capital acquired from a clergy upbringing was operative in respondents' accounts of their professional and religious development. Just how did clergy sons and daughters appear to draw from their upbringing in constructing their professional and religious identities as adults? The data are rich and complex, so for the purposes of brevity, here I focus on a single pattern in the emergence of values, one that illustrates the interconnectedness between experiences of family in childhood and orientations to religion and professional life that emerge in adult life.

Many sociologists have developed Emile Durkheim's argument that the modern world is characterised by an increasing degree of differentiation. Institutions that were once interrelated are now relatively discrete, each serving a particular function and often existing as structurally separate from one another. Religion offers a prime example, and proponents of secularisation have often traced the decline in the social significance of religion with reference to the early modern church – which served an educational, welfare and health, as well as liturgical, function – contrasted with the contemporary church, which concerns itself primarily with matters of private faith. With significant consensus that the spheres of family, work and religion are mainly kept discrete among the citizens of contemporary Britain, it is interesting to note how, within the clerical household, the boundaries between these three spheres of life are frequently blurred so that each field of life experience invades into another. This is most evident in recollections by clergy children of the clerical home: a domestic space that was frequently compromised by its use by non-family-members, be they parishioners, other clergy or church officials, as if it were a public space. The vicarage was at the same time a home, their father's work-space, and a context for the pastoral care and spiritual guidance of the needy. This is presented as an ambiguous predicament, and while some recalled fondly encounters with interesting and influential individuals, others focused on their feelings of displacement and alienation. Indeed, we may expect this blurring of boundaries to have been experienced as problematic, especially during formative years, when clergy children begin to learn that this arrangement is abnormal and counter to the dominant – more differentiated – cultural norm. As has been noted in previous studies of youth, a recurring source of alienation is a sense of being different from the norm, apart from the crowd, and in light of this, one can appreciate the potential for this experience among clergy children on a number of levels.

Our analysis of interview data revealed that many clergy children adopted a particular strategy in making sense of their identities, focused on unravelling these boundaries and maintaining an arrangement that keeps them discrete. Spiritual capital is thereby negotiated in a way that harnesses its advantages, but within a life situation that maintains the home/religion/work boundaries these individuals have since learnt as socially normal. For example, some respondents had sought to separate their understanding of Christian faith from the institution of the Church of England. This allowed them to account for their negative experiences during childhood as consequences of a flawed church rather than lay them at the door of Christianity as a whole, something they were reluctant to do. In fact, the vast majority of our respondents affirmed Christianity as a positive social force, with almost all of the 75 per cent who claimed a religious identity also claiming to be Christian (whether that be Church of England, Roman Catholic, or without a particular denomination, for example). This strategy also allowed our respondents to separate pressures on the family from Christianity itself, by associating them with professional pressures brought to bear on their father by the church, thus freeing up Christianity as a positive spiritual resource for appropriation in adult life and within the upbringing of their own children.

A different example can be found among respondents who acknowledged the values they received because of their upbringing, and saw these as connected to their father's vocation as a clergyman. They also affirmed these values in their own lives, but made sense of their worth as moral, social or professional skills. They did their job as their father did his job as a vicar, even though they were a corporate manager, teacher or civil servant and even though, for some, they had no interest in the church and no sense of religious identity. Hence, what might be called 'Christian virtues' are reconceived as professional values, thus separating religion from professional life, while maintaining the spiritual capital acquired from being raised a clergy child. A sense of working out virtues through channels that are not explicitly Christian, or indeed religious at all, may also be found in the fact that almost three-quarters of our respondents had worked in the caring/nurture professions – e.g. teaching, nursing or social work – at some point in their lives; over half still did, and many traced their career choices to the values associated with the clergy household of their youth. One respondent commented on how her own experience of being raised in a clerical household had inspired her and her siblings to embrace moral causes in adult life, even though none had a strong connection to the church or a strong sense of Christian identity. As she commented:

> … a friend of mine … once sort of said 'you know you and your sisters do seem in love with dedicating yourselves to good causes, don't you?' And you know we took it for granted I suppose, that you should have moral principles and that they should lead you into actually doing something. And I think … all those Sunday services probably had their affect … and we've all stuck with it, one way or the other.

What difference do clergy families make?

These instances illustrate strategies for the negotiation of spiritual capital within the lives of individuals living in contemporary Britain. In accordance with Verter's understanding, they present spiritual capital as a multifaceted phenomenon, something capable of being transformed into other forms, but in dialogue with the boundaries established by early life experience. To take this observation further, one could argue that religious institutions enjoy a kind of social influence beyond the professed beliefs and practices of their members, channelled through the families of their leaders. One interpretation of this might refer to the secularisation of religious ideas – the reinterpretation of religious values learnt in childhood into more secular forms. But the high levels of affirmed religiosity among this group suggest that transformation, rather than erosion, may be a more appropriate description of this trend. Whether these transformed identities are likely to translate stated convictions into social action that has an identifiable religious dimension is less clear, and perhaps a comparative and longitudinal biographical study of the lives of clergy children is required before such questions can be answered with any justified confidence. What is clear is that the relationship between family upbringing and the negotiation of values in adult life is not simple, and calls for an analysis of the transmission of religious values that demands a renewed complexity in our understandings of religious identity and the life-course. Moreover, part of this understanding will need to take greater account than has been taken thus far of how religious identities evolve through adult life, and how this process often involves an ongoing conversation between individual agents and their memories of childhood, through which enduring ideas are forged.

Chapter 22

Protestant Confirmation in European Perspective

Leise Christensen, Duncan Dormor, Ida Marie Høeg,
Wolfgang Ilg and Kati Niemelä

Overview (Duncan Dormor)

One of the central anxieties for European churches is how religious identity, belief
and practices can be transmitted between the generations. One of the key 'links' in
this is the socialisation of adolescents through the rite of confirmation (Hervieu-
Léger, 2000; Davie 2000). In many of the Protestant countries of Europe, especially
Lutheran Scandinavia and the Protestant regions of Germany, a large proportion
of each cohort of adolescents is confirmed, and just as importantly, undergoes a
lengthy period of preparation. However there is a marked contrast between high
confirmation rates and low rates of regular church attendance. This gulf suggests
that in such countries, confirmation is experienced predominantly as a rite of
passage[1] with significant cultural and social significance for the individual, their
families and the wider peer group.

Such high rates of confirmation are in sharp contrast with the situation in the UK,
where currently about 4.5% of teenagers are confirmed within another Protestant
denomination, the Church of England.[2] Whilst there are clear historical differences
between their respective theologies and ecclesiologies, with Anglican practice
untouched by the emergence and spread of Pietism in the eighteenth century (the
key influence on Lutheran practice), such variation is more fully accounted for by
the seminal work of David Martin (1978, cf. 2005) on the varying character of the
relationship between church and state, and in particular, the degree of religious

---

[1] Perhaps the most striking evidence for this is the existence of humanist 'confirmation'
rites in the eastern part of Germany, Norway and to a very small extent in other Nordic
countries. In 2007 16% of all 15-year-old Norwegians underwent a 'confirmation' conducted
by the Norwegian Humanist Association.

[2] It is sometimes asserted that confirmation in the Church of England, is, or has
been, a rite of passage in a similar way. However, no more than one in four adolescents in
any given cohort has been confirmed in the Church of England over the last century, see
Church Information Office (1959) and various issues of the annual publication, the *Church
of England Yearbook*.

pluralisation within European countries. In the 'Nordic' model, confirmation preparation receives greater support from the main agents of socialisation (i.e. schools), but can also bring specific entitlements which are regarded as central to cultural and national identity. As the research below suggests, such a close alliance with the state may be double-edged. For example, for confirmation classes to take place within the school day, as is often the case in Denmark, ensures high levels of engagement by enlisting adolescents through natural peer groups (in effect an 'opt out' model) yet may also generate a climate in which the Christian faith is discussed 'objectively' rather than with a personal commitment in sight. The aim of this chapter is to explore the experience and understandings of confirmation amongst young people going through the process.

European Research (Leise Christensen, Ida Høeg, Wolfgang Ilg and Kati Niemelä)

Compared to other fields of education and youth work, confirmation preparation has seldom been investigated empirically. Niemelä (2008) and Schweitzer and Elsenbast (2009) are rare examples of work in this field. There exists no comprehensive survey to show how confirmation preparation is managed in the various European Protestant churches. For this reason, we decided in 2007 to carry out a large survey to clarify how such preparations are organised in a number of Europe's Protestant churches, how they are conducted and what actually happens in the course of the training, both from the confirmands' point of view and from the leaders' point of view.[3] Churches from seven countries have taken part in the survey so far – Germany, Switzerland, Austria, Denmark, Sweden, Finland and Norway. The empirical results discussed below are taken from this ongoing international study and draw on the data from four of the participating countries – Germany, Denmark, Finland and Norway (see www.confirmation-research.eu for more information).[4]

The percentage of young people being confirmed in Germany, Denmark, Finland and Norway varies. In Finland, the percentage is high – 89% of 15-year-old Finns were confirmed into the Church of Finland in 2007. Confirmation remains equally popular in some of the German regional Protestant churches; around 30% of all German 14 year-olds (which is more than 90% of Protestant young people) were confirmed in 2007 into the various Protestant regional churches. In Denmark 72% (2007) of all young people were confirmed into the Church of Denmark and 67% in Norway into the Church of Norway. The majority of the confirmands in these four countries are aged between 13 and 15.

---

[3]   The research was initiated by the German Lutheran and Reformed Churches and the University of Tübingen.

[4]   See Schweitzer et al. (forthcoming).

The ways in which the confirmation preparation is conducted in different countries also varies. In Denmark it is typically organised within school hours in a state school and lasts for almost one school year. The preparation may also be organised after school or during weekends as is most often the norm in Germany, Norway and in the area of the Danish capital. The main part of the training may also take place in a camp which is a very typical feature of Finnish confirmation training where 90% of confirmands attend training that is mainly in a camp form.

Methodologically, the investigation was quantitative. By means of questionnaires, confirmands were (among others) asked about their background, their reasons for attendance, their expectations, satisfaction towards the content and teaching methods used in their confirmation preparation. The participants received a four-page questionnaire at the beginning and at the end of the preparation process. A total of 20,000 confirmands from these countries completed the survey during the years 2007 and 2008.[5] The leaders (usually their parish ministers, in some countries also catechists, youth leaders, deacons, volunteers and so on) received a similar questionnaire at the same time. The purpose here was to be able to compare the confirmands' answers with their instructors' answers; to see whether the confirmands' views had changed in the course of the preparation; to see whether there were differences in the confirmands' satisfaction with the preparation according to which methods had been used on them; to see how the instructors had tackled the preparation pedagogically, didactically and regarding the teaching context – that is, classroom teaching, a combination of classroom teaching and 'confirmation camp', or camp only – and to see whether the instructors' intentions with their courses were fulfilled.

As the investigation is fairly comprehensive, it is not possible here to give a complete picture of its results. In this chapter, we concentrate on why young people in different countries want to be confirmed. Why do they attend and what do they gain from it? We also analyse some central tenets of Christian belief. We explore whether or not the confirmation training has a positive effect on the young people's faith and attitudes to Christianity.

Results

Motivation factors and experiences from the confirmation preparation course

The confirmands were asked why they had embarked on confirmation preparation. Eighteen possible reasons were given (plus some extra national options), ranging

---

[5]   Each of the churches/countries involved has endeavoured to ensure that the parishes taking part in the investigation are representative of the population as a whole in the country in question with regard to social groupings and geographical aspects – i.e. rural districts, towns, cities, the capital and its environs.

from the religious ('to learn more about God and faith') to the more prosaic ('to get money or presents at the end').

Table 22.1   Reason for registering for confirmation preparation course. (The confirmand: 'What is my background and reason for joining the course?')

I registered for confirmation time, ...	Germany	Norway	Denmark	Finland
because my friends did so as well.	29%	21%	14%	45%
because I was invited personally (e.g. by a letter).	36%	19%	15%	58%
because it is a good old tradition.	32%	52%	47%	60%
because I was baptised when I was a child.	53%	60%	55%	81%
because I felt obliged to take part.	10%	24%	26%	14%
because my parents wanted me to do so.	25%	30%	26%	57%
because my grandparents wanted me to do so.	10%	19%	10%	43%
because I had been told that confirmation training is fun.	38%	20%	11%	72%
because I see myself as a Christian.	-	33%	-	52%
because I want to be able to get married in the church.	-	-	-	73%
because I want to be allowed to be a godparent.	-	-	-	60%
because I want to attend a camp	-	-	-	76%

In cases of a blank space the question was not asked in these countries.

Motivation factors for becoming a confirmand

Table 22.2   Motivation factors for becoming a confirmand. (The confirmand: 'Where do I want to go with regard to being a confirmand?')

I registered for confirmation preparation course, ...	Germany	Norway	Denmark	Finland
to learn more about God and faith.	46%	29%	43%	24%
to experience community in the confirmation group.	47%	53%	35%	41%
to come to my own decision about my faith.	48%	37%	39%	39%
to make an important step in growing- up.	38%	38%	34%	48%
to meet and get to know friends.	44%	44%	32%	73%
to think about what is good or bad for me and my life.	31%	28%	19%	34%
to be strengthened in my faith.	42%	28%	32%	25%
to have a beautiful celebration with family and friends on the day of confirmation.	54%	58%	69%	54%
to get money or presents at the end.	53%	52%	54%	72%
to receive a blessing on the day of confirmation.	50%	35%	47%	45%

The results show that young people are not independent of tradition (see Table 22.1). What has happened earlier in life, what kind of family they have been raised in, and what kind of society they are part of, are important factors for the choices they make. Many confirmands' choice of confirmation is motivated by the fact that they have been baptised and that they view confirmation as a good old tradition. Confirmands' friends do not have the same influence on their choice. What their friends think about confirmation and what kind of choice their friends make about confirmation do not, according to the confirmands, have the same degree of influence on their own choice of confirmation as do tradition and the guidance from their infant baptism 15 years earlier or, in most countries, even their parents' wish.

In Finland, by attending confirmation training young people get rights – they get the right to get married in the church, a right to be a godparent and the right to vote in parish elections. These rights are regarded as important and for many they are among the most important reasons for attending. Almost three out of four confirmands sees the right to get married in the church and 60% the right to be a godparent as an important reason for registering on the confirmation course. However, the most important reasons for young Finns to attend confirmation training are that they were baptised as a child and most of them wanted to go to a camp. Confirmation training also has a positive image: the young people want to attend because they are told that the training is fun.

Other reasons such as 'to learn more about God and faith'; 'to come to my own decision about my faith'; 'to think what is good or bad for me and my life' did not score quite as well (see Table 22.2). One could sum up by saying that the confirmands had generally not joined the preparation courses for the more religious reasons, but for the more 'relational' reasons – parties and friends – and financial reasons – to get money and presents at the end. The Danish and German confirmands deviate slightly by giving the confirmation blessing high priority. The fact that the social/relational element (meeting new friends and so on) is not rated as highly by the Danish confirmands is probably due *not* to their having less interest in this aspect than young people in the other countries, but to their confirmation classes being made up largely of the same pupils as their school classes, so that in most cases they will know their fellow confirmands already.

When we asked the confirmands a few weeks before confirmation about their experiences with their confirmation time, the young people indicated they had got more out of their confirmation preparation than they had expected – both with regard to the faith-related questions and the non faith-related.

But what was the position with the more faith-related questions? Had the confirmation preparations done anything fundamentally to alter the confirmands' views on the central tenets of Christian belief? The confirmands were asked to state their opinion concerning Christian faith and the Protestant church with the same items at the beginning and at the end of confirmation time (see Table 22.3).

Statements of faith at the beginning of the confirmation preparation course and at the end

What the primary aim of confirmation preparation is or should be, is the subject of continued debate. Is it the passing on of concrete knowledge, is it Christian preaching, or should it be a mixture of the two with the teacher being left to decide where the emphasis is laid? If it is the passing on of knowledge, then confirmation preparation in Denmark would seem to have good prospects. The Danish confirmands' personal standpoints seem little inclined to budge when it comes to central Christian beliefs regarding God as creator, God as a helper in difficult situations, or Jesus being raised from the dead. Any changes which may occur are under 5%. But on the question of whether or not confirmands feel they know what Christian faith entails, there is indeed a big shift. At the end of the course, no fewer than 26% more of the Danish confirmands feel than they *do* now know what it entails.

Table 22.3   Statements of faith at the beginning of the confirmation preparation course and at the end

What do you think about the following statements?	Germany		Norway		Denmark		Finland	
	Beginning	End	Beginning	End	Beginning	End	Beginning	End
God created the world.	49%	+1	37%	+2	34%	0	37%	+11
There is life after death.	51%	+7	52%	+2	53%	+5	41%	+16
God loves all humans and cares about each one of us.	64%	+2	58%	+3	56%	+3	50%	+19
Jesus has risen from the dead.	52%	+6	38%	+5	39%	+5	38%	+18
I am not sure what I should believe.	30%	+1	37%	0	34%	-3	37%	+3
I often talk about God with other people.	14%	+3	8%	+6	7%	+3	8%	+2
Faith in God helps me in difficult situations.	35%	+3	23%	+4	18%	+2	21%	+11
I believe in God.	67%	+2	45%	+2	62%	-1	40%	+11
I know what the Christian faith entails.	54%	+14	49%	+13	44%	+26	46%	+23
I try to live according to the Ten Commandments.	22%	+4	23%	+5	20%	+6	33%	+15

The Norwegian confirmands by and large resemble the Danes. This is hardly surprising given the two countries' history and close association. The Norwegian confirmands, like those in the other countries, get 'more of everything' – if we can put it that way – in the course of their preparation, but the jump with regard to faith-related statements is between 2% and 5%, so there is not as great a 'development' as with the Finns. The Norwegians, too, acquire a great deal of knowledge about Christianity during their preparation (+ 13%), but it is not possible to say whether this affects their degree of faith in either one direction or the other.

The German confirmands appear to be more likely to hold traditional religious views in comparison with other European confirmands when beginning their confirmation preparation. In connection with the great majority of the faith-related statements on the questionnaire, they have a more positive attitude than their counterparts in the other countries, and this development continues throughout the preparation course, though the changes are not as marked as is the case with the Finns. The German confirmands also seem to acquire a good portion of factual knowledge along the way considering the rise in agreement with the statement 'I know what the Christian faith entails.'

The findings from Finland present a quite different picture. The Finnish confirmands seem at first sight to resemble their peers elsewhere in Europe, though they are generally more sceptical about 'dogmatically correct' statements. Only 40% believe in God when they begin the confirmation process, for example, which is considerably fewer than in Denmark, Norway and Germany. But by the end of the confirmation preparation courses, this figure has risen by 11%. The same is the case with the statement 'Jesus has risen from the dead.' The Finnish young people are sceptical to begin with, 38% of them believing it to be so, but by the end of the course, this figure is 56%. One might also highlight 'There is a life after death', where there is a corresponding 16% rise in the number subscribing to the belief. The Finnish confirmands, like their Danish counterparts, are also given a lot of information/knowledge in the course of their preparation for confirmation, but they are to a greater extent than the Danes influenced in their personal beliefs regarding central articles of Christian faith. The Finns have a two-figure percentage rise on almost all parameters. One could draw the conclusion that the Finnish confirmation preparation has more emphasis on faith than knowledge than the other countries in the survey and that it chooses a pedagogy and course structure which supports this aim.

Conclusions

As mentioned above, this study of the confirmand preparation in the Protestant churches of some European countries has not been completed as yet, but this chapter gives an overall impression of the work being done. A deeper analysis of the data contained in the survey will show in detail the chances and the problems of this substantial area of Protestant approaches to young people. There is no doubt that young people appreciate confirmation because of its long tradition. Nevertheless, a good confirmation preparation will not succeed just by continuing the traditional ways of teaching. In order to keep confirmation work on a successful path a lot of innovative ideas are needed. The comparison of the different results in the countries involved shows that the pedagogical methods used in confirmation work do make a difference as to how young people experience their confirmation time. An international cooperation on didactics and pedagogical methods within confirmation work might offer valuable insights for the future.

PART VI
Researching Youth Religion

Many of the chapters in this volume are rich in their descriptions of the method and approach the authors used to gather the data upon which their arguments rest. This final section highlights some of the different methods at our disposal as researchers spanning both the quantitative (Voas) and qualitative approaches including 'visual methods' as one that might work particularly well in this field (Dunlop and Richter). Attention to method is vital since there are particular issues to consider when researching religion and young people (Collins-Mayo and Rankin). The very youth of those we study raises questions as to how to ensure they are involved in the research in an ethical manner – by consent rather than coercion. Issues of sensitivity to research subjects on the part of the researcher are all the more critical when there is an age gap between researcher and subject. Further methodological complexity is introduced in relation to the researcher's status as an 'insider' or 'outsider' to the communities of which young people are a part (Abramson). The diversity of youth populations also needs recognition. It is all too easy to talk of 'young people' as if they constitute a homogenous group. Young people's experiences of, and engagement with religion, varies according to ethnicity, class, ability, sexual orientation and, as Aune and Vincett explore, gender.

Chapter 23

A Question of Belief

Sylvia Collins-Mayo and Phil Rankin

This chapter is concerned with some of the issues researchers face when trying to represent young people's religious and spiritual beliefs. Our reflections are based on experiences in the field and draw particularly on my work with 11–23 year old young people in educational settings and youth clubs (Collins 1997; Savage et al. 2006) and Phil Rankin's work with teenagers and young adults in public places (Rankin 2005). Some of the issues we discuss are pertinent to any research on religion; some are more specific to the practicalities of working with young people.

Giving young people voice

Becker's classic 1967 article makes the point that research is not without prejudice – the key thing is deciding whose side we are on. For ourselves there are three points of reference: our commitment to academic research, our own faith allegiances and our ideological stance regarding young people. We shall return to the first two when discussing the implications of research. Regarding the latter, youth studies scholars are increasingly moving away from seeing young people as the 'objects' of research to being actors in their own right, and developing research initiatives which aim to benefit the young people they study. We, like many researchers in this area, are wholly committed to giving voice to young people in the adult world. The question is how best to do this authentically and ethically? A number of issues present themselves. The main motivation for our researches has been to describe and understand the 'everyday' religious and spiritual beliefs of young people in Britain to find out what forms they take and what, if any, significance they have. We have chosen not to focus on youth congregations or specific religious movements, since relatively few young people are part of these. The type of religiosity we are interested in is less visible – it may involve institutional affiliation and occasional attendance at a place of worship, but not necessarily. Given the nature of our research focus our methodological orientation has been towards qualitative or mixed methods designs which offer enough flexibility to allow young people to express themselves as far as possible in their own terms and to clarify their meaning. Thus we have had extended conversations around questions such as 'How aware are you of God in your life?', 'How likely are you to pray?' (Collins-Mayo 2008), 'Would you perceive yourself to be spiritual?' and

'What do you think the word spiritual means?' (Rankin 2005, 26). Our research therefore reflects what young people think and say about their religious beliefs and practices. Despite the richness and usefulness of the data collected through this method, flexibility in the questioning technique does not guarantee young people engage in free self-expression in their answers. For this at least two things are required. First, that the young person has an opinion they can articulate verbally. Secondly, that the young person feels physically and emotionally safe and trusts the interviewer enough to be willing to share their thoughts.

Articulating beliefs

Religious ideas are often ambiguous and difficult to put into words. Theologians and artists alike, struggle with the complexities of expressing religious meaning. We should not, therefore, be too surprised if young people also have trouble articulating their thoughts on the matter, especially if they have not given it much consideration beforehand. Towler warns:

> When you ask the question 'Do you believe in an afterlife?' what you may actually be asking is 'When you stop and consider it, even though you have never done so before, do you believe in any sort of afterlife?' And that is an entirely different matter. (1974, 159)

Under these circumstances a structured approach which helps young people find words to express inchoate ideas, or approximate what they might think, can be a useful, if a somewhat blunt, prelude to more in-depth conversations. One young person, for example, wrote at the end of a questionnaire:

> I think the questionnaire is good because you can show your real feelings about God and ethical questions. The questions are good because they make you think about what you are writing on the paper. (Collins 1997, 41).

On the other hand, youth studies scholars are increasingly advising researchers not to underestimate young people. Raby (2007) cautions against being too bound by developmental models in our methodological ambitions since they can give somewhat jaundiced expectations of young people's levels of cognitive, emotional and (we can add) spiritual sophistication at different ages. Clark (2004) argues that even the youngest children can give articulate accounts of meaning if methods are developed which play to their strengths rather than weaknesses.

   Whatever method is used to help young people express their views, there is always the possibility that responses are simply an artefact of the questioning process. If this is the case, what status should we give the data in terms of understanding of young people's religiosity? Unstructured interview methods are just as susceptible to this criticism as structured approaches, the only advantage is that the 'working out' is more readily apparent in the contradictions and clarifications running through a conversation than they are on tick-box questionnaires. Ethnomethodologists have long argued that the real job of sociology is to consider the discursive practices which lead to the construction of meaning in situ, rather than concern itself with the articulation of beliefs and attitudes as if they are realities in their own right. Few studies on youth religion, however, have taken such a radical social constructionist perspective. In *Making Sense of Generation Y* (Savage et al. 2006) my colleagues and I wanted to explore the spiritual dimension of young people's world view in relation to popular culture without deliberately leading them into discussion. Ethnographic observation was not a feasible option because the type of data we required would have taken too long to collect, and because as middle-aged researchers we would have struggled to 'fit in' with the young people's social settings. Instead, we chose to use semi-structured group interviews in which we presented to young people a series of stimuli from popular art and culture, some of which hinted at spiritual and religious ideas to see whether the young people of their own volition would discuss the religious/spiritual dimensions of the stimuli or draw on religious concepts more generally. On the whole, traditional religious language was largely absent from the resulting discussions, which suggests that religious thinking is not a salient part of everyday life for many young people, at least amongst peers. Had we used a belief inventory or asked young people directly about their religious ideas we might have ended up overemphasising the day-to-day relevance of such beliefs to young people.

Trust and power

Trust between researcher and participant is important in any study. When researches include young people, however, there are extra dimensions to consider. Significantly, studies involving young people under 16 years old normally require the researcher to inspire the trust of adult gatekeepers as well as the young people themselves in order for the study to go ahead.[1] This means that young people's voices can be 'silenced' from the outset by adults who refuse access to them regardless of the young people's own preferences (Leonard 2007). Once physical access has been granted, the researcher then has to build enough trust with the young people to win social access. This involves negotiating the complex power dynamics which exist between adult researchers and young people.

Whilst the researcher is always responsible for the research process and its ethical implementation, amongst other things, the power relations vary depending on age differential, access to resources and location of the research. A key indicator of the power balance is how easy it is for young people to decline participation in a study. At one end of the spectrum an adult researcher administering a questionnaire

---

[1]   In the UK a clean Criminal Records Bureau check is normally a required indicator of 'trustworthiness' on the part of the researcher.

in a classroom during a lesson has a great deal more power than the young people. Young people are used to following instructions in school whether or not they want to, and they may be afraid to refuse participation in case it attracts punishment. This means that in addition to ensuring the study is explained to young people in such a way as to enable *informed* consent, the choice to say 'no' must be a real one. Some researchers distance their self by dress and manner from the role of teacher or adult authority figure to make dissent easier, and other activities are made available as an alternative to the research.

Youth clubs provide a mid-way point on the power spectrum. Youth workers are generally viewed differently from teachers – they are 'softer' authority figures, mentors and 'critical friends'. Young people's involvement in a youth club also tends to be voluntary in contrast with the compulsory nature of schools, and activities more youth-led. Consequently the power balance is more equitable if still ultimately in the adult's favour. A researcher new in this environment is usually reliant on the sponsorship of a trusted youth worker vouching for them. In these circumstances it is my experience that young people are often happy to talk to a researcher. However, it could be argued that whilst young people in this situation are not coerced into participation, their relationship with the youth worker is to some extent exploited in so far as they may not be so willing to participate were it not for the fact of doing their youth worker a favour.

At the other end of spectrum are studies such as Phil's which take place on young people's own 'turf'. Here it is the young people who decide the rules and they can easily refuse participation if they want to. In these cases the power balance is somewhat reversed. Phil notes his apprehension at approaching groups of older teens and young adults in streets and parks he did not know, in order to talk about spirituality. There was plenty of scope for his actions to be misconstrued by the young people, offence taken and allegations made.

With knowledge and experience gained elsewhere, Phil was acutely aware of the potential impact of his approach to young people. Just as with the school setting, dressing in a certain way can have an effect but so can accent, physical appearance and so forth, and these are things that cannot be changed. Indeed Phil's own apprehension about making the initial contact had an impact, no matter how small, on any future interview or conversation. As particular examples, Phil was aware that his Northern Irish accent could create assumptions in the minds of young people he engaged with, as could his physical appearance and approach if engaging with a group of young women in a public place. Operating unethically a researcher could use these types of factors to manipulate and advantage themselves in the process of data collection, so it is vitally important to recognise the impact of these factors and the power that can sit with the adult researcher. A sharp sense of personal and professional boundaries and a keen self-awareness are required to negotiate such potentially difficult situations. An advisory/monitoring panel can also be invaluable to the research as it needs to be shown that the researcher has given due diligence to the safeguarding of young people, the research method and their own protection.

Research setting

Trust is also affected by features of the location where the study takes place. It is normal practice, for example, to reassure young people that their views will remain anonymous thereby protecting the confidentiality of the young person. However, it is difficult to guarantee this in certain settings. For example, following the administration of a questionnaire in school which was supposed to be completed on an individual basis, my field notes describe how a discussion struck up amongst class members about their answers:

> One girl in the class had made it clear to those on her table that she did not believe in God, yet she still answered the question about heaven by saying that there was such a place. A boy on her table picked up on what appeared to him to be a contradiction of belief: 'You believe in heaven?' he queried, to which the girl replied defiantly ''Course I do, but there ain't no God up there!'

The only way to ensure confidentiality in this case would have been to adopt exam conditions, which potentially would have been problematic in terms of how the questionnaire was understood.

In another instance, a young man being interviewed in an office adjacent to a classroom stopped the interview abruptly when he suddenly became self-conscious of his disclosures. 'They can't hear us next door, can they?' he asked. His anxiety was real; being 'religious' is not always regarded in the best light by peers and can be the source of teasing. Facilitating a 'safe' environment for research therefore needs to be conscious of the physical setting in which the research is conducted. Phil's method of interviewing young people in their own space had the advantage of reducing the impact of people overhearing personal information and the scope for negative peer pressure.

Which young people?

Researchers who want to give young people voice also have to consider the question of 'which young people?' Few researchers have the resources to provide exhaustive representation of all groups of young people, particularly if those studies aim to secure rich data which is labour intensive in its collection. Accessing young people outside of schools and institutional settings is particularly difficult and time consuming. Phil's 'detached youth work' strategy for meeting young people in their own public settings was an interesting attempt to do this and potentially gave him access to otherwise 'hard to reach' young people who are normally excluded from studies of youth religion. Even then, however, personal characteristics, inclination and chance affected the types of contacts which could be made. As a white male researcher, for example, Phil did not feel he would get sufficient acceptance to conduct interviews in areas dominated by black and minority ethnic young people.

In addition to sampling, there is a matter of representation in the analysis. Youth studies have had a tendency to focus on 'spectacular' young people because the exotic makes interesting reading. Within the sociology of youth religion this penchant for the spectacular can translate to studies of unusual new religious movements or young people of fundamentalist persuasion. More mundanely it can also manifest itself in the preference for the colourful quote, the dramatic story or the most articulate responses being represented in reports. This means that the more commonplace or hesitant voices of young people are not heard directly.

Who's listening?

If research gives voice to young people, who is listening and how are they listening? Three constituencies are important from our perspective – the academic community, practitioners and funders – and each impact on the question of whose side we are on. Our commitment to academic research and our contribution to sociological understandings rest on our ability to recognise but then bracket out our personal sympathies, including our own religious commitments. Failure to do this will be met with resistance by the academic community since whilst it is accepted that the subjective cannot be scripted out, 'methodological atheism' (Berger 1967) remains the orthodoxy for sociological research and the researcher's personal religious affiliations a matter of disquiet if suspected of introducing bias. The strength of sociological research techniques and theories is that they provide the means whereby we might approximate objectivity provided we are self-aware and, to use Becker's words, 'limit our conclusions carefully' (1967, 247). Nevertheless tensions still arise. For example, discussions around spirituality encourage a high degree of self-reflection which may raise more questions for a young person than they can answer. One young woman concluded an interview with Phil by saying 'You've made me realise I need to find God.' It is not the job of the researcher, nor was it his intention, to trigger this need. But is it ethical to 'open up a can of worms' and then walk away? And if not, who should pick up her expressed need and how?

The tension between one's own religious inclination and a sociological agenda can be stretched further by practitioners and funders who want to go beyond limited, careful conclusions to look at the practical implications of research for their own work – in the case of the sociology of youth religion this may include anything from improving support for young people through outreach and mission to a more proselytising agenda. The reading of research and the implications drawn from it may well be out of the researcher's control once it has been published (this can be frustrating if findings are taken out of context or the nuances of argument lost), but in other cases funders may require researchers to stipulate policy implications upfront in their reports. In this case a researcher, particularly if in sympathy with the funder's agenda, may find himself or herself walking the line between the sociology of religion and religious sociology. An applied sociology of youth religion is then forced to recognise that we may be on various sides and we have to tread carefully between our allegiances.

Chapter 24

Quantitative Methods

David Voas

Introduction

One might imagine that youth religion is too complex to measure in numbers. The words we could use instead, though, refer to qualities that people possess to a greater or lesser degree. While it is true that quantification simplifies what has been observed, such methods force us to be clear about what we are studying. The act of selecting and defining variables imposes a rigour and an openness to criticism that can more easily be escaped in discursive treatments of the same phenomena.

We need quantitative data in order to discuss big issues, such as the alleged growth in alternative spirituality, the supposed persistence of Christian belief among non-churchgoers, the apparent strength of evangelical and charismatic congregations, the religious indifference of most young men, and the degree of commitment of young European Muslims, to name just a few. Unless we are content with guesswork, we have to collect information from representative groups of people through social surveys. Without empirical evidence of this kind, we have nothing but case studies, the representativeness of which would be impossible to judge.

Survey research allows us to say who is religious and how committed they are, by age, sex, ethnicity, partnership status, class and so on. It tells us how far religion and religiosity are associated with values, attitudes and behaviour in domains including politics and prejudice, morality and delinquency, marriage and family, and education and employment. Quantification often provides the best or only way of testing theories about the causes and consequences of religious affiliation and involvement. It is the natural perspective to use in discussing trends, and it facilitates international comparisons.

Surveys of representative samples of individuals (or congregations or anything else) are important because they allow us to generalize. Information about a few people, or for that matter about a thousand people not selected at random, only tells us about those individuals. In trying to discover what is happening and (broadly) why, there is no substitute for investigating the population as a whole via sample surveys.

Measuring religion

It would be a mistake to think that religion itself – Catholic, Anglican, Hindu, Buddhist – is necessarily the key variable in this domain. For some people, affiliation is purely nominal; others will have a serious personal commitment, seeing faith as important in their lives. What matters may be not only or even mainly one's notional identity or affiliation, but instead one's degree of religious commitment, or 'religiosity'. (This term is used non-pejoratively to mean the quality of being religious, not – as often in common usage – the display of excessive or affected piety.) Religiosity is bound up with attitudes, behaviour and values, while religion per se is arguably more like ethnicity, something that for most people is transmitted to them rather than being chosen by them.

These two concepts lead to quite separate questions. On the one hand there is the issue of the social significance of being Methodist, Mormon or Muslim relative to having some other affiliation, or none; on the other, the issue is how far degree of religiosity matters. Change over time may be a matter either of growth or decline in particular denominations or in the commitment shown by those involved.

We have various indicators of 'being religious' but no real measure, and the quality may be multi-dimensional. A crucial issue from the outset of rigorous empirical investigation has concerned how best to 'operationalize' religion. The challenge, in other words, has been to find variables that capture enough of what we mean by 'religious commitment' (or related concepts) that we can justifiably use them in research.

In recent years it has become conventional to focus on three aspects of religious involvement: belief, practice and affiliation. The first two dimensions seem fundamental, representing the distinction between the internal (belief in creeds, knowledge and acceptance of doctrine, affective connection) and the behavioural (participation in services, private devotion and communal activity). Belief (in God, an afterlife, a transcendent moral order, specific articles of faith or, less directly, in the importance of religion) is a basic sign of religious commitment, and profession of faith or agreement with some specific statements of belief may be a good index of personal religiosity. Actual religious behaviour, such as frequent prayer or attendance at services, may be an even stronger sign of religious commitment. Of course some people attend for personal, family or social reasons in the absence of faith or even affiliation, but in general one can reasonably assume (with good evidence) that religious practice in the modern world implies belief.

Although affiliation is simply what Americans label 'religious preference' rather than a measure of commitment, the growth (particularly outside the USA) in the number of those who say that they have no religion has ironically turned the simple willingness to accept a denominational label into an indicator of religiosity. Objective measures of religious affiliation (e.g. baptism) now tend to be less important than self-identification. Identity has become a major topic in contemporary sociology, and religion is still capable of being an aspect of personal identity that does not depend on active participation, official membership or even agreement with basic doctrine.

Measuring change

Most surveys collect data on a cross-section of the population at a single point in time (e.g. see Mason, chapter 7 herein). The resulting data give us a snapshot of the situation, and just as with a picture we can place people and their surroundings in relation to each other. We may find it more difficult, however, to see whether someone has been or will be moving, and in what direction. For many purposes, such as studying social change, we would really like a series of pictures rather than a snapshot – but can surveys provide it?

There are various ways to generate data on change. One is to go back to the same people year after year, decade after decade, to find out what is new and what has stayed the same. These are 'panel' or 'longitudinal' surveys. Such studies require a large investment over a very long period, and there are relatively few of them. The 'birth cohort studies' – large samples of individuals born in particular weeks in 1946, 1958, 1970 and 2000/2001 – are valuable, though only limited information is available on religion. The British Household Panel Survey (BHPS) is widely used in the UK, and although it focuses on adults, special questionnaires were given to adolescents in a few years. More recently, the Longitudinal Study of Young People in England (LSYPE), organized by the Department for Children, Schools and Families, has generated interesting findings on youth and religion (Noble and Moon 2009). In the USA , the National Longitudinal Survey of Youth 1979 (NLSY79) covers individuals born 1957–64; the respondents were aged 14–22 when first interviewed in 1979. A separate study of the children of women from that sample started in 1986, which has produced an exceptional intergenerational dataset. Finally, the NLSY97 is a survey of people born in the early 1980s who were 12–17 when first interviewed in 1997. Also in the USA, the National Study of Youth and Religion (Smith, chapter 5 herein) was extended to include two follow-up surveys of the respondents originally interviewed in 2002.

Alternatively, a survey may be conducted every year or two with many of the same questions appearing each time. The sample is not the same from one year to the next, and hence there is an additional source of uncertainty: if there are differences, is it because things have changed or simply because new people have been interviewed? Nevertheless these repeated cross-sectional surveys often give us the best information we possess about trends. The Teenage Religion and Values Survey in England and Wales (Robbins and Francis, chapter 6 herein) provides an example. Unfortunately the major national and international surveys (such as the British Social Attitudes survey, the European Social Survey, the US and Canadian General Social Surveys or the European and World Values Surveys) sample only people aged 18 and above. Some quantitative information on youth and religion is available in aggregated form from the census of population and the English and Scottish Church Censuses conducted by Christian Research (Brierley 2006).

There are also ways of creating a time series other than through contemporaneous data collection. Respondents can be asked to reconstruct their family, education or work histories. Such retrospective data are also useful with religion; one can ask about religion of upbringing, attendance at certain ages, when churchgoing stopped or started, and so on. Other questions related to childhood concern the religious affiliation or practice of the respondent's mother and father at that time. Indeed, respondents may answer questions about parents, partners and (if applicable) children, serving in effect as proxies for them in supplying data on entire families.

Data collection issues

Many of the difficulties in collecting data on youth religion for quantitative analysis are those faced by survey researchers in any field. For example, in order for a sample to be drawn, one needs a list of some kind – a 'sampling frame' – of individuals in the relevant population. If the aim is to study members of a minority religious group, there may be no such lists available. Similarly, there are common problems of representativeness.

It is unlikely that merely phoning, knocking on doors or stopping people in the street will produce a representative sample. Those who are at home or out at any given time of the day tend to have special characteristics, which is why the best surveys often involve repeated attempts to interview specific individuals selected for the sample. Surveys conducted via the internet have become common, but again there are many problems of representativeness. Even assuming that everyone has equal access to the questionnaire, those who complete it will be essentially self-selected. A related problem exists even when investigators approach specific individuals selected from a good sampling frame: not all will agree to participate. The issue of non-response bias – the effect on the results of losing those who refuse to do the survey – is a constant concern for quantitative researchers.

Even surveys using the best sampling techniques may not produce representative data if the samples are too small. Size is rarely a problem in looking at simple frequencies for the key variables – most serious surveys have at least a thousand respondents – but it quickly becomes an issue as one attempts to break down the totals by other characteristics. Hence it may be possible to discover (within an acceptable margin of error) what proportion of young people believe that our destiny is written in the stars, but it may be impossible to say anything meaningful about how they differ from their peers.

Religion can be a sensitive subject, though it falls a long way short of some others (e.g. sex, drug use) in difficulty. Members of minority groups may be reluctant to identify themselves for fear of persecution. Others may be reluctant to answer questions about what they see as personal matters. Social desirability can infect responses, so that people may not want to admit to unusual beliefs or practices and conversely might exaggerate their orthodoxy or frequency of churchgoing. These effects may be stronger in personal interviews than on more anonymous written questionnaires or even telephone surveys.

Some questions may not be clear to people. Answers on specific doctrines or religious ideas, such as the Trinity or reincarnation, may be difficult to interpret if the concepts are not understood by everyone. The same problem arises when using a word like 'belong': how formal does the belonging have to be? If the way such questions are understood varies systematically by age, class or culture then the results may be especially misleading. Comparisons over time and cross-nationally are particularly hazardous.

The variables that purport to capture religion or religiosity may not be reliable or valid, or may not relate to those dimensions that are relevant to our purpose. Obtaining fully satisfactory data on religion – whether affiliation, attendance or belief – is difficult. Indeed, the following 'law' is at least semi-serious: a quarter of responses to any question on religion are unreliable. Various cases in point are described in Voas (2007).

Uses of survey data

Notwithstanding these difficulties, it remains possible to obtain useful data on religion. Such data are valuable in helping us to understand the nature and sources of religiosity on the one hand, and the consequences of religious affiliation and commitment on the other.

Often we are interested in explaining the relative prevalence of religion or religiosity in different times and places. In statistical terms it is the *dependent variable*, so called because its level is assumed to be dependent on the values of the explanatory (or independent) variables. Many of the main theories of religion aim to account for the success or failure of the religious enterprise in relation to other factors.

Social scientists are also concerned with the impact of religion on other aspects of life – what are often referred to as 'outcomes'. Religion can affect age at marriage, marital stability, attitudes to family planning and desired family size, health and morbidity, education, economic activity, social equality, crime, alcohol use, social attitudes and any number of other traits. In studying these topics religion or religiosity would be *independent variables*, the variation in which may help to explain the levels of something else.

One needs to be wary in looking at the alleged effects of religion on other social phenomena. Perhaps religion is simply a proxy for other variables. The existence of an association between religiosity and health, for example, does not necessarily mean that religion per se is the proximate determinant or has any causal effect. Religion often acts through or is correlated with lifestyle or other variables, and part of the challenge in this field is to identify such mediating or confounding factors. It may also be the case that religiosity and these various characteristics are influenced by common factors, so that any association is only apparent.

Selection bias may confuse us about the direction of causation. Does religion cause good outcomes, or do people likely to experience good outcomes tend to be religious? The association between churchgoing and success among inner-city youth in the United States might imply that compulsory church attendance would be beneficial – or alternatively could come about simply because socially dysfunctional people do not go to church while families that favour work and discipline do (Freeman 1986). Recent research suggests that there are genuinely causal connections between religion and various outcomes, but the issue is clearly an important one (Regnerus and Smith 2005).

Detecting new manifestations of spirituality

Many scholars argue that spirituality based on personal experience and well-being is growing and even displacing conventional religion (Heelas and Woodhead 2005; Houtman and Aupers 2007; Roof 1999). Efforts to assess the scale, nature and significance of alternative spirituality are sorely needed, especially as the size, projected growth, novelty and permanence of this phenomenon are vigorously debated (Voas and Bruce 2007; Heelas 2007).

It is not always easy to say what 'spiritual' means; the label is used to flatter anything from earnest introspection to beauty treatments, martial arts to support groups, complementary medicine to palm reading. Moreover the descriptions of spirituality given by respondents seem to have little to do with the supernatural or even the sacred; it appears to be a code word for good feelings, the emotional rather than the material. Not even a quarter of those from a sample in Kendal, England defined their core beliefs about spirituality in terms that were either vaguely esoteric ('being in touch with subtle energies') or religious ('obeying God's will'). The rest said that it was love, being a decent and caring person, or something similarly terrestrial (Heelas and Woodhead 2005). A proportion even described it as 'living life to the full', on which basis some pop stars might qualify as spiritual masters.

Sociologists need to try to distinguish between the different constituencies currently considered under the holistic banner. Some people are undoubtedly attracted to metaphysical spirituality, but others are mainly interested in physical and mental methods of stress relief, or in alternative forms of healing, or in spa-type bodywork, or in self-expression and psychological support. How the numbers break down, how much overlap there is between them, whether and when the connections reflect a shared conception of the sacred rather than simply mutual sympathy or common practice – these are the questions to address.

Alternative spirituality may turn out to be even more complex than conventional religiosity. We can use the standard indices: self-identification (e.g. as 'spiritual but not religious'), belief (in characteristic ideas such as past lives or the sacredness of the self) and practice (of activities like astrology or alternative medicine, where they are personally important). The resulting overlap can be quite small (Voas and Crockett 2004). Whereas there is still a reasonably close connection between mainstream religious belief, affiliation and attendance, the realm of spirituality is considerably more diffuse; it is very difficult to predict what people believe, do, or call themselves on the basis of any of the other pieces of information.

Datasets for secondary analysis

Every investigator dreams of working with data from high quality, purpose-built sample surveys. In practice it is so expensive and time consuming to conduct good surveys that most quantitative work is done on existing data collected for uses not specifically related to religion. Such 'secondary analysis' is often frustrating, principally because questionnaires typically contain far fewer questions on religion than one would like, but the approach does allow a great deal to be done quickly and cheaply.

Regular national surveys are conducted for the purposes of social research in many developed countries. These datasets are typically archived and made available to scholars within a year or two after fieldwork is completed. Most are repeated cross-sectional surveys, and religious affiliation and frequency of attendance at services often feature among the core questions that are asked routinely.

For cross-national comparisons, a number of surveys are conducted in many countries at approximately the same time. The International Social Survey Programme questionnaires have focused on religion in 1991, 1998 and 2008. The European and World Values Surveys provide good coverage of religious topics. The European Social Survey is more recent and includes only a few questions on religion, but the quality of the data is high. Eurobarometer and similar studies provide regular surveys of attitudes, with at least basic information about religious affiliation and practice.

Many other surveys are catalogued at websites such as British Religion in Numbers (http://www.brin.ac.uk), the Association of Religion Data Archives (http://www.thearda.com), and the UK Data Archive (http://www.data-archive.ac.uk).

The surveys so far named aim to provide representative samples of the adult populations and hence are not ideal for studying youth. (The youngest respondents are typically 18 and only a fraction of respondents will be less than 30.) Some surveys, however, do target young people specifically; the best known is perhaps the National Study of Youth and Religion mentioned above (see chapter 5 in this volume), with others from the USA listed on its website (at http://www.youthandreligion.org/resources/surveys.html). In addition, from time to time there are small (and sometimes not so small) surveys that touch on religion conducted by opinion pollsters, churches, academics and public agencies. Often only summary statistics are released; the datasets themselves are not generally available for use. Nevertheless the figures can be of value to researchers interested in religion and youth.

Chapter 25
Visual Methods

Sarah Dunlop and Philip Richter

The Facebook/YouTube Generation inhabit an image-saturated world and are savvy consumers of visual images. So it seems particularly appropriate to use visual research methods to understand their religiosity. In this chapter we explore some of the emergent theory and practice relating to visual research methods, with particular reference to young people's religiosity.

Since the invention of the portable camera anthropologists have used photographs as visual field notes to substantiate their observations (e.g. see the work of Evans-Pritchard http://southernsudan.prm.ox.ac.uk/biography/pritchard/). Over time the methods of using images within research have been refined and developed by both anthropologists and sociologists. (For a summary of the history of visual research see Pink 2007, 9–17.) Recently, the advent of affordable digital cameras and high-resolution camera-phones has both democratised the medium and enabled sociologists economically to incorporate visual methods into their research.

Visual sociology is, arguably, a more vital, sensuous and affective means of representing society than conventional sociology. As such, its methods seem particularly appropriate for researching *religion and youth*, and equal to the vitality of what is being represented. Photographic images can operate on a subconscious level to elicit responses about meaning, identity and spirituality. Working on a connotative level with images can allow research to dig beneath the surface of a social situation. But it also guards against too exclusive a focus on young people's thought forms and beliefs, and takes proper account of the observable behaviours, emotions and rituals of religion. Photography can be one means, amongst others, of paying attention to the embodiment of religious tradition – the inscription of tradition in 'distinctive bodily practices' and the 'ceaseless interplay between the messages of bodies and the messages of explicit discourse' (McClintock Fulkerson 2007, 50).

Photography was, however, famously critiqued by Susan Sontag who claimed that taking photographs is a hostile act, that the camera is a predatory weapon, that the photographer aggressively objectifies others, and that 'to photograph people is to violate them … it turns people into objects that can be symbolically possessed' (1979, 14). On the face of it, were photography, as Sontag suggested, merely a form of dissociative, objectifying seeing, it would seem to sit uneasily with religious research. However, although her claims may be true of some photography, at some times, by some people, these are not necessarily defining features of the medium. Photographic seeing is not reducible to a single objectifying gaze, and photography can entail reciprocity between photographer and subject, as was evidently the case in the photography by, say, the contemplative monk, Thomas Merton (Richter 2006).

Young people use and consume symbols and intertextual references in many different kinds of visual media. Youth are adept at 'reading' images, which is evident in how they consume and recycle images within popular culture (Willis 1990). Therefore, visual research methods open opportunities for creative lines of conversation with young people. Images operate on a subconscious, intuitive level, which means they are often able to transcend religious language and lead to fruitful discourse about spirituality and belief. This is precisely what Rosalind Pearmain discovered in her study of young people's sense of spiritual aspects of the self. She argues that visual material, due to its ability to evoke embodied experience, allows a 'bigger space' for talking about spiritual experience with young people than the traditional interview question-and-answer format within qualitative research (2007).

Visual methods have begun to feature significantly in youth research. Photographers Andrew Dewdney and Martin Lister established a community youth project in South London (1988). Through taking photographs, the young people explored various subjects, such as self-identity, values and objects that represent what is important or meaningful to them. The 50,000 photographs that they accumulated between 1978 and 1984 formed an invaluable archive of sociological data about the everyday lives of these young people. Eleanor Nesbitt studied the religious experience of 8–13 year-olds in Coventry between 1986 and 1996 (2000a, 2000b). She brought photographs of places of worship to the interviews and used them, as well as images that she found on the walls of the child's home, as visual stimuli for the children's responses. She found that during the interviews the images enabled the children to talk freely about their religious experiences. Sara Savage, Sylvia Collins-Mayo and Bob Mayo conducted research among young people in the UK and used images from popular culture to elicit responses from young people about their worldview (Savage et al. 2006).

Sarah Dunlop used a variety of visual ethnographic methods to study the search for spirituality among students in Eastern and Central Europe (2008). Given that religious affiliation in this region is closely tied to national identity and conversations about personal religious beliefs are a social taboo, a social remnant of the enforced atheism during the time of the Soviet Union, Dunlop discovered that images provided a non-confrontational means for exploring issues of belief and spirituality with young people. Conversations with youth about the images on their wall provided a particularly rich source of data. Dunlop also gained insightful information through asking the students to spend a week photographing what is 'significant' to them and then interviewing them about the images produced.

Figure 25.1   'The organisation of life' painted by an 18 year-old in Kiev, Ukraine.[1] Photograph by Dunlop, Kiev, 2002

When Lorraine Young and Hazel Barrett conducted research among young people living on the streets of Kampala, they developed a method that was sensitive to the role that young people have as meaning-makers and important social actors. They found that using four different visual research methods, including photo diaries, gave these socially excluded young people a high level of participation in the research (2001). Horst Niesyto (2000) also sees the importance of enabling young people to make meaning within research, and argues that since media has an increasing influence on young people and how they experience reality, it is fruitful for researchers to provide opportunities for youth to create audio-visual self-productions: see, for example, the 'Children in Communication about Migration' project (2001-5) - http://www.chicam.org/reports/download/chicam_final_report.pdf.

[1]   The 18-year-old young person who painted this picture explained. 'At the beginning of life there are just pieces, but then they develop into many lines and finally these lines make the whole form that we have in all of life, everything in life and relationships begins with a small, small drop. Of course there is some power in the world, in you, and in the general world. Faith is mysterious because it organises reality in such a precise way.' .

Recently, a team of researchers from the UK, Germany and Norway, led by Roger Hewitt, have set out to study the religious perceptions of young people in three urban settings. This project, 'The Architecture of Contemporary Religious Transmission', includes photography workshops and photo elicitation interviews, based on informants' own photographs often taken on a camera phone. The research process has also itself been video-recorded (http://www.relemerge. org/project_02).

There are various ways of using images in research. For example, visual research can become an aspect of studies of material culture when the research seeks to discover how people use various types of images in everyday life, such as in art, pop culture, media, public space and the internet. In *The Visual Culture of American Religions*, David Morgan and Sally Promey argue that religion and the visual frequently come together in society, and thus argue for more studies of the visual nature of religion (2001, xi). Visual culture includes folk and official art, architecture, illustration, mass-produced images and objects of everyday use.

Museums, historical records and personal photo albums all contain archives of images from a specific point in time. An analysis of these images is useful for comparing then and now, and studying changing demographics (Edwards 2007, 1992). Douglas Harper has combined archival image research with photo elicitation (2001). A weakness of using historical archival images for research is that at times it is difficult to discern staged images from impromptu pictures. Furthermore, if the story of who is pictured and why the photographer is taking the picture is lost, then the photograph's usefulness is limited to content analysis (see below).

The documentary photography approach entails the researcher photographing aspects of social life (Becker 1998). Researchers spend a period of time with a group and take pictures of what they observe. The images are intended to be un-staged since they are recording visual field notes of the research context. In this type of study, the images are the main source of data. The strength of this method is that it is sensitive to the visual nature of social life and usually produces photographs that are good enough to be used for publication. The drawback is that the researcher, not the research subject, is framing the photographs and then narrating them based on observations of the social group.

Using photos during an interview to spark conversation is referred to as 'photo elicitation' (Hurworth 2003). One of the strengths of photo elicitation is that it is a non-confrontational interview technique. The focus of conversation is on the pictures, directing the gaze of the interviewee and interviewer to the images, not to each other. Using an archive of images provided by the researcher means that the same images could be used in each interview, giving a measure of consistency and ability to compare reactions to a given image across the sample. However, when the researcher provides the images, sometimes the interviewee may not relate to the image or valuable conversation time might be taken up with questions about the origin of the photograph.

The researcher can overcome this by inviting participants to take photographs or film that illustrate some aspect of their lives. When combined with an interview about the images, this method is called 'reflexive photography'. The main strength of this approach is that there is a high level of collaboration between the researcher and the participants. The main drawback is that the researcher cannot control the quality of the images produced (see below).

The taking of photographs, especially of children, can be subject to legal and/ or ethical constraints. Researchers working with young people under the age of 17, unaccompanied by their parents, should have relevant Criminal Records Bureau clearance (or the equivalent elsewhere). In terms of legality, there are no legal restrictions in the UK on photography in most public spaces, except in certain prohibited areas. Neither is there a presumption of privacy for individuals when in public. Photographs taken, without permission, on private land may constitute trespass and represent an invasion of privacy (see http://www.sirimo.co.uk/ukpr. php). The dissemination of photographs may raise other legal issues. Where research involves photography by the subjects themselves, copyright resides with the image creator, unless copyright is waived and passed to the researcher. In other countries different laws apply (e.g., for the USA see: http://www.kantor. com/useful/Legal-Rights-of-Photographers.pdf).

There are also ethical issues to consider when taking and publishing photographs. The 'physical, social and psychological well-being' of subjects should not be put at risk and research participation should be based on 'freely given informed consent'; in the case of children, the consent of parents *and* child should be elicited (http://www.visualsociology.org.uk/about/ethical_statement. php). Sometimes the identities of subjects may need to be concealed, for instance, by photographing from behind. Covert photography usually runs counter to the principle of informed consent, so is rarely justified. Occasionally, covert methods may be employed if subjects are likely to alter their behaviour once they realise they are being photographed: permission can then be sought afterwards from the subjects to 'keep', rather than 'take', the images. Use of a large, easily visible, camera can help ensure that photography is overt.

Equally, there are issues of control and potential exploitation. Research may exploit and disempower the subjects, if images are 'taken' or 'stolen', rather than 'given'. The researcher may also consciously or unconsciously attempt to control what their reader sees, for instance, in terms of how a photograph is cropped. The researcher's own interpretation of the data, as well as aesthetic considerations, may dictate close cropping of the image, whereas the reader might read the data differently were they able to see what was happening beyond the frame; framing creates connections between components of the image which do not necessarily exist (Edwards 2006, 107). Captions can attach a spurious sense of objectivity to photographic images, especially if they are couched in general terms and give the impression of depicting a more widespread category or phenomenon. However, these difficulties can be minimised if captions are expressed in more specific terms, for instance, specifying the precise location and date of the photograph.

Some researchers have deliberately placed their captions in an unconventional manner, for example, superimposed on the image, in order to alert readers to the caption and invite the reader to 'speculate about its function in relation to the image ... and [entertain] a range of interpretations' (Chaplin 1994, 271). Greater autonomy can also be lent to photographs by separating them from written text, for instance, by printing them on opposite pages to the text, as in Bateson and Mead's *Balinese Character* (1942).

Collaborative projects, involving research subjects as 'participants' in their own representation, can help obviate these risks (Pink 2007, 57). Sarah Pink has identified a variety of collaborative approaches, including: 'direction' of the ethnographer's own photography by informants; interviews focused on the ethnographer's photographs or the informants' own (pre-existing) photographic collections; viewing displays, exhibitions and archives with informants; and informant-produced images and photo-interviews (2007, 75–94). Once in collaborative mode, portraits of subjects may then, for instance, be made quite differently: the researcher's preference for an un-posed naturalistic shot may give way to a deliberately posed image in which subjects have intentional control over how they represent themselves. Where collaboration involves subjects taking photographs themselves this may diminish the quality of the research's photographic data, because of, for instance, obstructed lenses, camera shake, inaccurate focus, unintentional cropping or failure to 'fill the frame'. However, projects can intentionally include photographic skills training, which can empower subjects with transferable skills useful beyond the research project (see http://www. photovoice.org/). The extent of collaboration can, however, vary. For instance, the VIA (video intervention/prevention assessment) Project at The Children's Hospital, Boston, USA, empowers children and adolescents to create visual narratives of their 'illness experiences and needs', in order to inform clinicians about patients' issues and needs and to enhance clinical practice (http://www.viaproject.org/ home/). But, although in many respects highly innovative, this patient–clinician partnership model only hands the processes of observation over to the patients, and does not include the patients in the processes of data analysis.

The analysis and interpretation of visual data varies according to the aims of the research and the type of research method used. The simplest approach is content analysis. For example, a study of the images on young people's walls would mean the researcher counts the number of posters of pop stars, religious images or photographs of friends and family. But photographs can also be interrogated as social documents. An ethnographic approach to analysing visual data entails an empathetic study of the meanings of the images for the person viewing the image. A cultural studies approach involves an emphasis on the medium, the production of the image and the function of the image in social life. This perspective would analyse how images are used in meaning-making as well as in everyday life. Since visual research methods often include those being researched as collaborators, it can be very fruitful to additionally involve the participants in the analysis of the data.

Visual researchers occasionally find it useful to employ semiotic tools for analysis of visual data (Hall 2000). The images produced by a social group or images used and consumed by the group are studied to discover the symbols within the images and to reveal the significance of the symbols to the people being studied. This approach to the analysis of visual data focuses on the image itself and discovering all of the possible readings of a symbol (Van Leeuwen 2001). A weakness of this approach is that although it studies the public meaning of images and symbols, it may not uncover the personal, private meaning that the image evokes in individuals.

In this chapter we have argued that visual sociology, itself a relatively young sub-discipline, can offer helpful new tools for researching religion and youth. Visual research methods are not intended as a substitute for written text and discursive argument. But photographic images have the power to not only complement and illustrate the written text, but, potentially, to enable the viewers to interrogate the visual data on the basis of what they themselves see. Hence, social analysis can be enhanced by the photography, just as the observation of the photograph can be enhanced by the accompanying social analysis. Each, as it were, can comment on the other in a 'marriage of text and image' (Banks 1995) and each can form 'not a complete record of the research but a set of different representations and strands of it' (Pink 2007, 120).

Figure 25.2 'Young woman at Italian Sunday market, Gavignano, 2007', from Philip Richter, 'Sunday – soul of the other days?' (http://www.stets.ac.uk/sunday/)[2]

---

[2] In this Photo Essay Philip Richter compares and contrasts contemporary attitudes towards Sunday in three European locations.

   Photography has inherent limitations as a research tool: it is a snapshot of time that may or may not be representative of other moments; it cannot, on its own, communicate the complexities of social relationships; its images are not simply a transparent reflection of reality – they are framed, produced and sometimes manipulated; and its images are ambiguous – different viewers/readers will give the images different meanings (Pink 2007, 152–5). But these limitations also apply, to greater or lesser extents, to more conventional social research methods. As we have seen, visual research methods also present important advantages. They take proper account of the embodiment of religiosity. They, as it were, pluralise the observer and empower subjects to represent their own religiosity. And they connect with young people's saturation by, and expertise in reading, visual images in contemporary society.

Chapter 26

Gender Matters: Doing Feminist Research on Religion and Youth

Kristin Aune and Giselle Vincett

Introduction

Feminism – that is, belief and actions supportive of gender equality and rejecting women's subordination – has increasingly shaped researchers' questions, topics, theories and methodologies, especially from the 1970s onwards.

Feminists noted that studies of 'youth' were predominantly studies of young men in public spaces (McRobbie and Garber 1975). Girls and young women were marginal to the analyses – standing chatting at the side of the youth club where young men's games were the focus – and their unequal status was not critiqued. So researchers began to study girls, seeking to understand the structures constraining them, such as limited career opportunities and pressure because of the 'sexual double standard' to keep their sexual reputations intact (McRobbie 1978). To get close to young women, researchers had to enter their private worlds, where girls spent more time than boys. More recently, feminist structural analyses have given way to a focus on the influence of culture and media in shaping young women's identities (Harris 2004b; Aapola et al. 2005). Additionally, researchers study masculinity from a feminist perspective, noting that young men exhibit different versions of masculinity, and that some are privileged (Frosh et al. 2002) – an area we explore in our case study below.

Gender and methods

Feminist research methods are diverse – there is no such thing as a single feminist method. Nevertheless, feminists have been influential in developing research that is *participatory* (seeing those studied not as subordinate 'subjects' but as equal participants), *reflexive* (involving the researcher reflecting deeply and personally on the research process) and *uses theory to identify and critique gender inequalities*. Feminists often do qualitative (detailed, often small-scale) research, believing that it facilitates an in-depth examination of beliefs, practices and processes. Feminists have also argued that quantitative methods can dichotomise gender difference without revealing the complexity of gender identities or the process of gender identity formation. Quantitative methods may also marginalise those who do not fit into categories on survey forms – for example, those of mixed ethnicity or with unorthodox religious commitments.

It is worth introducing and critiquing participatory methods here because the research project discussed in our case study was partly conducted using this method. Participatory methods aim to foster a collaborative approach in which informants shape the research through flexible discourse methods (Pain 2004). Interrogation of, reflection upon and reshaping of subjectivities are at the heart of participatory methods and may be a particularly good fit for young people, whose subjectivities are especially in flux.

However, it can be dangerous to assume that such methods really give voice to everyone. The reality, say critics, 'all too often boil[s] down to situations in which only the voices and versions of the vocal few are raised and heard' (Cornwall 2003, 1325). This is because 'power relations reproduce themselves, regardless of how "participatory" or "democratic" a setting is, unless a conscious, sustained effort is undertaken to alter them' (Connell 1997, 251–2). In qualitative group work with youth, this can mean that girls and gender-'marginal' boys (Cornwall 2003, 1337) are silent or silenced. Gender-marginal participants (whether girls or boys) may be constrained by social limitations about gender roles and abilities and by the 'absence of a "critical mass"' of gender marginal participants (Cornwall 2003, 1329). The post-feminism of many youth (discussed below) may exacerbate these restrictions by producing a situation where gender is unexamined.

Gender in youth and religion research

Existing literature on youth and religion contains little acknowledgement of how gender matters. The exception is some quantitative research on gender differences in youth religiosity (see below). A brief search in the indexes of the main texts about youth religion (e.g. Flory and Miller 2000; Smith 2005; Heft 2006) reveals a couple of pages mentioning gender. But these are generally minor asides and are not integral to the argument. Perhaps this is because gender differences and inequalities have become less pronounced and are thus considered to merit less discussion. This is partly so, since one hallmark of youth religion is its inclusiveness and support for opening positions of religious authority to women (a point made briefly in Flory and Miller 2000). Nevertheless, since gender is a central component in everyday life, it is crucial that gender questions are integrated into analyses of young people and religion.

Equally, research on youth and gender neglects religion and spirituality. In an important recent text, religion is conspicuously absent from the list of social divisions shaping young women's lives – a list that included ethnicity, class, race, sexuality, ability and nationality (Aapola et al. 2005, 1).

But gender matters in youth and religion research. This is so, we argue, for two principal reasons: first, because there are differences between young men and women's religiosity and these are declining in response to changes in society;

second, because youth religion is an arena where gender identities are negotiated and performed. We explore each of these in turn, before presenting a case study from recent research on young Christians in Scotland.

Gender differences in youth religiosity

There are differences between young men and women's religiosity. For both, religious commitment is declining. The data suggest that the gender difference evident among twenty- and thirty-something adults, or Generation X (see figures in Wuthnow 2007, 62–70), is declining amongst teenagers (also known as 'Generation Y' or the 'millennial generation'). But even amongst teenagers and students, females are somewhat more inclined than males to classify themselves as religiously committed, and to practice religion. In the 2002–3 US National Survey of Youth and Religion, 44 per cent of females and 37 per cent of males aged 13–17 attended a religious service at least once a week and 72 per cent of females compared with 58 per cent of males prayed alone at least once a week (Smith 2005, 279). In the UK, Francis and Robbins' (2005, 62–3) survey of 23,400 young people (aged around 13–15) in urban areas in the late 1990s revealed a lower level of religious practice but a similarly gendered pattern: 40 per cent of males and 46 per cent of females said they believed in God. If it is rarer for boys to describe themselves as religious, it is also more costly and counter-cultural for them. While piety has historically been associated with femininity, until at least the mid-twentieth century masculinity was 'the antithesis of religiosity' (Brown 2001, 88). Even today, the activities advocated as central to masculinity within popular culture (alcohol consumption, lewd behaviour and sexual exploration) are activities eschewed by religious communities.

But gender differences seem to be declining. For instance, church censuses conducted by the UK organisation Christian Research reveal a reduced gender imbalance in religiosity, especially among younger age groups. The 2005 English Church Census demonstrated that for the first time young men aged 15–19 outnumbered young women as church attendees (Brierley 2006, 130–1).

Additionally, the erosion of religious commitment is happening at a faster rate for females than males (Brierley 2006, 130–6). Partly, this is because with the rise of female employment in the public sphere, where religion is least evident and nurturing religiosity is harder, women's behaviour is becoming more like men's. Young women are less likely to be (or remain) conventionally religious because they are spending considerable time working and studying, and their egalitarian values and diverse family and sexual relationships are incompatible with the traditional values and family patterns of religious institutions (Aune et al. 2008).

While some young people have embraced feminism for themselves, forming a new feminist 'wave' (Dicker and Piepmeier 2003), the majority have not. Most young people take gender equality for granted, especially those yet to enter full-time employment and parenthood (where gender injustices often begin being felt). Young people are often 'post-feminist': that is, they are familiar with feminist ideas and support gender equality but see feminism as something that belongs in the past since 'everybody is equal now'.[1] For religious youth, gender issues may similarly lie unexamined, and the gendered status quo in different religious groups may remain unchallenged. However, the assumption that men and women are equal can mask or even encourage older – and new – gender inequities.

Negotiating gender in youth religion

Religion provides a space where gender identities are negotiated and performed. Gender identities may be traditional for young people involved in some more popular forms of religion (for example evangelical Christianity or Islam). This is a complex area, however, for even those who adopt what outsiders might see as gender-traditional roles or modes of dress do so in modern, contemporary ways. For instance, the adoption of the *hijab* by many younger Muslim women post 9/11 might be seen as evidence that they are embracing traditional feminine roles. Yet by selecting fashionable hijabs from online stores and explaining their veiling as a challenge to the oppressively sexualised Western culture women are subjected to, it becomes clear that the label 'gender traditional' is inadequate.

The gender identities negotiated within religion are, therefore, changeable and multiple as young people negotiate different areas of life (family, education, friends, leisure, work and so on) and as they intersect with other social divisions like ethnicity, sexuality and class. Gender identities constructed through involvement in religion may be normative or non-normative in relation to the religious group and/or to mainstream society. A gender identity approved of by a religious group may be considered deviant or ridiculed in mainstream society, for instance. Some non-religious young people too may see their secularism as part of their gender identity – for instance if they adopt values or lifestyles antithetic to mainstream religion.

Concerns which have traditionally occupied sociologists of religion (religion in modernity, secularisation, the origin and structure of religious organisations, New Religious Movements) are giving way to those that better reflect the shape of younger people's involvement in religion (including: post-modernity, the growth of spirituality, and religion and popular and cyber culture). The gender issues in these areas are somewhat different. Popular culture plays a significant role in young people's lives – indeed, Beaudoin (1998, 21) claims that popular culture functions as the 'surrogate clergy' of Generation X – so a gendered analysis of the popular culture's representation of religion and spirituality is salient.

---

[1]   It is arguable that post-feminist society is not an equal society, given pay gaps, high rates of domestic violence, sexualised media images and punishing beauty ideals.

Youth, gender and religion in Scotland

Our case study is drawn from recent research examining the religious lives and meaning making of young Christians in Glasgow, Scotland.[2] Participants were between the ages of 16 and 27, from diverse denominational and socio-economic backgrounds. Young people were first asked to participate in group work, which was designed to be participatory, so that young people could shape and direct the encounter. Later, volunteers participated in two interviews: one with a parent or guardian to investigate religious transmission and identity formation, and one with the young person alone to examine the young person's belief and meaning-making systems.

For post-feminist youth, direct questioning about gender issues may be a false or leading method. Though a question on gender was included in interviews with young people, the post-feminist nature of young participants made the question feel awkward. To the question, 'Do you think it's harder to be a girl or a boy in the church today?', young people generally responded in one of two ways. Either they claimed that they didn't see much difference, or they said that it was harder for boys because being Christian was not seen as an acceptable (or 'cool') identity for boys. Young people framed this difficulty in terms of normative gender performance. Being male and Christian was perceived as a marginal gender performance, though one which young men said occasionally garnered them respect for its 'authenticity' (that is, others respected that they stuck to their beliefs despite the fact that it marginalised them socially).

Several young men indicated that religion can aid in the construction of a non-normative or marginal gender identity. For example, Jack is 17, he has finished school and works at a shipbuilding yard. He does not attend a traditional church, but considers the Boys' Brigade youth group his church.

Interviewer: I remember you said that if you hadn't been involved in the Boys' Brigade you would have been a very different person.

Definitely.

Interviewer: What is it about the Boys' Brigade that's made you a certain way?

I think one of the major things for me was the officers were such a big influence because they had faith, but they were having a laugh at the same time. And as a youngster, going to church it was just full of serious faces ... And seeing these sort of ... young officers having fun ... you know, having a social life and still believing and having faith, It was just a sort of reality check that that's just what

---

2   The project was funded by the AHRC/ESRC under the 'Religion and Society' programme. The research team consisted of Elizabeth Olson, Giselle Vincett, Peter Hopkins and Rachel Pain.

I want. And another reason why I said ... em ... I'd be a totally different person is just seeing people who live so close to me ... there's a guy that lives round the corner from me and. I'm pretty sure he's got the same background as me, but he's just a nightmare. He smokes, he drinks ... he hangs about late at night. He's up to no good ... and he didn't go to the BB.

Interviewer: Do you think it was important that the officers are young guys?

Yeah, I thought that was very important ... because it gives you something to look up to.

Interviewer: It would have been different if they were young women?

Yeah. I mean, I'm not a sexist, but ... like ... it's just the fact that I can relate to it so closely simply because they're male.

Young men stressed that being a Christian allowed for relationality and emotional expression. As Peter (age 22) put it, as a Christian male you are 'allowed' to be happy, rather than being 'the cool person who sort of mopes about'. Peter also pointed out that as a young Christian male, he does not have to buy into what he identified as a culture of 'sexual propaganda' and glorified violence.

At the same time, religion can support the performance of normative gender identities. For example, Robin is 16 and loosely affiliated with the Church of Scotland. During her interview, she spoke about the expectation of being 'hard' (i.e. tough) as a man in Glasgow, which placed her in a difficult position with relation to her father. Robin explained that her Dad is in the Orange Order, which she associates with religious 'bigotry' and sectarian violence. His membership, she claims, is mainly 'because his father done [it] and all his brothers have done it. ... And now he's started getting some of my step-brothers and that in it as well now.' Young people thus also spoke about the way past religious or sectarian practices continued to exert influence on gender performances.

In group work with nominally Christian youth, young people's body postures, group dynamics, gendered discourse and gendered use of space mirrored normative gender constructions and confirmed what the young people themselves claimed about the pressures on boys to act in a certain way. That is, boys slouched in their seats, made jokes, swore for effect, and otherwise demonstrated how they were still 'cool' despite being involved with a Christian youth group. Other boys talked about being laughed at by others for attending a Christian youth group. The church was clearly identified as 'not cool' which meant, in effect, 'feminine' or not appropriate for a 'real' man. At the same time, it was precisely the 'feminine' qualities of relationality and emotional expression which young men identified as allowed by and desirable in the church.

Some female participants in the research pointed to the way that gender performances for girls may differ according to class and be changing more broadly.

Maia is 16, from an area of Glasgow in which violence amongst girls is common. She constructed her participation in fights as outside of proper Christian behaviour ('I'm not as good a Christian as I could be'). She claims that being a Christian is teaching her to 'try and sort [things] out' without violence, which she likes and finds she can be good at. The difference in her behaviour has been noticed by her secular friends, who now call her a 'wee goody goody'. Maia is thus caught between her social location and the gender performances of girls in that position, and her desire to be Christian, in which very different gender performances are expected.[3]

It was clear that young people often used religion in the construction of gender identities or subjectivities. This was particularly obvious with young men because their gender identity was in contradistinction to the norm. Except for those girls from parts of Glasgow where girls' gender identity has moved closer to a male 'hard man' performance, most young women found that their religious gender identity fitted well with prevailing gender performances for girls. The churches were thus still perceived as 'feminine', as the 'not cool' for boys stigma reveals. The church may, however, offer an alternative gender identity for young men, not through Jesus (who rarely came up in these conversations) or traditional teachings per se, but through the modelling of non-normative gender performances by Christian men.

Conclusion

As scholars and students of religion, we cannot ignore the ways in which gender and religion interact in conscious and unconscious ways, in the individual and society. As King has written, religion and gender are 'deeply embedded' (2005, 3) in one another. Though we have only had space for a few examples, the embeddedness of gender in religion shows itself in many other ways, from the recent admittance of girls as altar attendants in the Catholic church, to who makes and cares for religious artefacts, to religious body markers such as veiling or circumcision. What is more, religions can accommodate multiple, even conflicting, gender performances: from the non-normative 'feminised', relational male to the historically normative 'hard man' of Glasgow Protestantism (the Orange Order). Although the lines of connection between religion and gender may be 'subtle and often invisible' (King 2005, 3), they are no less complex or important. The fact that in the Glasgow project, gender at first seemed inconsequential, was important in itself and signalled a generational change. For as King (2005, 3) points out, the 'pattern' of religion and gender is 'dynamic'; the patterns of the past will not be the

---

[3]   Maia also spoke about how Christianity has allowed her to revalue her body even though she does not fit hegemonic standards of 'beauty', as God 'loves us all'. The body is an important site in constructing gendered subjectivities, though we have not had space to examine this in detail here.

patterns of today – and the patterns of different generations will not be the same as those of today.

The rapidly shifting subjectivities of young people require researchers to choose methods that can capture those subjectivities. But researchers must also be alert to how the research methods used can highlight or obscure gender issues in the study of religion.

We are all gendered beings, and all of us negotiate gender through multiple lenses (historical period, society, ethnicity, class and so forth) every day; this means that gender matters in a fundamental way. Researchers have shown how gender has mattered in religion historically and for older generations; today, an important task is to show how it continues to matter, and how it matters differently, for younger generations. Understanding this will help us to grasp the ways religion is changing and the forms it may take in the future.

Chapter 27

Insider-Desire: Coveting Insider Status and Its Consequences

Sarah J. Abramson

In the great encounter at the burning bush, Moses' second question to G-d was 'Who are you?' His first was 'Who am I?'

(Sacks 1997, 79)

I began my PhD research with the utmost confidence in myself, or at least in my ability to act as a 'responsible feminist researcher' whilst studying conceptions of Jewish authenticity within youth movements. I felt particularly at ease about researching a group of people with whom I identified. I am a 'Jew' and, as such, considered myself at least somewhat 'inside' the British-Jewish community, even as my American citizenship, researcher position and other identifications made it impossible to claim full insider status. Naively, I assumed that my position as 'the researcher' afforded me a special right to claim any status, so long as I was careful to acknowledge the 'politics of my location' (Rich 1986). However, after starting my fieldwork it became apparent that my self-defined location was not always congruent with how those whom I encountered in my research located me (Mullings 1999).

My right to claim even partial insider status was often called into question, for reasons including my family heritage and admitted cultural, rather than religious, connection to Judaism. Ultimately my experience of this disjuncture – between my own understanding of self and how the young people taking part in my fieldwork understood me – shaped my findings and my feelings in ways that I had not anticipated. In the end, my research experience was as much about the difficulties involved in enacting feminist and social science ethical research principles as it was about the topic I originally set out to study.

My dissertation began as a study of Jewish authenticity, or what makes an Anglo-Jew 'real' to himself or herself, to other Jews and to non-Jews. I was certainly not alone in my desire to analyse intersections among 'authenticity', identity and 'Judaism' (Charme 2000; Lederhendler 2001; Cheng 2004; Barack Fishman 2007). However, I was the first academic researcher to study the concept of authenticity in the context of Anglo-Jewish youth movements.

Jewish youth movements have historically formed the backbone of continuity within British Judaism and these groups are still important sites for the dissemination of information about Judaism, Jewishness, religion, culture and tradition (Bunt 1975; Kahane 1997; Smith 2002; Chazan 2003). Whilst there is a growing body of research on formal faith schooling,[1] the importance of *informal* education in Jewish identity construction is often overlooked (Chazan 2003). Accordingly, my research was the first qualitative study to explore the processes by which young people become recognized as authentically Jewish subjects within Anglo-Jewish informal education settings.[2]

Each youth movement that I studied subscribes to a different conception of Judaism, and the boundaries of Jewish identity are contested between movements (Cooper and Morrison 1991; Charme 2000; Stratton 2000; Lederhendler 2001; Valins 2003). Debates include: what, or which, Judaism is necessary for Anglo Jewish continuity? Are Jews 'ethnic'? A 'race'? Or are Jews 'just' a religious group? Is Judaism definable by impervious borders and, if so, is some Judaism 'fake' rather than 'authentic' or 'genuine'? Who has the authority to define Judaism and Jewishness? As Susie Orbach asks, 'What is the significance of naming oneself a Jew?' (Orbach 1993, ix).

These questions were fundamental to my research. From the outset, I was interested in why, and by which processes, young people come to name themselves 'Jews', and what 'being Jewish' means in different youth movements. Yet it soon became clear that I could not answer these questions without first examining the significance of *me* naming *myself* a Jew.

The right to be Jewish: emerging insider desire

As I began my participant-observation research within Anglo-Jewish youth movements, I eagerly attempted to communicate a sense of camaraderie with the young people I met. As a 'fellow Jew', I wanted them to consider me as part of a universal 'Jewish community'. I tried to locate myself as an insider, or someone who shares the history, interests and beliefs of those taking part in my project.

My need for camaraderie exposed my tendency to fix the 'Jewish community' as a static entity, unchanging across place and time. Yet significantly, I did not conceptualize Anglo-Jewish youth movements as a monolithic entity, and took pains to describe the differences in philosophies and programmes among the many movements. However in my quest to be accepted as an insider by *all* of these

---

[1]   Important work on faith schooling in the UK includes Cush (2003) and Grace (2003). Important work on Jewish faith schooling in the UK includes Zisenwine and Schers (1997), Miller (2001) and Valins (2003).

[2]   I have, however, come across a number of short articles which have examined similar issues, most notably: 'Bagels, Schnitzel and McDonalds-'Fuzzy Frontiers' of Jewish Identity in an English Jewish Secondary School' (Scholefield 2004) and 'On Being Jewish: A Qualitative Study of Identity among British Jews in Emerging Adulthood' (Sinclair and Milner 2005).

different movements, I ultimately reduced the insider–outsider research dynamic to a binary, unchanging relationship (even though feminist sociologists have called this duality into question many times). As Nancy Naples has written:

> The bipolar construction of insider/outsider also sets up a false separation that neglects the interactive processes through which 'insiderness' and 'outsiderness' are constructed ... by recognizing the fluidity of 'outsiderness/insiderness', we also acknowledge the three key methodological points: as ethnographers we are never fully outside or inside the 'community'; our relationship to the community is never expressed in general terms but is constantly being negotiated and renegotiated in particular, everyday interactions; and these interactions themselves are located in shifting relationships among community residents. These negotiations simultaneously are embedded in local processes that reposition gender, class, and racial-ethnic relations among other socially constructed distinctions. (1996, 84)

Despite such warnings, I continued to ascribe particular importance to being accepted as 'one of them'. During the beginning stages of my research, I was focused less on making the movements comfortable with me as a *researcher*, and more on trying to make them accept me as *Jew*. Yet this task was harder than I imagined, as it had never occurred to me that the groups I studied would call into question my own definition of Judaism, and consequently my right to call myself a Jew.

I am the child of a Jewish father and a convert-from-Protestantism-to-Reform-Judaism mother. I was active in my synagogue and youth movement as a child and young adult; I went to Hebrew school two days a week, and also to Sunday school (and later taught these classes). I had a *Bat Mitzvah*, and went on to be confirmed and even post-confirmed. Although I grew up near large Jewish communities, I spent my childhood in a town with an overwhelmingly Christian majority, and any expression of Judaism was considered distinctively exotic. In the public imagination of my surroundings, all Jews were one and the same, since we all fell outside of the mainstream and prevailing system of beliefs. In a sense, I think I adopted this view – that indeed, I held a certain indescribable 'something' in common with all other Jews. That 'something' included a shared sense of history, and a shared sense of 'otherness' within an overwhelmingly Christian nation (whether the United States or Britain).

However, I faced culture shock when moving to the United Kingdom, where modern Orthodoxy is often regarded as the normative expression of authentic Anglo-Judaism by powerful communal organizations. Accordingly, in the eyes of many British Jews (due to the *halachic* [religious] laws of Orthodoxy)[3] I am a 'non-Jew' since my mother converted to Reform (and not Orthodox) Judaism. Although I was aware of *halachah*, I never considered religious law an

---

3   *Halachic*, or religious, law determines 'Jewishness' based on matrilineal descent.

insurmountable barrier to my own Jewishness. I assumed that since I was accepted as a Jew while growing up in the United States, my ability to call myself a Jew would not be questioned in the United Kingdom.[4]

In retrospect, I am amazed that I did not anticipate this dilemma. After all, I considered myself well versed in the late-twentieth-century feminist research that warns of the inherent risks in denying the historical and social contexts of shifting identifications (Hill Collins 1990; Hooks 1999, 1983). By ignoring these important issues, I began to produce a piece of research which discounted monumental turns in feminist research about the 'standpoint of the researcher' and the importance of re-evaluating static and fixed categories of group identifications (Hartsock 1987; Haraway 1991; Harding 1991). As Adrienne Rich notes: '[i]f we have learned anything in these years of late twentieth-century feminism, it's that "always" blots out what we really need to know: When, where, and under what conditions has the statement been true' (1986, 214). These are questions I would have expected other feminist researchers to answer, but my desire for insider-status made them seem less important for my work.

My answer 'yes' to the question 'Are You Jewish?' was often questioned and at times refuted. My 'yes' was called into question in a variety of ways: some people – both leaders and movement members –asked me point-blank about my 'Jewish status', others asked me what – if any-synagogue did I attend? – and more people subtly asked me about my opinions on intermarriage and the importance of Jewish continuity. I was often caught off guard by the blunt nature of the questions posed to me; as I was negotiating access to their organizations, movement members and leaders qualified these questions by characterizing them as necessary for knowing how to introduce me to other people, and knowing how much background information I would require. While I was only once refused any type of access, my answers did impact on what *type* of access I managed to negotiate, and whether or not I was regarded as 'similar' (in the case of Liberal and Reform youth movements) and granted widespread access, or 'different' (*Masorti*[5] and Orthodox groups) and granted limited or less extensive access.

However, even after I realized the consequences of locating myself as a Reform Jew in Anglo-Jewry, I continued to struggle with an understanding of British Jewry as a shifting, changing entity. Interestingly, I would *never* have assumed that all women, poor, or disabled people share the same standpoint or politics of location, yet I *still* tried to convince those taking part in my research that we shared some indescribable similarity, simply due to the fact we all called ourselves 'Jews' (even if we mean different things). This realization proved eye opening, as it made clear

---

[4]   I am specifically referencing instances when I engaged with modern Orthodox Jews. My self-identification as a Jew was accepted by most Reform and Liberal people, thereby highlighting the contingent nature of self-representation and the interpretation of positionality.

[5]   *Masorti* Judaism is the name given to Conservative Judaism in the United Kingdom (and in Israel).

that the theoretical grasp of a concept does not necessarily translate into the easy enactment of this principle during research. In a final attempt to overcome my insider-desire, I forced myself to take a closer look at other factors contributing to the ways in which people viewed, and responded to, me as an outsider.

Researching youth and religion: compounded positionality

My attempts to claims of some sort of insider status were additionally thwarted by the age gap between those taking part in my research and myself. Anglo-Jewish youth movements accept 'youth' from 8 to 18; leaders of the movements generally range in age from 18 to 24. I began my research confident that I was still young enough to avoid being seen as an adult or authority figure since I was 'only' 26 when I finished my fieldwork.[6] While my age alone might have been surmountable, my status as a researcher pursuing a high level of education was not, especially since my role as participant-observer easily distinguished me from the movement participants.[7]

My age and non-movement affiliation firmly located me as an adult-researcher-outsider. As such, I needed to account for ethical questions about representations of youth and young people, questions such as: '[w]hat claims to represent children's voices can adult researchers legitimately make? And what meanings may we unwittingly reinforce as we make such public re/presentations?' (Alldred in Ribbens and Edwards 1998, 147). As Pam Alldred noted, researchers often write about young people as if they exist in a distinct world, one that has little in common with the researchers' own adult one. Yet divorcing the world of children from the world of adults risks presenting children and young people as 'other' to the 'norm' of adult existence (1998, 152); '[f]or contemporary childhood research there is surely a tension between studying children simply as people, and giving them research (or political) attention because they are currently marginalized, which then risks reinforcing the idea of them as a "special case"' (1998, 152).

The blurred boundaries between child, teenager and adult in Anglo-Jewish youth movements further complicate the category of 'youth'. Most movements are autonomous spaces in which young people aged 16 to (roughly) 24 become

---

[6]   Again, here is another example of a situation in which I assumed how I viewed myself (as relatively young) would be shared by all those taking part in my research. Yet for the 8 year-olds and others, 26 rooted me firmly in the category of 'older' and 'adult', causing them to view me differently than I viewed myself.

[7]   Many movement members described the organizations as extended families; movement members have known, or will know, each other for years and much growing-up takes place within the movements. Since I was a newcomer in my mid-twenties, I was easily identifiable as an outsider who lacked the requisite insider knowledge of day-to-day movement activities, assumptions and principles.

the 'adults' of the movements;[8] 16–22 year-olds who run the movement with little to no input from people outside of the movement or anyone older than they. These leaders set up movement councils, trips abroad, judiciary boards, as well as weekly meetings and month-long summer camps. They also embody the role of caretakers for young people when on trips or camps, and the role of disciplinarians towards those who violate the organization's rules. Accordingly, thinking about all young people within a movement as distinctly 'non-adults', and simply 'youth', distorts the unusual hierarchies of age-related power operating within movement settings.

The question of how to best give voice to young people becomes even more complicated when religion is involved. As Lynn Davidman has argued, it is important to 'take seriously' religious peoples' choices, and not reduce them to social pressures, misguided authority or psychological neediness (1991). Yet in relation to religiously based youth movements, the question arises as to whether or not young people accept the religious beliefs promoted by the youth movements because they 'actually' believe in them, or because they recognize that these beliefs are necessary for inclusion within the youth movement organization.[9] Accordingly, the religious aspect of the youth movements must be carefully weighed against other factors (such as sociability, cultural affiliation and parental influence) when determining its role in shaping members' identification with Judaism. At the same time, the researcher must 'take seriously' the ways in which young people themselves talk about their relationship with the religion in question.

Towards a reconciliation of theory and practicality

My research has prompted two major ethical dilemmas: namely, a dilemma of representation of myself as I have described, and also a dilemma of 'best representation' for those taking part in my research.[10] Whilst my struggle for self-representation was important, I did feel a deep commitment to representing the young people who took part in my research as much through their own voices as through mine.

In order to best represent the young people within Anglo-Jewish movements, I decided to conceptualize youth as 'a widely debated and increasingly contested

---

[8]   In this case, adult is understood as a person in charge and in a position of power.

[9]   Of course, religious belief is not only taught by youth movements. Many of the movement participants come from religious homes, and receive information about Judaism from their parents, or from their schools if they attend a faith school. Yet youth movement organizations each have a particular way of enacting Judaism, and members must tailor their previous beliefs so as to be congruous with those supported by the movement.

[10]   Both of these dilemmas shed light on the serious issue of deception in the research process: deception to self as a researcher, deception to the people involved in the research, and deception in the way the research is portrayed to a wider audience, see Shaffir and Stebbins (1991) for a discussion on this point.

term … a discursive construct and consequently, a term overlain with multiple and, in many cases, conflicting meanings' (Bennett 2007, 23). In particular, Sunaina Maira and Elisbeth Soep's definition of youth was helpful. For Maira and Soep, youth is best conceptualized as a '*scape*', meaning a 'shifting circuit of people who occupy a given social world' (2005, xvii). The term 'youth' is still a useful umbrella term, but implies an understanding of youth as a 'deeply ideological category', rather than as a homogenous unit (2005, xvii). Maira and Soep's definition of a *youthscape* captures the inherent intersectionality between childhood, teenage years, youth and young adulthood. 'Youthscapes' captured the full range of movement participants, from the oldest (24) to the youngest (8), regardless of whether or not they could also be described as (embodying the roles of) children, teenagers or young adults.

However, theoretical concepts cannot fully 'theorize away' fundamental issues of consent, compliance, privacy and confidentiality. As Gill Valentine has written, 'the authority that adults have over children at home and at school generates a further minefield of ethical problems around the issues of privacy and confidentiality' (1999, 146). I thus chose to conduct my research with young people in the same way I would have done with adults. Whilst I adhered to all legal protocols for working with young people (such as parental consent), I also replicated these requests with the young people themselves. Each person I spent time with and/or interviewed signed a consent form specifically designed for a person of his or her age. I made sure to relay my findings back to the young people themselves, and allowed them complete freedom to self-exclude from any part of the research which made them feel uncomfortable.

Conclusion: research and the self

I attempted to create a research project based on an ethics of responsibility to both my research participants and myself. I first had to admit that my quest for insider status was distorting many issues fundamental to quality feminist research. After this admission, I tried to self-consciously represent my struggle to 'take seriously' the opinions of my research participants, whilst simultaneously refusing to allow my participants to undermine my own right to a certain identity.

I remained vigilant about these ethics of my self-representation. For example: when asked 'Are you Jewish?' I could have answered with a simple 'yes'. Yet for me, this answer was only 'true' when the people asking the question shared my conception of authentic Judaism. I therefore forced myself to remain (uncomfortably) aware of my responsibilities to my research participants. In order to 'take seriously' people's different conceptions of authentic Judaism, I often chose to share the specific details of my relationship to Judaism so my participants could gauge for themselves how to locate me. This strategy was awkward at times as it required me to acknowledge that my definition of being Jewish was often not sufficient for other people. However, I slowly realized that allowing some people to disagree with my right to a certain identification does not undermine my relationship with that identity – or in this case, my continued positioning of myself as an 'authentic' Jew.

Against my initial wishes, my fieldwork was successfully conducted from a variety of locations – insider, outsider, and somewhere in between. Undoubtedly, boundaries between the insider and the outsider, the young and the old and the ethical and the deceptive are never as clear as we might wish and shifting between these changing identifications can prove emotional and ungainly. Yet in my case, moving back and forth along the spectrum of insider and outsider afforded me the opportunity to maintain my own location while also not denying or hiding the discrepancies between this position and how many participants in my research located me. The experience of this back-and-forth tug of war over location and positionality drove home the potential emotional consequences of researching a community with which you (somewhat) identify.

Conclusion

Pink Dandelion

Sylvia Collins-Mayo started this book by outlining some of the preoccupations of sociologists of religion regarding age and religion. She noted that:

> young people growing up in late modern Western societies tend to be less religious than older people, at least in terms of institutional religion. Young people are less likely to identify with any one religious tradition than their older contemporaries, less likely to subscribe to the creed of a major world religion and less likely to attend a place of worship on a regular basis (Davie 2000; Voas and Crockett 2006). This observation immediately raises questions. The first is concerned with the extent to which an interest in religion may be dependent on the life cycle. Is it the case that young people are 'naturally' less religious than older people because religion tends to deal with 'ultimate concerns' and experiences that are more likely to arise later in life – in the words of Cyndi Lauper, do 'girls just wanna have fun'? Perhaps with the accumulation of significant life events non-religious young people will become religious older people. Or is it the case that young people generation on generation are 'losing their religion'? A second question follows. If there is a generational trend away from institutional religion, are young people basically succumbing to the forces of secularisation (a perspective that seems to have gone out of fashion), or are there sacralising influences running parallel which are changing the way young people relate to religion thereby keeping the sacred alive and meaningful? If the latter, then what significance does religion in its new forms have both for the individual and for wider society? A third set of questions relates to the transmission of faith. If young people are less religious than older people is it because older people have failed to pass faith on effectively?

Some of the chapters in this volume, particularly those in Parts I and II, directly address these questions. Indeed, these are questions that continue to challenge researchers and which will surely form much of the future research agenda, especially for those concerned with secularisation and the future of institutional religion. They are questions about the future of the past and present, questions about change. They are in a sense questions from an adult society wondering what the next generation will bring.

What this collection shows is that youth religion and spirituality, particularly in 'the West', is not playing to the same tune as 'adult' religiosity. Denton Smith may find 'moralistic therapeutic deism' operating as a framework for teenager belief in the USA but for large numbers of young people, whether merely innovating as per Richard Flory and Donald Miller's analysis or virtualising faith in Tom Beaudoin's terms, religiosity is configured and constructed in radically different ways from earlier manifestations of faithfulness. Seeker churches, emergent and convergent faith, all technologically tethered, all exhibit new ways of being church that selects and discards from the toolbox of the traditions. There is nothing new in this pattern of radical reinvention of religion – each revival consists in the same tropes (including that of Liberal religion and its rationalistic reinvention of faith at the end of the nineteenth century which sociologist Steve Bruce sees as so decidedly terminal in the twenty-first (Bruce 2002)), but in terms of agency, youth reinvention is new. The democratisation of the access to technology and the advent of disposable income for teenagers have created whole new networks and markets which can drive new options for youth-designated and ultimately youth-designed spirituality. The Manga Bibles and comic book prophets of the 1990s were temporary icons of a fading print culture, but easily transferred to highly portable 'personal electronic devices', which carry self-selected tunes and text side by side, a concordance or a Koran or just a comic at each hip.

For me, what comes out of this collection are not the continuing agendas linked to change in what life used to be like, but questions arising out of the experience of the young people themselves. In many ways, that voice (of youth) is largely missing here, but we can catch glimpses of what their concerns and agendas might be. More important than the detail of those agendas is the need for us, as those researching and studying youth religion, to become aware of them. One study that has particularly helped me in this regard is Simon Best's work on teenage Quaker religiosity in Britain (2008a, 2008b).

In the same way that I spent my doctoral years studying adult Quaker religiosity in Britain in the early 1990s, Best spent five years researching teenage Quaker religiosity. I had concluded that British Quakerism operated a 'double culture' of a liberal or permissive belief culture and a conformist and conservative 'behavioural creed'. Belief was marginal and diverse to the point of it being impossible to label the group as simply Christian, but the group found coherence in the way it did things, in its form of worship and of conducting its business (which Quakers do without voting, claiming instead to 'seek the will of God'). Changes in normative patterns of belief had taken place under the mask of the emphasis given silence in worship and the de-emphasis given speech, what I termed the 'culture of silence' (Dandelion 1996).

Simon Best ran surveys, group interviews, and individual interviews with 418 teenage British Quakers attending residential events and set to analyse his data. Every sociological concept I had coined for the adult Quaker group was challenged by his findings and his subsequent conceptualisation of how teenage Quakers operationalised their identity and manifested their spirituality.

These were committed Quakers, 85 per cent stating that their involvement in Quakerism was either quite important or very important to them. However, nearly 60 per cent also said that other adolescents were the group of Quakers they felt most affinity with. Meeting together at residential events was thus key for the nurture and affirmation of this faith identity, technology allowing those networks to be sustained between-times across the miles, what Best calls a 'continuing community' (2008a, 195).

Worship and ritual was very important to these young Quakers. It is based in silence and seated in a circle as it is for the adult group, but without some of the formalisation of the worship process developed by the adults such as standing to 'offer ministry' or the role of (only) the Elders to end worship. Young Quakers hardly ever stood up to speak and the formal handshake at the end of adult worship was replaced by hugs and the whole group joining hands. Worship ritual is thus less differentiated between participants. It is also more fluid in its form and gave more place to dance, song and music generally. Unlike the adult group, speech or non-silence is given equal value to silence. Best concludes that a 'culture of contribution' operates rather than a 'culture of silence'.

This culture of contribution affects patterns of believing. Rather than belief being a marginal and often invisible category as in the older Quaker group, only uncovered when sociologists run belief surveys, the freedom to share belief-stories increases the acceptance and knowledge of theological diversity. Changes in theology are overt. Belief is not so much marginal as not relevant as a discrete category of conversation. Adolescent Quakers in this sense are not post-Christian but post-doctrinal (and as it happens non-Christian). Of the 41 per cent who claimed they believed in God and the 40 per cent who said they were not sure, participants gave 27 different descriptions of God in response to a single survey question. Questions of belief, so enthusiastically discussed by sociologists of adult Quakerism, become irrelevant in the study of youth Quakerism. Key terms to older Quakers such as the idea of 'that of God in everyone' have been reinterpreted into new ir/relevance.

Values have taken the place of belief in the creation of Quaker identity for these young people but these are also individualised. Only the value of being committed to pacifism or peace was shared by more than 25 per cent of the participants. However, their mutual well-being was a key value shared by all and Best has developed the concept of a 'community of intimacy' to describe the social dynamic within the group:

> The core features of a Community of Intimacy are that: 1) the members of the group feel a sense of belonging and affiliation to the group; 2) the group has a set of shared values which are expressed in internal and external behaviour; 3) this behaviour contributes to feelings of difference between the Community of Intimacy and other group which it is juxtaposed to; 4) this results in the group occupying separate physical and psychological spaces. (2008a, 192)

Community is highlighted and encouraged to create a self-identity which is self-policed and is perceived as counter-cultural or non-worldly, potentially world-rejecting (Wallis 1984).

This sense of sectarian difference is shared with the older Quaker group but, critically, these young Quakers also feel different from adult Quakers, who, of course, are no longer bullied for their beliefs and who, to the younger Quakers, do not live their faith so openly or radically. It appeared as if the habitus of older Quakers was less differentiated from wider society and less developed in discrete terms than the younger Quaker one. Older Quakers went to Meeting (worship) and talked about God, younger Quakers lived their ideas and beliefs in everyday networked community. As Best writes:

> The adolescent Quaker group has both a high level of internal integration and a high degree of differentiation from other groups (Fenn 1997, 41). Adolescent ritual involves the creation of a separate space that reflects an ideal social order and the transformation of individuals to being members of the adolescent Quaker group, the Community of Intimacy. (Best 2008a, 209)

Whilst older Quakers operate a double culture, Best identifies a 'triple culture' amongst the younger group formed by 'ritual, 'networked community' and 'narrative and behaviour'. This triple culture creates and preserves a sense of separate space and maintains and sustains the community of intimacy. Thus adolescent Quakers are not Quakers by reference to their older co-religionists but with reference to their own sense and creation of a distinctive Quaker identity. They are Quaker because they say they are.

Thus an adult Quaker research agenda does not ask the right questions of the younger Quaker group. Sociologists of the world beware! We must not imagine or assume that the study of youth religion should follow the same questions and categories which we apply to religion more broadly or the religion of today or yesterday.

Equally we should not approach the study of youth religion by reference to the 'parent institution' even when that institution claims that its youth wing is part of the broader group. In other research, Best shows that both older and younger Quaker groupings operate sect-like characteristics in relation to the world, but that the adolescent group is more demanding, more sectarian and maintains a sectarian attitude even towards the adult group – it is not just world-rejecting but parent-body rejecting. It is a 'hidden sect', a sect within a sect (Best 2008b, 112). However, this sectarian attitude is hidden from the parent body and potentially from outside investigation by the rhetoric of the older group claiming that youth and adults are part of the same large group, that the young are the future Quakers of tomorrow.

Unless the young change their ways of being Quaker, or unless Quakerism shifts into a culture constructed around a communities of intimacy and contribution, this is patently not the case. Rather, Best argues, the older Quaker group idealises 'their' young as part of the same cultural and doctrinal formation without listening to the concerns and aspirations of these young people. Best called this process 'empty co-option' (2008b, 110). It is easy, Best argues, for sociologists to misread the relationship between youth and adult parts of the group:

> If there is to be meaningful research of youth religion, especially in situations where the youths meet separately, then there needs to be primary research with adolescents and participant observation of occasions when the two groups operate in the same space or overlap in order to get a full picture of the group. (Best 2008b, 111)

Thus we can identify two major strands of future research agenda. There are those questions, symbolised by longitudinal surveys but also evident in the secularisation questions rehearsed at the beginning of the chapter which locate youth religion in terms of deviation. However, there are also the research projects driven by the self-understanding of youth themselves.

The value of the former type of study is in determining the nature and rate of change and the dynamic between tradition and innovation. We can also, using this kind of work, start to investigate potential causal connection, and offer predictive models.

We can also see in this collection other strands which take youth on its own terms and ask what it tells us about the nature of youth and the nature of youth religion. This may be initially less fruitful in modelling social change but it helps build the conceptual apparatus for future location and direction of research into youth and religion. It helps us identify the wholly new.

If there is to be meaningful research of youth religion, especially in situations where the youth meet separately, then there needs to be primary research with adolescents and participant observation of occasions when the two groups operate in the same space or overlap in order to get a full picture of the group. Eileen Barker's work on 'Moonie' children (2008) is a compelling example of this and we can see excellent examples of this kind of work in Parts III and IV of this volume.

First, of course, we need to ensure that religion is firmly situated as part of the agenda of youth studies. As Collins-Mayo points out in the introduction, this has been far from the case and in this regard, this volume is both timely and innovative. We can see from the essays here just how complex and fruitful and area of research youth and its connection with religion is. We can also see how far the study of religion needs to account in a dramatically more explicit way for the vitality of youth religion in its summaries of the triumphs, tribulations and trends of popular religiosity. This volume brings together two crucial aspects of social life in a concentrated way that to the shame of the Western academy is all too rare. We are very pleased to have managed to bring such a rich collection of international scholarship together to redress this erstwhile lack of balance.

As such, we also trust that this volume can lay out some of the markers for future research in the connection between these fields. There are gaps in terms of the traditions represented – this volume over-emphasises Christianity, reflects only a little of what is happening within Islam, and points to the difficulty in trying to source much work on other religions. A key area for further research – which in a global society is likely to be central – is sociology of youth religion in non-Western countries from local researchers (i.e. not just Western scholars speaking about non-Western youth). One of the strengths of this volume is that it includes the section on methods and we hope and trust this will assist those keen to take this agenda forward.

Cutting across types of religiosity and between different national and ethnic contexts, we can see the exciting range of youth identity and experience. However, we can also see in this collection many of the commonalities, for example the tensions between 'youth' and 'adult' variants of faith in terms of beliefs, faith identity and its interpretation, resources, lifestyle and the importance of peer networks. Finally we are pleased that this collection mixes some of the 'old heads' of the disciplines of sociology and youth studies with some of the latest generation of researchers fresh from doctoral research. It is an important and powerful combination and one that models well the kind of academic inclusivity that we argue is so necessary if 'youth and religion' is not to continue to be marginalised.

Epilogue

Linda Woodhead

Once upon a time – not so very long ago – many people assumed that religion was transmitted down the generations. Parents would socialize their children into the faith in which they had themselves been raised by their own parents, and the cycle would repeat itself. Today, as so many of the chapters in this book remind us, this assumption is no longer tenable. It is not simply that such transmission has failed, but that conditions have changed. For one thing, there are many more influences which shape young people, including real and virtual social networks. And for another, we now inhabit societies in which it is no longer the done thing to do the done thing: indeed, it is the done thing *not* to do the done thing.

This spirit of rebellion became a trademark of 'youth culture' in the baby boom generation. When boomers rebelled against 'the establishment', religion was part of the package they rejected. Not only was Christianity the religion of their parents, it was seen to be integral to everything which was wrong with society: class hierarchy and snobbery, sexual repression and prudishness, patriarchy and paternalism. Far from being antinomian, many boomers had an intensely moral vision of the sort of society they wanted to create in place of the existing one: a more equal, more peaceful, more loving, more humanitarian and more liberated society. They also imagined it as more secular, or at least as less churchy and Christian.

Even if the boomers failed to realize their dream, there is no doubting that 'late modern' or 'postmodern' society is significantly different from what preceded, including in its values and 'habits of the heart'. Nor is there any doubt that the historic churches have suffered dramatic decline, and that Christianity since the 1960s has lost its cultural monopoly. The boomers who grew up to hold positions of power in the media, education and politics were often secular in their orientation, and as they have come to power they have imposed that preference on the institutions which they control.

There is nothing in the evidence presented in this volume to suggest that the children and grandchildren of the baby boomers have departed from their parents' commitment to personal choice and autonomy. None of the voices of young people recorded here defend duty and deference over individuality and authenticity. It is as much as an imperative to 'do your own thing' today as it was in the 1960s – and for much larger numbers. As the middle class has expanded, affluence and consumerism have grown, and many forms of gender inequality have diminished, more young people than ever before are able to answer the cultural invitation to forge their own 'unique' identities. What is new, however, is that for the current generation of young people, religion is no longer part of the status quo against which they must rebel in order to do so. For Generations X and Y, it is the secular society created by their parents which forms the backdrop for rebellion. And there is plenty for them to dislike: corrupt politicians, cynical marketing and public relations industries, unfettered capitalism, growing social inequality, post-colonial injustices and the destruction of the environment.

Does this suggest that the 'new' youth rebellion will be towards rather than away from religion? The contributions to this volume tell us that the answer is complex, and that it depends on whom you are talking to and about. They leave us in no doubt that it is no longer helpful to speak of 'youth' or 'youth culture' in an undifferentiated way. For some young people, religion will indeed be an important resource. For young Pagans, for example, religion is providing a means of critiquing gender expectations, helping to resource alternative identities and taking action for the environment. And for many young British Muslims, a rediscovery and reinterpretation of Islam is serving both as a means to rebel against aspects of their own cultural heritage (and their parents), and a means of rejecting the most unacceptable aspects of Western culture (including racism) whilst appropriating other aspects (like female equality). For others, however, religion has ceased to have relevance. Increasing numbers have little contact with religion. Their main 'source of significance' is more likely to be close family and friends than a religious community and its gods. Even those who come into contact with Christianity are unlikely to appropriate it in traditional ways. They may turn its rituals to their own purposes, including the sanctification of important life events and transitions, and they have little or no time for doctrine or clerical authority.

Thus even young people who are religious seem to be religious in new ways. The traditional markers of religion in Western societies – adherence to doctrines, membership of church-like communities, deference to religious elites – are precisely what has been rejected. This creates difficulties for those who are wedded to a view of religion which emphasizes just these features. From their point of view, what we are seeing is the decline and dilution of religion, rather than its transformation. From a different point of view, however, what we are witnessing is not so much the decline of religion as the decline of a particular form of (European) confessional Christianity *and* of those forms of secularism which represent a reaction to it. In an important sense, Richard Dawkins is as old-fashioned as the kind of religion he attacks. From this perspective, the rejection of historically-contingent kinds of religion and secularity, combined with the influence of new global flows of information and people, is resulting in the opening up of a richer array of religious and secular resources on which young people are drawing in new ways, inflected by ethnicity, class, gender and other variables.

Both perspectives are represented in this volume, which captures and advances a neglected field of study at an exciting point in its development. The conference which led to this volume was held in 2008, the same year that two UK research councils, the AHRC and ESRC, contributed £4m to fund research on youth and religion. This funding formed an extension to the existing £8m Religion and

Society research Programme, of which I am the Director. Some people thought that the extension was really about 'young Muslims', in the wake of the 7/7 bombings in London. It wasn't, as the research we commissioned shows.[1] But the fact that there were young people in Britain society who not only cared passionately about religion, but were prepared to kill and die for it, *was* important. It brought it home that the neglect of the topic of youth and religion was serious, and needed to be corrected.

The research showcased in this volume, and the research in the Religion and Society Programme, shows that strides are being taken. There are encouraging signs that interest is shifting away from questions which only make sense from the point of view of older generations and the institutions they grew up with or want to protect. Youth and religion is no longer a topic which is chiefly of interest to those concerned with the fate of the churches, and it has successfully resisted being harnessed to moral panics about cults, sects and extremists. Reading this book suggests that current work on youth and religion has an important contribution to make youth studies in general, as well as to our understanding of the direction of late modern society and culture. By moving beyond historically-contingent framings of religion and secularity, such work is now well placed to address the broader topics of where, how and why young people find meaning, value and purpose, how they symbolize and communicate it, and how this relates to their differing social positions and empowerment.

[1]   The projects cover a wide range of topics, including education (the largest single concentration of work), social deprivation, sexual identity, criminality, the decline of 'traditional' forms of religious practice, and the rise of new ones. Some projects look at the current situation, and some give perspective by looking at young people and religion in other times and places (for example, at religious dissent in the seventeenth and eighteenth centuries – and interesting earlier example of 'radicalization' and 'extremism'). For details see http://www.religionandsociety.org.uk

Bibliography

Aapola, S., Gonick, M. and Harris, A. (2005), *Young Femininity: Girlhood, Power and Social Change*, Basingstoke: Palgrave Macmillan.

Abercrombie, N., Baker, J., Brett, S. and Foster, J. (1970), 'Superstition and Religion: the God of the Gaps', in Martin, D. and Hill, M., eds, *A Sociological Yearbook of Religion in Britain*, London: SCM Press, pp. 93–129.

Adams, M. (2006), 'Hybridizing Habitus and Reflexivity: Towards an Understanding of Contemporary Identity?', *Sociology* 40: 511–28.

Alldred, P. (1998), 'Representing Voices in Ethnography and Discourse Analysis', in Ribbens, J. and Edward, R., eds, *Feminist Dilemmas in Qualitative Research: Public Knowledge and Private Lives*, London and Thousand Oaks, CA: Sage, pp. 147–70.

Allen, P. (2006), 'Drunk Britons Shatter the Peace of Lourdes', *The Sunday Telegraph*, 20 August, p. 5.

Alwin, D.F. (1996), 'Parental Socialization in Historical Perspective', in Ryff, C. and Seltzer, M.M., eds, *The Parental Experience at Midlife*, Chicago, IL: University of Chicago Press, pp. 105–67.

Anderson, T. and Kavanaugh, P. (2007), 'A Rave Review: Conceptual Interests and Analytical Shifts in Research on Rave Culture', *Sociology Compass*, 1: 499–519.

Anthias, F. and Yuval-Davis, N. (1992), *Racialized Boundaries: Race, Nation, Gender, Colour and Class and the Antiracist Struggle*, London: Routledge.

Anttonen, V. (1999), 'Uskonto ihmisen ajattelussa ja kulttuurissa', in Hyry, K. and Pentikäinen, J., eds, *Uskonnot maailmassa*, Helsinki: WSOY, pp. 32–42.

Anttonen, V. (2005), 'Space, Body, and the Notion of Boundary: A Category-Theoretical Approach to Religion', *Temenos* 41 (2), 153–84.

Arnett, J.J. (2000), 'Emerging Adulthood: A Theory of Development from the Late Teens through the Twenties', *American Psychologist*, 55 (5): 469–80.

Asad, T. (1993), *Genealogies of Religion: Discipline and Reasons of Power in Christianity and Islam*, Baltimore: Johns Hopkins University Press.

Ashworth, J. and Farthing, I. (2007), *Churchgoing in the UK*, Teddington: Tearfund.

Astley, J. (2005), 'The Science and Religion Interface within Young People's Attitudes and Beliefs', in Francis, L.J., Astley, J. and Robbins, M., eds, *Religion, Education and Adolescence: International Empirical Perspectives*, Cardiff: University of Wales Press, pp. 39–54.

Aune, K., Sharma, S. and Vincett, G., eds (2008), *Women and Religion in the West: Challenging Secularization*, Aldershot: Ashgate.

Bader, C.D. and Desmond, S.A. (2006), 'Do as I Say and as I Do: The Effects of Consistent Parental Beliefs and Behaviors upon Religious Transmission', *Sociology of Religion*, 67: 313–29.

Badone, E. and Roseman, S.R. (2004), *Intersecting Journeys: The Anthropology of Pilgrimage and Tourism*, Urbana, IL: University of Illinois Press.

Bailey, E. (1990), 'Implicit Religion: A Bibliographical Introduction', *Social Compass*, 37: 499–509.

Banks, I. (2000), *Hair Matters: Beauty, Power and Black Women's Consciousness*, New York: New York University Press.

Banks, M. (1995), 'Visual Research Methods', *Social Research Update*, http://sru.soc.surrey.ac.uk/SRU11/index.html, accessed 1 October 2009.

Banks, M. (2001), *Visual Methods in Social Research*, London: Sage.

Barack Fishman, S. (2006), *The Way into the Varieties of Jewishness*, Woodstock, VT: Jewish Lights Publishing.

Barker, E. (2008), 'Blessed Children: Second-Generation Adults Raised in the Unification Church', paper presented at the BSA Sociology of Religion Study Group Conference, Birmingham.

Basow, S.A. (1992), *Gender Stereotypes and Roles*, 3rd edn, Pacific Grove, CA: Brooks/Cole.

Bateson, G. and Mead, M. (1942), *Balinese Character: A Photographic Analysis*, New York: New York Academy of Sciences.

Bauman, Z. (1993), *Postmodern Ethics*, Oxford: Blackwell.

Bauman, Z. (2004), *Identity, Themes for the 21st Century*, Oxford: Polity.

Beaudoin, T. (1998), *Virtual Faith: The Irreverent Spiritual Quest of Generation X*, San Francisco, CA: Jossey-Bass.

Beck, U. (1992), *Risk Society: Towards a New Modernity, Theory, Culture and Society*, London and Newbury Park, CA: Sage.

Beck, U. and Beck-Gernsheim, E. (2002), *Individualization*, London: Sage.

Becker, H.S. (1967), 'Whose Side Are We On?', *Social Problems*, 14: 239–47.

Becker, H.S. (1974), 'Photography and Sociology', *Studies in the Anthropology of Visual Communication*, 1: 3–26.

Becker, H.S. (1998), 'Visual Sociology, Documentary Photography and Photojournalism: It's (Almost), All a Matter of Context', in Prosser, J., ed., *Image-based Research*, London: Routledge, pp. 84–96.

Bellah, R. (1967), 'Civil Religion in America', *Daedalus*, Winter: 1–21.

Bellah, R., Madsen, R., Sullivan, W., Swidler, A. and Tipton, S. (1985), *Habits of the Heart: Individualism and Commitment in American Life*, Berkeley, CA: University of California Press.

Bellamy, J., Black, A., Castle, K., Hughes, P. and Kaldor, P. (2002), *Why People Don't Go to Church*, Adelaide: Openbook.

Bengtson, V.L., Biblarz, T.J. and Roberts, R.E. (2002), *How Families Still Matter: A Longitudinal Study of Youth in Two Generations*, Cambridge: Cambridge University Press.

Bennett, A. (2000), *Popular Music and Youth Culture: Music, Identity, and Place*, Basingstoke: Macmillan.

Bennett, A. (2007), 'As Young as You Feel: Youth as a Discursive Construct', in Hodkinson, P. and Deicke, W., eds, *Youth Cultures: Scenes, Subcultures, and Tribes*, London: Routledge, pp. 23–36.

Berger, H.A. and Ezzy, D. (2007), *Teenage Witches: Magical Youth and the Search for the Self*, New Brunswick, NJ: Rutgers University Press.

Berger J. (2004), 'Re-sexualizing the Epidemic: Desire, Risk and HIV Prevention', in Heywood M., ed., *HIV and AIDS in Southern Africa: From Disaster to Development? Development Update* 5 (3): 17–44.

Berger, P. (1967), *The Sacred Canopy: Elements of a Sociological Theory of Religion*, Garden City, NY: Doubleday.

Berger, P. (1971), *A Rumour of Angels: Modern Society and the Rediscovery of the Supernatural*, Harmondsworth: Penguin.

Berger, P. (1999), *The Desecularization of the World*, Grand Rapids, MI: Eerdmans.

Berger, P.L. and Luckmann, T. (1991), *The Social Construction of Reality: A Treatise in the Sociology of Knowledge*, Harmondsworth: Penguin.

Best, S. (2008a), 'Adolescent Quakers: A Community of Intimacy', in Dandelion, P. and Collins. P., eds, *The Quaker Condition: The Sociology of a Liberal Religion*, Newcastle: Cambridge Scholars Press, pp. 192–215.

Best, S. (2008b), 'Adolescent Quakers: A Hidden Sect', *Quaker Studies*, 13: 103–13.

Biddulph, M. (2006), 'Sikh attacked', *Oxford Mail*, 31 May, http://www.oxfordmail.net/news/headlines/display.var.776820.0.sikh_attacked.php, accessed 5 December 2007.

Biggart, A. and Walther, A. (2006),'Coping with Yo-Yo Transitions: Young Adults' Struggle for Support, between Family and State in Comparative Perspective', in Leccardi C. and Ruspini E., eds, *A New Youth*, Aldershot: Ashgate, pp. 41–62.

Blackman, S. (2005), 'Youth Subcultural Theory: A Critical Engagement with the Concept, its Origins and Politics, from the Chicago School to Postmodernism', *Journal of Youth Studies*, 8: 1–20.

Blackman, S.J. (2007), '"Hidden Ethnography": Crossing Emotional Borders in Qualitative Accounts of Young People's Lives', *Sociology*, 41: 699–716.

Blaylock L. and Williams, P. (2005), 'Seventeen Year Olds: More Spiritual Than Religious, Less Atheistic Than You May Have Thought' *Resource, the Journal of NATRE*, 28 (1): 7–12.

Blaylock, L. and Williams, P. (2007), 'Explaining the Beliefs of 16–19 Year Olds: Respect, Spirituality, Human Rights Life After Death', *Journal of Chaplaincy in Further Education*, 3 (1): 17–29.

Bonacci, M. (1996), *We're on a Mission from God: The Generation X Guide to John Paul II, the Catholic Church and the Real Meaning of Life*, Ft Collins, CO: Ignatius Press.

Borhek, J.T. and Curtis, R.F. (1975), *A Sociology of Belief*, New York: John Wiley and Sons.

Bose, M. (2005), 'Difference and Exclusion at Work in the Club Culture Economy', *International Journal of Cultural Studies*, 8: 427–44.

Botros, G. (2006), 'Religious Identity as an Historical Narrative: Coptic Orthodox Immigrant Churches and the Representation of History', *Journal of Historical Sociology*, 19: 174–201.

Bouma, G. and Mason, M. (1995), 'Baby Boomers Downunder: The Case of Australia', in Roof, W.C., J. Carroll, J. and Roozen, D., eds, *The Postwar Generation and Establishment Religion: Cross-cultural Perspectives*, San Francisco, CA: Westview Press, pp. 59–86.

Bourdieu, P. (1977a), *Outline of a Theory of Practice*, Cambridge: Cambridge University Press.

Bourdieu, P. (1977b), 'Cultural Reproduction and Social Reproduction', in Karabel, J. and Halsey, A.H., eds, *Power and Ideology in Education*, Oxford: Oxford University Press, pp. 487–511.

Bourdieu, P. (1984), *Distinction: A Social Critique of the Judgment of Taste*, London: Routledge and Kegan Paul.

Bourdieu, P. (1986), 'The Forms of Capital', in Richardson, J.G., ed., *Handbook of Theory and Research for the Sociology of Education*, New York: Greenwood Press, pp. 241–58.

Bourdieu, P. (1991), 'Genesis and Structure of the Religious Field', *Comparative Social Research*, 13: 1–44.

Brierley, P. (2006), *Pulling out of the Nosedive: A Contemporary Portrait of Churchgoing – What the 2005 English Church Census Reveals*, London: Christian Research.

Brokaw, T. (1998), *The Greatest Generation*, New York: Random House.

Brown, C. (2001), *The Death of Christian Britain*, London: Routledge.

Bunt, S. (1975), *Jewish Youth Work in Britain: Past, Present, and Future*, London: Bedford Square Press.

Bruce, S. (1995), *Religion in Modern Britain*, Oxford: Oxford University Press.

Bruce, S. (2001), 'Christianity in Britain, R.I.P.', *Sociology of Religion*, 62: 191–203.

Bruce, S. (2002), *God is Dead: Secularization in the West*, Oxford: Blackwell.

Bushnell, H. (1967), *Christian Nurture*, New Haven, CT: Yale University Press.

Caputo, J. (2001), *On Religion*, London: Routledge.

Carr, D. and Landon, J. (1999), 'Teachers and Schools as Agencies of Values Education: Reflections on Teachers' Perceptions. Part Two: The Hidden Curriculum', *Journal of Beliefs and Values*, 20: 21–9.

Carrette, J. and King, R. (2005), *Selling Spirituality: The Silent Takeover of Religion*, London: Routledge.

Cavalli, A. (2004), 'Generations and Value Orientations', *Social Compass*, 51: 155–68.

Celek, T., Zander, D. and Klampert, P. (1996), *Inside the Soul of a New Generation*, Grand Rapids, MI: Zondervan.

Chaplin, E. (1994), *Sociology and Visual Representation*, London: Routledge.

Charme, S. (2000), 'Varieties of Authenticity and Jewish Identity', *Jewish Social Studies*, 6: 133–55.

Chatterton, P. and Hollands, R. (2002), 'Theorising Urban Playscapes: Producing, Regulating and Consuming Youthful Nightlife City Spaces', *Urban Studies*, 39: 95–116.

Chatterton, P. and Hollands, R. (2003), *Urban Nightscapes: Youth Cultures, Pleasure Spaces and Corporate Power*, London: Routledge.

Chaucer, G. (1951), *The Canterbury Tales*, translated by N. Coghill, Harmondsworth: Penguin.

Chaumeil, J.-P. (1983), *Voir, Savoir, Pouvoir: Le Chamanism chez les Yagua du Nord-est Péruvien*, Paris: EHSS.

Chazan, B. (2003), 'The Philosophy of Informal Jewish Education', *The Encyclopedia of Informal Education*, http://www.infed.org/informaljewish education/informal_jewish_education.htm, accessed 1 October 2009.

Cheng, V. (2004), *Inauthentic: The Anxiety over Culture and Identity*, New Brunswick, NJ: Rutgers University Press.

Church Information Office (1959), *Facts and Figures about the Church of England*, London: Central Board of Finance of the Church of England.

Clark, A. (2004), 'The Mosaic Approach and Research with Young Children', in Lewis, V., Kellett, M., Robinson, C., Fraser, S. and Ding, S., eds, *The Reality of Research with Children and Young People*, London: Sage, pp. 142–61.

Clark, L.S. (2003), *From Angels to Aliens: Teenagers, the Media and the Supernatural*, New York: Oxford University Press.

Clark, L.S. (2007), 'Religion, Twice Removed: Exploring the Role of Media in Religious Understandings among "Secular" Young People', in Ammerman, N., ed., *Everyday Religion: Observing Modern Religious Lives*, New York: Oxford University Press, pp. 69–81.

Clunis, A. (2006), 'Sikhs Suffer Terror Backlash', *The Voice*, 21 August, http://www.voice-online.co.uk/content.php?show=9888, accessed 5 December 2007

Clydesdale, T. (2007), *The First Year Out: Understanding American Teens after High School*, Chicago, IL: University of Chicago Press.

Cohen, E., Ben-Yehuda, M. and Aviad, J. (1987), 'Recentering the World: The Quest for Elective Centres in a Secularised Universe', *Sociological Review*, 35: 320–436.

Coleman, J. (1988), 'Social Capital in the Creation of Human Capital', *American Journal of Sociology*, 94: 95–120.

Coleman, S. and Eade, J. (2004), *Reframing Pilgrimage: Cultures in Motion*, London: Routledge.

Coleman, S. and Elsner, J. (1995), *Pilgrimage: Past and Present: Sacred Travel and Sacred Space in the World Religions*, London: British Museum Press.

Coleman, S. and Lindquist, G. (2008), 'Against Belief?', *Social Analysis*, 52: 1–18.

Collier, J. and Collier, M. (1986), *Visual Anthropology: Photography as a Research Method*, Albuquerque, NM: University of New Mexico Press.

Collins, S. (1997), 'Young People's Faith in Late Modernity', unpublished PhD thesis, University of Surrey.

Collins-Mayo, S. (2008), 'Young People's Spirituality and the Meaning of Prayer', in Day, A., ed., *Religion and the Individual*, Aldershot: Ashgate, pp. 33–46.

Collins-Mayo, S., Mayo, B. and Nash, S. with Cocksworth, C. (forthcoming), *The Faith of Generation Y*, London: Church House Publishing."

Community Agency for Social Equity (2000), *South African Youth Survey*, http://www.case.org.za/Youth, accessed March 2007.

Connell, D. (1997), 'Participatory Development: an Approach Sensitive to Class and Gender', *Development in Practice*, 7: 248–60.

Conselho Nacional de Educação (1999), *Resolução CEB Nº 3, de 10 de novembro de 1999. Fixa Diretrizes Nacionais para o funcionamento das escolas indígenas e dá outras providências*, Art 3º. http://portal.mec.gov.br/cne/arquivos/pdf/CEB0398.pdf; accessed 14 May 2009.

Cooper, H. and Morisson, P. (1991), *A Sense of Belonging: Dilemmas of British Jewish Identity*, London: Weidenfeld and Nicolson.

Cornwall, A. (2003), 'Whose Voices? Whose Choices? Reflections on Gender and Participatory Development', *World Development*, 31: 1325–42.

Coupland, D. (1992), *Generation X.*, London: Abacus.

Coupland, D. (1994), *Life After God*, London: Simon and Schuster.

Coupland, D. (2009), *Generation A*, London: William Heinemann.

Cox, K. (1998), *GenX and God: A GenX Perspective*, Chanhassen, MN: Tekna Books.

Crockett, A. and Voas, D. (2006), 'Generations of Decline: Religious Change in Twentieth-Century Britain', *Journal for the Scientific Study of Religion*, 45: 567–84.

Cunningham, S. (2006), *Dear Church: Letters from a Disillusioned Generation*, Grand Rapids, MI: Zondervan.

Cush, D. (1997), 'Paganism in the Classroom', *British Journal of Religious Education*, 19: 83–94.

Cush, D. (2003), 'Faith School Debate: Should the State Fund "Schools with a Religious Character?" The Recent Debate about "Faith Schools" in England', *Resource: The Journal of the Professional Council for Religious Education*, 25 (2): 10–15.

Cush, D. (2007a), 'Consumer Witchcraft: Are Teenage Witches a Creation of Commercial Interests?', *Journal of Beliefs and Values*, 28: 45–53.

Cush, D. (2007b), 'Wise Young Women: Beliefs, Values and Influences in the Adoption of Witchcraft by Teenage Girls in England', in Johnston, H.E. and Aloi, P., eds, *The New Generation Witches: Teenage Witchcraft in Contemporary Culture*, Aldershot: Ashgate, pp. 139–60.

Cush, D. (2007c), 'Should Religious Studies be Part of the Compulsory State School Curriculum?', *British Journal of Religious Education*, 29: 217–27.

Dandelion, P. (1996), *A Sociological Analysis of the Theology of Quakers: The Silent Revolution*, Lampeter: Edwin Mellen Press.

Darvall, S.L., ed. (2002), *Contractiarianism, Contractualism*, Oxford: Blackwell Publishing.

Dasgupta, S.D. (1998), 'Gender Roles and Cultural Continuity in the Asian Indian Immigrant Community in the U.S.', *Sex Roles*, 38 (11/12): 953–74.

Davidman, L. (1991), *Tradition in a Rootless World: Women Turn to Orthodox Judaism*, Berkeley, CA: University of California Press.

Davie, G. (1994), *Religion in Britain since 1945: Believing Without Belonging*, Oxford: Blackwell.

Davie, G. (2000), *Religion in Modern Europe: A Memory Mutates*, Oxford: Oxford University Press.

Davie, G. (2002), *Europe, the Exceptional Case: Parameters of Faith in the Modern World*, London: Darton, Longman and Todd.

Davies, D. and Guest, M. (2007), *Bishops, Wives and Children: Spiritual Capital Across the Generations*, Aldershot: Ashgate.

Davis, E. (1998), *Techgnosis: Myth, Magic and Mysticism in the Age of Information*, New York: Harmony Books.

Davis, E. (2004), *Hedonistic Tantra: Golden Goa's Trance Transmission*, in St John., G., ed., *Rave Culture and Religion*, London: Routledge, pp. 256–72.

Day, A. (2006), 'Believing in Belonging: A Case Study from Yorkshire', unpublished PhD thesis, Lancaster University.

Day, A. (2008), 'Wilfully Disempowered: a Gendered Response to a Fallen World', *European Journal of Women's Studies*, 15: 261–76.

Day, A. (2009a), 'Researching Belief Without Asking Religious Questions', *Fieldwork in Religion*, 4 (1): in press.

Day, A. (2009b), 'Believing in Belonging: An Ethnography of Young People's Constructions of Belief', *Culture and Religion*, 10 (3): 263–78.

Day, A. (2011), *Belief and Social Identity in the Modern World: Believing in Belonging*, Oxford: Oxford University Press.

Dean, K.C. (2004), *Practicing Passion: Youth and the Quest for a Passionate Church*, Grand Rapids, MI: Eerdmans.

Dent, H.J. (1947), *The Education Act 1944: Provisions, Possibilities and Some Problems*, 3rd edn, London: University of London Press.

Denton, M. and Smith, C. (2001), 'Methodological Issues & Challenges in the Study of American Youth & Religion', *National Study of Youth and Religion*, Chapel Hill, North Carolina, 2001, http://www.youthandreligion.org/docs/methods.pdf, accessed 12 October 2007.

Devadason, R. (2007), 'Constructing Coherence? Young Adults' Pursuit of Meaning through Multiple Transitions between Work, Education and Unemployment', *Journal of Youth Studies*, 10(2): 203–21.

DeVries, M. (1994), *Family-Based Youth Ministry: Reaching the Been-There, Done-That Generation*, Downers Grove, IL: InterVarsity Press.

Dewdney, A. and Lister, M. (1988), *Youth, Culture and Photography*, Basingstoke: Macmillan Education.

Dicker, R. and Piepmeier, A., eds (2003), *Catching a Wave: Reclaiming Feminism for the 21ˢᵗ Century*, Boston: Northeastern University Press.

Drury, B. (1991), 'Sikh Girls and the Maintenance of an Ethnic Culture', *New Community*, 17: 387–99.

Dunlop, S. (2008), *Visualising Hope: Exploring the Spirituality of Young People in Central and Eastern Europe*, Cambridge: YTC Press.

Durkheim, E. (2001), *The Elementary Forms of Religious Life*, Oxford: Oxford University Press.

Edgell, P. (2006), *Religion and Family in a Changing Society*, Princeton, NJ: Princeton University Press.

Edwards, E. (1992), *Anthropology and Photography 1860–1920*, New Haven, CT: Yale University Press.

Edwards, E. (2007), 'Samuel Butler's Photography: Observation and the Dynamic Past', in Paradis, J., ed., *Samuel Butler: Victorian Against the Grain*, Toronto: University of Toronto Press, pp. 251–86.

Edwards, S. (2006), *Photography: A Very Short Introduction*, Oxford: Oxford University Press.

Elkind, D. (1998), *All Grown Up and No Place to Go: Teenagers in Crisis, Reading*, MA: Addison-Wesley.

Ellingson, S., Van Haitsma, M., Laumann, E.O. and Tebbe, N. (2004), 'Religion and the Politics of Sexuality', in Laumann, E.O., Ellingson, S., Mahay, J., Paik A. and Youm, Y., eds, *The Sexual Organization of the City*, Chicago, IL, University of Chicago Press, pp. 309–48.

English, S. (2006), 'Sikh Boy's Hair Cut Off in Racist Attack by Knife Gang', *The Times*, 16 November, http://www.timesonline.co.uk/tol/incomingFeeds/article1087410.ece, accessed 22 July 2007.

Eysenck, H.J. and Eysenck, S.B.G. (1991), *Manual of the Eysenck Personality Scales*, London: Hodder and Stoughton.

Ezzy, D. (2003), 'New Age Witchcraft? Popular Spell Books and the Re-enchantment of Everyday Life', *Culture and Religion*, 4: 47–65.

Ezzy, D. (2006), 'White Witches and Black Magic: Ethics and Consumerism in Contemporary Witchcraft', *Journal of Contemporary Religion*, 21: 17–37.

Faulkner, Andrew (1997), *Knowing Our Own Minds*, London: Mental Health Foundation.

Fiorenza, E.S. (1992), 'Women in the Early Christian Movement', in Christ, C. and Plaskow, J., eds, *Womanspirit Rising: A Feminist Reader in Religion*, New York: HarperCollins, pp. 161–74.

Flory, R. and Miller, D.E., eds (2000), *GenX Religion*, New York: Routledge.

Flory, R. and Miller, D.E. (2004), 'Expressive Communalism', *Congregations*, 30 (4): 31–5.

Flory, R and Miller, D.E. (2007a), 'The Millennial Generation', *Worship Leader*, 16 (6): 20–24.

Flory, R and Miller, D.E. (2007b), 'The Embodied Spirituality of the Post-Boomer Generations', in Flanagan, K. and Jupp, P.C., eds, *A Sociology of Spirituality*, Aldershot: Ashgate, pp. 201–18.

Flory, R. and Miller, D.E. (2008), *Finding Faith: The Spiritual Quest of the Post-Boomer Generation*, New Brunswick, NJ: Rutgers University Press.

Forbes, B. and Mahan, J., eds (2000), *Religion and Popular Culture in America*, Berkeley, CA: University of California Press.

Ford, R. (2008), 'Is Racial Prejudice Declining in Britain?', *British Journal of Sociology*, 59: 609–36.

Forman, R. (2004), *Grassroots Spirituality*, Boston: Academic Imprint.

Foucault M. (1978), *History of Sexuality*, New York, Vintage Books.

Francis, L.J. (2005b), 'Prayer, Personality and Purpose in Life among Churchgoing and Non-churchgoing Adolescents', in Francis, L.J., Robbins, M. and Astley, J., eds, *Religion, Education and Adolescence: International Empirical Perspectives*, Cardiff: University of Wales Press, pp. 15–38.

Francis, L.J. (1982), *Youth in Transit: A Profile of 16–25 Year Olds*, Aldershot: Gower.

Francis, L.J. (1984), *Teenagers and the Church: A Profile of Church-Going Youth in the 1980s*, London: Collins Liturgical Publications.

Francis, L.J. (2000), 'The Relationship between Bible Reading and Purpose in Life among 13–15 Year Olds', *Mental Health, Religion and Culture*, 3: 27–36.

Francis, L.J. (2001a), *The Values Debate: A Voice from the Pupils*, London: Woburn Press.

Francis, L.J. (2001b), 'Religion and Values: A Quantitative Perspective', in Francis, L.J., Astley, J. and Robbins, M., eds, *The Fourth R for the Third Millennium: Education in Religion and Values for the Global Future*, Dublin: Lindisfarne Books, pp. 47–78.

Francis, L.J. (2001c), 'The Social Significance of Religious Affiliation among Adolescents in England and Wales', in Ziebertz, H.-G., ed., *Religious Individualisation and Christian Religious Semantics*, Münster: Lit Verlag, pp. 115–38.

Francis, L.J. (2001d), 'God Images, Personal Wellbeing and Moral Values: A Survey among 13–15 Year Olds in England and Wales', in Ziebertz, H.-G., ed., *Imagining God: Empirical Explorations from an International Perspective*, Munster: Lit Verlag, pp. 125–44.

Francis, L.J. (2002a), 'Catholic Schools and Catholic Values: A Study of Moral and Religious Values among 13–15 Year old Pupils Attending Non-denominational and Catholic Schools in England and Wales', *International Journal of Education and Religion*, 3: 69–84.

Francis, L.J. (2002b), 'The Relationship between Bible Reading and Attitude Toward Substance Use among 13–15 Year Olds', *Religious Education*, 97: 44–60.

Francis, L.J. (2003), 'Religion and Social Capital: the Flaw in the 2001 Census in England and Wales', in Avis, P., ed., *Public Faith: The State of Religious Belief and Practice in Britain*, London: SPCK, pp. 45–64.

Francis, L.J. (2004), 'Empirical Theology and Hermeneutical Religious Education: A Case Study Concerning Adolescent Attitudes Toward Abortion', in Lombaerts, H. and Pollefeyt, D., eds, *Hermeneutics and Religious Education*, Leuven: Peeters, pp. 355–73.

Francis, L.J. (2005a), 'Independent Christians Schools and Pupil Values: An Empirical Investigation among 13–15 Year-old Boys', *British Journal of Religious Education*, 27 (2): 127–41.

Francis, L.J. (2008a), 'Family, Denomination and the Adolescent Worldview: An Empirical Enquiry among 13–15 Year-old Females in England and Wales', *Marriage and Family Review*, 43: 185–204.

Francis, L.J. (2008b), 'Self-assigned Religious Affiliation: A Study among Adolescents in England and Wales', in Spalek, B. and Imtoual. A., eds, *Religion, Spirituality and the Social Sciences: Challenging Marginalisation*, Bristol: Policy Press, pp. 149–61.

Francis, L.J. and Kay, W.K. (1995), *Teenage Religion and Values*, Leominster: Gracewing.

Francis, L.J. and Robbins, M. (2004), 'Belonging Without Believing: A Study in the Social Significance of Anglican Identity and Implicit Religion among 13–15 Year Old Males', *Implicit Religion*, 7: 37–54.

Francis, L.J. and Robbins, M. (2005), *Urban Hope and Spiritual Health: The Adolescent Voice*, Peterborough: Epworth.

Francis, L.J. and Robbins, M. (2006), 'Prayer, Purpose in Life, Personality and Social Attitudes among Non-churchgoing 13–15 Year-olds in England and Wales', *Research in the Social Scientific Study of Religion*, 17: 123–55.

Fraser, S., Lewis, V., Ding, S., Kellett, M., Robinson, C., eds (2004), *Doing Research with Children and Young People*, London: Sage and Open University.

Frazer, E. (1988), 'Teenager Girls Talking about Class', *Sociology*, 22: 343–58.

Frazer, E. (1989), 'Feminist Talk and Talking about Feminism: Teenage Girls' Discourse of Gender', *Oxford Review of Education*, 15: 281–90.

Freeman, R.B. (1986), 'Who Escapes? The Relation of Churchgoing and Other Background Factors to the Socioeconomic Performance of Black Male Youths from Inner-city Tracts', in Freeman, R.B. and Holzer, H.J., eds, *The Black Youth Employment Crisis*, Chicago, IL: University of Chicago Press, pp. 353–76.

Frosh, S., Phoenix, A. and Pattman, R. (2002), *Young Masculinities: Understanding Boys in Contemporary Society*, Basingstoke: Palgrave.

Fuller, R. (2001), *Spiritual but not Religious: Understanding Unchurched America*, Oxford: Oxford University Press.

Fulton, J. (1999), 'Young Adult Core Catholics', in Hornsby-Smith, M.P., ed., *Catholics in England 1950–2000: Historical and Sociological Perspectives*, New York: Cassell, pp. 161–81.

Fulton, J. (2000), 'Young Adult Catholics in England', in Fulton, J., Abela, A. M., Borowik, I., Dowling, T., Long Marler, P. and Tomasi, L., eds, *Young Catholics at the New Millennium: The Religion and Morality of Young Adults in Western Countries*, Dublin: Dublin University College Press, pp. 137–59.

Furlong, A. and Cartmel, F. (1997), *Young People and Social Change: Individualization and Risk in Late Modernity*. Buckingham: Open University Press.

Galbraith, M. (2000), 'On the Road to Częstochowa: Rhetoric and Experience on a Polish Pilgrimage', *Anthropological Quarterly*, 73(2): 61–73.

Gane, N. (2002), *Max Weber and Postmodern Theory: Rationalization versus Re-enchantment*, New York, Palgrave.

Garland, D.R. (1999), *Family Ministry: A Comprehensive Guide*, Downers Grove, IL: InterVarsity Press.

Garner, R (2000), 'Safe Sects? Dynamic Religion and AIDS in South Africa', *The Journal of Modern African Studies*, 38: 41–69.

Garnett, J., Grimley, M., Harris, A., Whyte, W. and Williams, S., eds (2006), *Redefining Christian Britain: Post-1945 Perspectives*, London: SCM Press.

Germond, P. and Dooms, T. (2008), 'Religion and Adolescent Sexual Wellbeing: A Case Study of Christian Youth in Potchefstroom, South Africa', Paper presented at the meeting of the British Sociological Association Sociology of Religion Study Group Conference, Birmingham.

Giddens, A. (1984), *The Constitution of Society: Introduction of the Theory of Structuration*. Berkeley, CA: University of California Press.

Giddens, A. (1991), *Modernity and Self Identity: Self and Society in the Late Modern Age*, Oxford: Polity.

Good, B.J. (1994), *Medicine, Rationality, and Experience*, Cambridge: Cambridge University Press.

Gow, P. (1991), *Of Mixed Blood: Kinship and its History in Peruvian Amazonia*, Oxford: Clarendon Press.

Grace, G. (2003), 'Educational Studies and Faith Based Schooling – Moving from Prejudice to Evidence-Based Argument', *British Journal of Educational Studies*, 51: 149–67.

Grady, John (2008), Visual Research at the Crossroads [74 paragraphs]. *Forum Qualitative Sozialforschung / Forum: Qualitative Social Research*, 9(3), Art. 38, http://nbn-resolving.de/urn:nbn:de:0114-fqs0803384, accessed 1 October 2009.

Greeley, A. (1991), 'American Exceptionalism: the Religious Phenomenon', in Shafer, B.E., ed., *Is America Different? A New Look at American Exceptionalism*, New York: Oxford University Press, pp. 94–115.

Greener, T. and Hollands, R. (2006), 'Beyond Subculture and Post-Subculture? The Case of Virtual Psytrance', *Journal of Youth Studies*, 9: 393–418.

Grennan, S. (2001), 'Irish Sikhs Abandon Traditional Turbans', *Irish Independent*, 28 October, http://www.independent.ie/national-news/irish-sikhs-abandon-traditional-turbans-511233.html, accessed 29 November 2007.

Griffin, C., Measham, F., Moore, K., Morey, Y. and Riley, S. (2008), 'Editorial: The Social and Cultural Uses of Ketamine', *Addiction Research and Theory*, Special Issue on the Social and Cultural Uses of Ketamine, 16: 205–7.

Gross, R. (1993), *Buddhism after Patriarchy: a Feminist History, Analysis and Reconstruction of Buddhism*, Albany, NY: State University of New York Press.

Grossberg, L. (1997), *Dancing in Spite of Myself: Essays on Popular Culture*, Durham, NC: Duke University Press.

Gruber, J. and Hungerman, D. (2008), 'The Church vs. the Mall: What Happens When Religion Faces Increased Secular Competition?', *Quarterly Journal of Economics*, 123: 831–62.

Guttmacher Institute (2009), 'Sex and STI/HIV Education', *State Policies in Brief*, February 1.

Hadaway, C.K., Marler P.L. and Chaves, M. (1993), 'What the Polls Don't Show: A Closer Look at U.S. Church Attendance', *American Sociological Review*, 58: 741–52.

Hall, J. (2004), 'Why do Young People Choose to Become Witches?' Unpublished MA dissertation, Bath Spa University.

Hall, K. (2002), *Lives in Translation: Sikh Youth as British Citizens*, Philadelphia, PA: University of Pennsylvania Press.

Hall, S. (1996), 'Introduction: Who Needs Identity?', in Hall, S. and Gay, P. Du, eds, *Questions of Cultural Identity*, Thousand Oaks, CA: Sage, pp. 1–17.

Hall, S. (2000), 'Encoding, Decoding', in During, S., ed., *The Cultural Studies Reader*, London: Routledge, pp. 507–17.

Haraway, D. (1991), 'A Cyborg Manifesto: Science, Technology, and Socialist-feminism in the Late Twentieth Century', in Haraway, D., ed., *Simians, Cyborgs and Women: The Reinvention of Nature*, New York: Routledge.

Harding, D.J. and Jencks, C. (2003), 'Changing Attitudes Toward Premarital Sex: Cohort, Period, and Aging Effects', *Public Opinion Quarterly*, 67: 211–26.

Harding, S., ed. (1987), *Feminist Research and Methodology: Social Science Issues*, Bloomington, IN: Indiana University Press.

Harding, S. (1991), *Whose Science? Whose Knowledge?: Thinking from Women's Lives*, Ithica, NY: Cornell University Press.

Harding, S. (2004), *The Feminist Standpoint Theory Reader: Intellectual and Political Controversies*, London: Routledge.

Harper, D. (1998), 'An Argument for Visual Sociology', in Prosser, J., ed., *Image-based Research*, London: Falmer Press, pp. 24–41.

Harper, D. (2001), *Changing Works: Visions of a Lost Agriculture*, Chicago, IL: University of Chicago Press.

Harper, D. (2002), 'Talking about Pictures: A Case for Photo Elicitation', *Visual Studies*, 17: 13–26.

Harrington, M. (2007), 'The Perennial Teen Witch: A Discussion of Teenage Interest in Modern Pagan Witchcraft', in Johnston, H.E. and Aloi, P., eds,

The New Generation Witches: Teenage Witchcraft in Contemporary Culture, Aldershot: Ashgate, pp. 25–55.

Harris, A. (2004a), *Future Girl: Young Women in the Twenty-first Century*, London: Routledge.

Harris, A., ed. (2004b), *All about the Girl: Culture, Power, and Identity*, London: Routledge.

Harris, R. (1999), *Lourdes: Body and Spirit in the Secular Age*, Harmondsworth: Penguin.

Hart, R. and Kafka, E. (2006), 'Trends in British Synagogue Membership 1990–2005/2006', London: Board of Deputies of British Jews.

Hartsock, N. (1998), *The Feminist Standpoint Revisited and Other Essays*, Boulder, CO: Westview Press.

Hay, D. (2006), *Something There: The Biology of the Human Spirit*, London: Darton, Longman and Todd.

Heath, S., Brooks, R., Cleaver, E. and Ireland, E. (2009), *Researching Young People's Lives*, London: Sage.

Hebdige, D. (1979), *Subculture: the Meaning of Style*, London: Routledge.

Heelas, P. (1996), 'On Things not Being Worse, and the Ethic of Humanity', in Heelas, P., ed., *Detraditionalization*, Oxford: Blackwell, pp. 200–218.

Heelas, P. (2000), 'Expressive Spirituality and Humanistic Expressivism: Sources of Significance Beyond Church and Chapel', in Sutcliffe, S. and Bowman, M., *Beyond New Age: Exploring Alternative Spirituality*, Edinburgh: Edinburgh University Press, pp. 237–54.

Heelas, P. (2002), 'The Spiritual Revolution: from "Religion" to "Spirituality"' in Woodhead, L., Fletcher, P., Kawami, H. and Smith, D., eds, *Religions in the Modern World*, London: Routledge, pp. 357–77.

Heelas, P. (2007), 'The Holistic Milieu and Spirituality: Reflections on Voas and Bruce', in Flanagan, K. and Jupp, P., eds, *A Sociology of Spirituality*, Aldershot: Ashgate, pp. 63–80.

Heelas, P. and Woodhead, L., with Seel, B., Szersynski, B. and Tusting, K. (2005), *The Spiritual Revolution: Why Religion is Giving Way to Spirituality*, Oxford: Blackwell.

Heelas, P., Lash, S. and Morris, P. (1996), *Detraditionalization: Critical Reflections on Authority and Identity*, Oxford: Blackwell.

Heft, J.L., ed. (2006), *Passing on the Faith: Transforming Traditions for the Next Generation of Jews, Christians, and Muslims*, New York: Fordham University Press.

Hervieu-Léger, D. (1998), 'The Transmission and Formation of Socioreligious Identities in Modernity', *International Sociology*, 13: 213–28.

Hervieu-Léger, D. (2000), *Religion as a Chain of Memory*, Cambridge: Polity Press.

Heynes, J. (2008), 'An Exploration of Girls' Perceptions of, and Views on, the Representation of Women and Gender in Religious Education', unpublished PhD thesis, University of Manchester.

Hill Collins, P. (1990), *Black Feminist Thought: Knowledge, Consciousness, and the Politics of Empowerment*, London: Routledge.

Hill, J. (1993), *Keepers of the Sacred Chants: The Poetics of Ritual Power in an Amazonian Society*, Tucson: University Press of Arizona.

Hill, P.C. and Hood, R.W. (1999), *Measures of Religiosity*, Birmingham, AL: Religious Education Press.

Hiltebeitel, A. and Miller, B.D. (1998), *Hair: Its Power and Meaning in Asian Cultures*, New York: State University of New York Press.

Hobbs, D., Hadfield, P., Lister, S. and Winlow, S. (2003), *Bouncers: Violence and Governance in the Night-time Economy*, Oxford: Oxford University Press.

Hodkinson, P. (2002), *Goth: Identity, Style and Subculture*, Oxford: Berg.

Hodkinson, P. (2005), '"Insider Research" in the Study of Youth Cultures', *Journal of Youth Studies*, 8: 131–49.

Hoge, D.R.; Petrillo, G.H. and Smith, E.I. (1982), 'Transmission of Religious and Social Values from Parents to Teenage Children', *Journal of Marriage and the Family*, 44: 569–80.

Holland, J. and Ramazanoglu, C. (1994), 'Coming to Conclusions: Power and Interpretation in Researching Young Women's Sexuality', in Maynard, M. and Purvis, J., eds, *Researching Women's Lives from a Feminist Perspective*, London: Taylor and Francis, pp. 125–48.

Hollands, R. (2002), 'Divisions in the Dark: Youth Cultures, Transitions, and Segmented Consumption Spaces in the Night-time Economy', *Journal of Youth Studies*, 5: 153–71.

Hollands, R. and Chatterton, P. (2003), 'Producing Nightlife in the New Urban Entertainment Economy: Corporatisation, Branding, and Market Segmentation', *International Journal of Urban and Regional Research*, 27: 361–85.

Hooks, b. (1984), *Feminist Theory: From Margin to the Centre*, Boston, MA: South End Press.

Hooks, b. (1999, 1983), *Ain't I a Woman: Black Women and Feminism*, London: Pluto Press.

Hoover, S. (2006), *Religion in the Media Age*, London: Routledge.

Hoover, S. and Clark, L.S., eds (2002), *Practising Religion in the Age of the Media: Explorations in Media, Religion and Culture*, New York: Columbia University Press.

Hoover, S. and Lundby, K., eds (1997), *Rethinking Media, Religion and Culture*, London: Sage.

Hoover, S., Clark, L.S. and Alters, D. (2004), *Media, Home and Family*, London: Routledge.

Houtman, D. and Aupers, S. (2007), 'The Spiritual Turn and the Decline of Tradition: the Spread of post-Christian Spirituality in 14 Western Countries, 1981–2000', *Journal for the Scientific Study of Religion*, 46: 305–20.

Hughes, P., Thompson, C., Pryor, R. and Bouma, G. (1995), *Believe It or Not: Australian Spirituality and the Churches in the '90s*, Melbourne: Christian Research Association.

Hull, J.M. (1984), *Studies in Religion and Education*, Lewes: Falmer Press.

Hundeide, K. (2004), 'A New Identity, A New Lifestyle', in Perret-Clermont, A.-N., Pontecorvo, C., Resnick, L.B., Zittoun, T. and Burge, B., eds, *Joining Society: Social Interaction and Learning in Adolescence and Youth*, Cambridge: Cambridge University Press, pp. 86–106.

Hunt, S. (2005), *Religion and Everyday Life*, London: Routledge.

Hurworth, R. (2003), 'Photo-Interviewing for Research', *Social Research Update*, http://sru.soc.surrey.ac.uk:80/SRU40.html, accessed 1 October 2009.

Hutton, F. (2006), Risky Pleasures: Club Cultures and Feminine Identities, Aldershot: Ashgate.

Iannaccone, L. (1991), 'The Consequences of Religious Market Structure: Adam Smith and the Economics of Religion', *Rationality and Society*, 3: 156–77.

Inglehart, R. (1977), *The Silent Revolution: Changing Values and Political Styles among Western Publics*, Princeton, NJ: Princeton University Press.

Inglehart, R. (1990), *Culture Shift in Advanced Industrial Society*, Princeton, NJ: Princeton University Press.

Inglehart, R. (1997), *Modernization and Post-Modernization*. Princeton, NJ: Princeton University Press.

Inglehart, R. and Welzel, C. (2005), *Modernization, Cultural Change and Democracy: The Human Development Sequence*, New York: Cambridge University Press.

Inglis, T. (2007), 'Catholic Identity in Contemporary Ireland: Belief and Belonging to Tradition', *Journal of Contemporary Religion*, 22: 205–20.

Jackson, P. (2004), *Inside Clubbing: Sensual Experiments in the Art of Being Human*, Oxford: Berg.

Jackson, R. and Nesbitt, E. (1993), *Hindu Children in Britain*, Stoke-on-Trent: Trentham.

Jenkins, R. (1992), *Pierre Bourdieu*, London: Routledge.

Johnson, R., Chambers, D., Raghuram, P. and Tincknell, E. (2004), *The Practice of Cultural Studies*, London: SAGE.

Johnston, H.E. and Aloi, P., eds (2007), *The New Generation Witches: Teenage Witchcraft in Contemporary Culture*, Aldershot: Ashgate

Kahane, R. (1997), *The Origins of Postmodern Youth: Informal Youth Movements in Comparative Perspective*, Berlin: Walter de Gruyter.

Kalra, V.S. (2005), 'Locating the Sikh Pagh', *Sikh Formations*, 1: 75–92.

Kalsi, S.S. (1997), 'Sacred Symbols in British Sikhism', DISKUS 2:2, http://web.uni-marburg.de/religionswissenschaft/journal/diskus/kalsi.html, accessed 10 July 2007.

Karlsson Minganti, P. (2007), *Muslima: Islamisk väckelse och unga kvinnors förhandlingar om genus i det samtida Sverige* [Muslima: Islamic Revival and Young Women's Negotiations on Gender in Contemporary Sweden], Stockholm: Carlsson Bokförlag.

Karlsson Minganti, P. (2008), 'Becoming a "Practising" Muslim: Reflections on Gender, Racism and Religious Identity among Women in a Swedish Muslim

Youth Organisation', *Elore*, 15/1. http://www.elore.fi/arkisto/1_08/kam1_ 08.pdf, accessed 1 October 2009.

Kaufman, S.K. (2005), *Consuming Visions: Mass Culture and the Lourdes Shrine*, Ithaca, NY: Cornell University Press.

Kay, W.K. and Francis, L.J. (1996), *Drift from the Churches: Attitudes Toward Christianity During Childhood and Adolescence*, Cardiff: University of Wales Press.

Kay, W.K. and Francis, L.J. (2001), 'Religious Education and School Assembly in England and Wales: What do Religious Minorities Think?', in Heimbrock, H.-G., Scheilke, C.Th. and Schreiner, P., eds, *Towards Religious Competence: Diversity as a Challenge for Education in Europe*, Munster: Lit Verlag, pp. 117–28.

Kay, W.K. and Francis, L.J. (2006), 'Suicidal Ideation among Young People in the UK: Churchgoing as an Inhibitory Influence?' *Mental Health, Religion and Culture* 9, pp. 127–40.

Keats, J. (1959), 'Letter to George and Thomas Keats [1817]', in Bush, D., ed., *Selected Poems and Letters*, Boston: Houghton Mifflin, pp. 260–61.

Khan, S. (2002), *Aversion and Desire: Negotiating Muslim Female Identity in Diaspora*, Toronto: Women's Press.

King. J. (2003), *Morals and Messaging in the Fight against HIV/AIDS*, Johannesburg, HIVAN Media team.

King, U. (2005), 'Introduction: Gender-Critical Turns in the Study of Religion', in King, U. and Beattie, T., eds, *Gender, Religion and Diversity: Cross-Cultural Perspectives*, London and New York: Continuum.

King, U. (2008), *The Search for Spirituality: Our Global Quest for a Spiritual Life*, New York: BlueBridge.

Kirchberg, V. (2007), 'Cultural Consumption Analysis: Beyond Structure and Agency', *Cultural Sociology*, 1: 115–35.

Knott, K. (2005), 'Spatial Theory and Method for the Study of Religion', *Temenos*, 41: 153–84.

Kohli, H.S (2006), 'Faked Attack that Exposes an Uncomfortable Truth', *The Times*, 31 December, http://www.timesonline.co.uk/tol/news/uk/scotland/ article1264988.ece, accessed 22 August 2007.

Kosmin, B and Keysar, A. (2009), 'American Religious Identification Survey' (ARIS 2008), Summary Report, Trinity College, Hartford, CT.

Kurien, P.A. (1998), 'Becoming American by Becoming Hindu: Indian Americans Take Their Place at the Multicultural Table', in Warner, R.S. and Wittner, J.G., eds, *Gatherings in Diaspora: Religious Communities and the New Immigration*, Philadelphia, PA: Temple University Press, pp. 37–70.

Kurien, P.A. (2007), *A Place at the Multicultural Table: The Development of an American Hinduism*, New Brunswick, NJ: Rutgers University Press.

Lagrou, E.M. (2001), 'Identidade e alteridade a partir da perspectiva kaxinawa', in Esterci, N., Fry, P. and Goldenberg, M., eds, *Fazendo antropologia no Brasil*, Rio de Janeiro: DPandA Editora, pp. 93–128.

Lamb, C. and Siedlecka, J. (2006), 'British Pilgrims to Lourdes at Record High', *The Tablet*, 5 August, p. 42.

Lambert, Y. (2004), 'A Turning Point in the Religious Evolution of Europe', *Journal of Contemporary Religion*, 19(4): 29–46.

Langdon, E.J.M. (1996), 'Introdução: Xamanismo – Velhas e novas perspectivas', in Langdon, E.J.M., ed., *Xamanismo no Brasil: Novas perspectivas*, Florianópolis: UFSC, pp. 9–17.

Lankshear, D.W. (2005), 'The Influence of Anglican Secondary Schools on Personal, Moral and Religious Values', in Francis, L.J., Robbins, M. and Astley, J., eds, *Religion, Education and Adolescence: International Empirical Perspectives*, Cardiff: University of Wales, Press, pp. 55–69.

Larsson, Göran (2006), *Muslimerna kommer! Tankar om islamofobi* [*The Muslims are Coming! Thoughts on Islamophobia*]. Göteborg and Stockholm: Makadam.

Lederhendler, E., ed. (2001), *Who Owns Judaism? Public Religion and Private Faith in America and Israel*, Studies in Contemporary Jewry Volume XVII, Oxford: Oxford University Press.

Leonard, M. (2007), 'With a Capital "G": Gatekeepers and Gatekeeping in Research with Children', in Best, A.L, ed., *Representing Youth: Methodological Issues in Critical Youth Studies*, New York: New York University Press, pp. 133–56.

Likert, R. (1932), 'A Technique for the Measurement of Attitudes', *Archives of Psychology* 140: 1–55.

Lopes, A. da Silva (2002), 'Pequenos "xamãs": crianças indígenas, corporalidade e esclarizaçao', in Lopes da Silva Macedo, A.V. and Nunes, Â., eds, *Crianças Indígenas. Ensaios Antropológicos*, São Paulo: FAPESP, pp. 37–63.

Lopez, D. (1998), 'Belief', in Taylor, M.C., ed., *Critical Terms for Religious Studies*, Chicago, IL: University of Chicago Press, pp. 21–3.

Lovheim, M. (2007), 'Virtually Boundless? Youth Negotiating Tradition in Cyberspace', in Ammerman, N., ed., *Everyday Religion: Observing Modern Religious Lives*, New York: Oxford University Press, pp. 83–100.

Luckmann, S. (1967), *The Invisible Religion: The Problem of Religion in Modern Society*, New York: Macmillan.

Luckmann, S. (2003), 'Going Bush and Finding One's "Tribe": Raving, Escape, and the Bush Doof', *Journal of Media and Cultural Studies*, 17: 315–30.

Luckmann, T. (1967), *The Invisible Religion*, New York: Macmillan.

Luz, P.F. (2002), 'O uso ameríndio do caapi', in Caiuby Labate, B. and Sena Araújo, W., eds, *O uso ritual da ayahuasca*, Campinas: Mercado de Letras, pp. 35–66.

Lynch, G. (2002), *After Religion: 'Generation X' and the Search for Meaning*, London: Darton, Longman and Todd.

Lynch, G., ed. (2008), *Between Sacred and Profane: Researching Religion and Popular Culture*, London: IB Tauris.

Lynch, G. (2009), 'Cultural Theory and Cultural Studies', in Lyden, J., ed., *The Routledge Companion to Religion and Film*, London: Routledge, pp. 275–91.

Lynch, G. and Badger, E. (2006), 'The Mainstream Post-rave Dance Scene as Secondary Institution: a British Perspective', *Religion and Culture*, 7: 27–40.

Lyon, D. (2000), *Jesus in Disneyland: Religion in Postmodern Times*, Cambridge: Polity.

MacKinnon I. (2003), 'Sikhs put Macho Image Back in Fashion', *The Times*, August 11, http://www.timesonline.co.uk/tol/news/world/article863990.ece, accessed 22 September 2009.

MacLaren, D. (2004), *Mission Implausible: Restoring Credibility to the Church*, Milton Keynes: Paternoster.

MacRae, E. (1992), *Guiado pela lua. Xamanismo e uso ritual da ayahuasca no Culto do Santo Daime*, São Paulo: Editora Brasiliense.

MacRae, R. (2004), 'Notions of "Us" and "Them": Markers of Stratification in Clubbing Lifestyles', *Journal of Youth Studies*, 7: 55–71.

Mahdavi, P. (2008), *Passionate Uprisings – Iran's Sexual Revolution*, Stanford, CA: Stanford University Press.

Mahedy, W. and Bernadi, J. (1994), *A Generation Alone: Xers Making a Place in the World*. Downers Grove, IL: InterVarsity Press.

Mahmood, C. and Brady, S. (1999), *The Guru's Gift: An Ethnography Exploring Gender Equality with North American Sikh Women*, Mountain View, CA: Mayfield.

Mahmood, S. (2005), *Politics of Piety: The Islamic Revival and the Feminist Subject*, Princeton, NJ: Princeton University Press.

Maira, S. and Soep, E. (2005), *Youthscapes: The Popular, the National, the Global*, Philadelphia, PA: University of Pennsylvania Press.

Malbon, B. (1999), *Clubbing: Dancing, Ecstasy, and Vitality*, London: Routledge.

Mannheim, K. 1952 [1928], 'The Problem of Generations', in P. Kecskemeti, ed., *Essays on the Sociology of Knowledge*, New York: Oxford University Press, pp. 276–322.

Manning, P. (2007), *Drugs and Popular Culture: Drugs, Media and Identity in Contemporary Society*, Cullompton: Willan.

Margo, J. (2008), *Make Me a Criminal: Preventing Youth Crime*, London: Institute for Public Policy Research.

Marler, P.L. (1995), 'Lost in the Fifties: The Changing Family and the Nostalgic Church', in Ammerman, N.T. and Roof, W.C., eds, *Work, Family, and Religion in Contemporary Society*, New York: Routledge, pp. 23–60.

Marler, P.L. and Hadaway, C. (2002), 'Being Religious or Being Spiritual in America, a Zero-sum Proposition?', *Journal for the Scientific Study of Religion*, 41: 289–300.

Martin, D. (1978), *A General Theory of Secularization*, Oxford: Basil Blackwell.

Martin, D. (2005), *On Secularization: Towards a Revised General Theory*, Aldershot: Ashgate.

Martinic, M. and Measham, F., eds (2008), *Swimming with Crocodiles: The Culture of Extreme Drinking*, London: Routledge.

Mason, M., Singleton, A. and Webber, R. (2007), *The Spirit of Generation Y: Young People's Spirituality in a Changing Australia*, Mulgrave: John Garratt Publishing.

Mattar, Y. (2003), 'Virtual Communities and Hip-Hop Music Consumers in Singapore: Interplaying Global, Local and Subcultural Identities', *Leisure Studies*, 22: 83–300.

Mayo, E. and Nairn, A. (2009), *Consumer Kids: How Big Business is Grooming our Children for Profit*, London: Constable.

McCallum, C. (2001), *Gender and Sociability in Amazonia: How Real People are Made*, Oxford: Berg.

McClintock Fulkerson, M. (2007), *Places of Redemption: Theology for a Worldly Church*, Oxford: Oxford University Press.

McConnell, S. (2009), *Multi-Site Churches: Guidance for the Movement's Next Generation*, Nashville, TN: B&H Publishing Group.

McLeod, W.H. (2001), 'The Turban: Symbol of Sikh Identity', in Singh, P. and Barrier, N.G., eds, *Sikh Identity Continuity and Change*, New Delhi: Manohar, pp. 57–67.

McNay, L. (1999), 'Gender, Habitus and the Field: Pierre Bourdieu and the Limits of Reflexivity', *Theory, Culture and Society*, 16 (1): 95–117.

McRobbie, A. (1978), 'Working Class Girls and the Culture of Femininity', in Women's Studies Group Centre for Contemporary Cultural Studies, eds, *Women Take Issue: Aspects of Women's Subordination*, London: Hutchinson, pp. 96–108.

McRobbie, A. and Garber, J. (1975), 'Girls and Subcultures', in Hall, S. and Jefferson, T., eds, *Resistance through Rituals*, London: Hutchinson, pp. 209–22.

Mead, G.H. (1930), 'Philanthropy from the Point of View of Ethics', in Faris, E., Laune, F. and Todd, A.J., eds, *Intelligent Philanthropy*, Chicago, IL: University of Chicago Press, pp. 133–48.

Measham, F. (2004a), 'The Decline of Ecstasy, the Rise of "Binge" Drinking and the Persistence of Pleasure', *Probation Journal*, 51: 309–26.

Measham, F. (2004b), 'Play Space: Historical and Socio-cultural Reflections on Drugs, Licensed Leisure Locations, Commercialisation and Control', *International Journal of Drug Policy*, 15: 337–45.

Measham, F. (2006), 'The New Policy Mix: Alcohol, Harm Minimisation and Determined Drunkenness in Contemporary Society', *International Journal of Drug Policy*, 17: 258–68.

Measham, F. and Brain, K. (2005), '"Binge" Drinking, British Alcohol Policy and the New Culture of Intoxication', *Crime, Media, Culture*, 1: 262–83.

Measham, F. and Moore, K. (2008), 'The Criminalisation of Intoxication', in Squires, P., ed., *ASBO Nation: Anti-social Behaviour – Critical Questions and Key Debates*, Bristol: Polity, pp. 273–88.

Measham, F., Aldridge, J. and Parker, H. (2001), *Dancing on Drugs: Risk, Health and Hedonism in the British Club Scene*, London: Free Association Books.

Melechi, A. (1993), 'The Ecstasy of Disappearance', in Redhead, S., ed., *Rave Off: Politics and Deviance in Contemporary Youth Culture*, Aldershot: Avebury, pp. 29–40.

Meyer, B. (2008), 'Religious Sensations: Why Media, Aesthetics and Power Matter in the Study of Contemporary Religion', in de Vries, H., ed., *Religion: Beyond a Concept*, New York: Fordham University Press, pp. 704–23.

Meyer, B. and Moors, A. (2006), *Religion, Media and the Public Sphere*, Bloomington, IN: Indiana University Press.

Mikkola, T., Niemelä, K. and Petterson, J. (2007), *The Questioning Mind: Faith and Values of the New Generation*, Tampere: Church Research Institute.

Miles, S. (2000), *Youth Lifestyles in a Changing World*, Buckingham: Open University Press.

Miller, B.D. (1998), 'The Disappearance of the Oiled Braid: Indian Adolescent Female Hairstyles in North America', in Hiltebeitel, A. and Miller, B.D., eds, *Hair: Its Power and Meaning in Asian Cultures*, New York: State University of New York Press, pp. 259–80.

Miller, H. (2001), 'Meeting the Challenge: The Jewish Schooling Phenomenon in the UK', *Oxford Review of Education*, 27 (4): 501–13.

Mitchell, J. and Marriage, S., eds (2003), *Mediating Religion: Conversations in Media, Religion and Culture*, London: Continuum.

Moore, K. (2003), 'E-Heads Versus Beer Monsters: Researching Young People's Music and Drug Consumption in Dance Club Settings', in Bennett, A., Cieslik, M. and Miles, S., eds, *Researching Youth*, Basingstoke: Palgrave, pp. 138–53.

Moore, K. (2004), 'A Commitment to Clubbing', *Peace Review: A Journal of Social Justice*, 16: 459–65.

Moore, K. (2006), '"Sort Drugs, Make Mates": The Use and Meaning of Mobiles in Dance Music Club Culture', in O'Hara, K. and Brown, B., eds, *Consuming Music Together: Social and Collaborative Aspects of Music Consumption Technologies*, Dordrecht: Springer, pp. 211–40.

Moore, K. and Measham, F. (2006), 'Ketamine Use: Minimising Harm and Maximising Pleasure', *Drugs and Alcohol Today*, 6(3): 29–32.

Moore, K. and Measham, F. (2008), '"It's the most fun you can have for twenty quid": Motivations, Consequences and Meanings of British Ketamine Use', *Addiction Research and Theory*, Special Issue on the Social and Cultural Uses of Ketamine, 16: 231–44.

Morgan, D. and Promey, S. (2001), *The Visual Culture of American Religions*, London: University of California Press.

Mullings, B. (1999), 'Insider or Outsider, Both or Neither: Some Dilemmas of Interviewing in a Cross-Cultural Setting', *Geoforum*, 30: 337–50.

Murji, K. (1998), 'The Agony and the Ecstasy: Drugs, Media and Morality', in Coomber, R., ed., *The Control of Drugs and Drug Users: Reason or Reaction*, Amsterdam: Harwood Academic Publishers, pp. 69–85.

Naples, N. (1996), 'A Feminist Revisiting of the Insider/Outsider Debate: the "Outsider Phenomenon" in Rural Iowa', *Qualitative Sociology*, 19: 83–106.

National Institute on Spirituality in Higher Education (2000–2003), online reports: http://spirituality.ucla.edu/results/index.html; http://spirituality.ucla.edu/results/Findings_Summary_Pilot.pdf; http://spirituality.ucla.edu/results/Longitudinal_00-03.pdf; http://spirituality.ucla.edu/spirituality/reports/FINAL_REPORT.pdf; all accessed 20 June 2009.

Needham, R. (1972), *Belief, Language and Experience*, Chicago, IL: University of Chicago Press.

Nesbitt, E. (1993), 'Gender and Religious Tradition: The Role-Learning of British Hindu Children', *Gender and Education*, 5: 81–91.

Nesbitt, E. (2000a), 'Researching 8 to 13 Year-olds' Perspectives on Their Experience of Religion', in Lewis, A. and Lindsay, G., eds, *Researching Children's Perspectives*, Buckingham: Open University Press, pp. 135–49.

Nesbitt, E. (2000b), *The Religious Lives of Sikh Children: A Coventry Based Study*, Leeds: Community Religions Project, University of Leeds.

Nesbitt, E. (2001), 'Religious Nurture and Young People's Spirituality: Reflections on Research at the University of Warwick', in Erricker, J., Ota, C. and Erricker, C., eds, *Spiritual Education Cultural, Religious and Social Differences: New Perspectives for the 21st Century*, Brighton and Portland: Sussex Academic Press, pp. 130–42.

Nesbitt, E. (2005), *Sikhism: A Very Short Introduction*, Oxford: Oxford University Press

Nesbitt, E. (2008), 'Religious Nurture', in Cush, D., Robinson, C. and York, M., eds, *Encyclopedia of Hinduism*, London: Routledge, pp. 677–9.

Niemelä, K. 2008. 'Does Confirmation Training Really Matter? A Longitudinal Study of the Quality and Effectiveness of Confirmation Training in Finland', Tampere: Church Research Institute.

Niesyto, H. (2000), 'Youth Research on Video Self-Productions', *Visual Studies*, 15: 135–53.

Norris, P. and Inglehart, R. (2004), *Sacred and Secular: Religion and Politics Worldwide*, New York: Cambridge University Press.

Northcote, J. (2006), 'Nightclubbing and the Search for Identity: Making the Transition from Childhood to Adulthood in an Urban Milieu', *Journal of Youth Studies*, 9: 1–16.

O'Murchu, D. (1997), *Reclaiming Spirituality*, Dublin: Gill and Macmillan.

Olivelle, P. (1998), 'Hair and Society: Social Significance of Hair in South Asian Traditions', in Hiltebeitel, A. et al., *Hair: Its Power and Meaning in Asian Cultures*, New York: State University of New York Press, pp. 11–49.

Orbach, S. (1993), 'Preface', in Baker, A. and Camping, J., eds, *Jewish Women in Contemporary Society: Transitions and Tradition*, New York: New York University Press.

Ovaleson, T. (2004), 'Connectedness and the Rave Experience: Rave as New Religious Movement?', in St John, G., ed., *Rave Culture and Religion*, London: Routledge, pp. 85–106.

Overing, J. (1988), 'Personal Autonomy and the Domestication of the Self in Piaroa Society', in Jahoda, G. and Lewis, I.M., eds, *Acquiring Culture: Cross Cultural Studies in Child Development*, New York: Routledge, pp. 169–92.

Pagan Federation (2009), http://www.paganfed.org, accessed 1 October 2009.

Pain, R. (2004), 'Social Geography: Participatory Research', *Progress in Human Geography*, 28 (5): 1–12.

Palmer, P.J. (2007), *The Courage to Teach: 10th Anniversary Edition*, San Francisco, CA: Jossey-Bass.

Parekh, B. (2000), R*ethinking Multiculturalism: Cultural Diversity and Political Theory*, Basingstoke: Palgrave.

Park, J.Z. and Ecklund, E.H. (2007), 'Negotiating Continuity: Family and Religious Socialization for Second-Generation Asian Americans', *The Sociological Quarterly*, 48: 93–118.

Parsons, T. (1962), 'Youth in the Context of American Society', *Daedalus*, Winter: 97–123.

Partridge, C. (2006), 'The Spiritual and the Revolutionary: Alternative Spirituality, British Free Festivals, and the Emergence of Rave Culture', *Culture and Religion*, 7: 41–60.

Pascoe, C. (2007), '"What If A Guy Hits On You?": Intersections of Gender, Sexuality and Age in Fieldwork with Adolescents', in Best, A.L., ed., *Representing Youth: Methodological Issues in Critical Youth Studies*, New York: New York University Press, pp. 226–47.

Pasierbek, W., Ziebertz, H.-G. and Riegel, U. (2006), 'Poland: Religious Individualisation among Youth', in Ziebertz, H.-G. and Kay, W.K., eds, *Youth in Europe II: An International Empirical Study about Religiosity*, Berlin: Lit Verlag, pp. 104–16.

Pearce, L.D. and Axinn, W.G. (1998), 'The Impact of Family Religious Life on the Quality of Mother–Child Relations', *American Sociological Review*, 63: 810–28.

Pearmain, R. (2007), 'Evocative Cues and Presence: Relational Consciousness Within Qualitative Research', *International Journal of Children's Spirituality*, 12: 75–82.

Pearson, J. (2002a), 'The History and Development of Wicca and Paganism', in Pearson, J., ed., *Belief Beyond Boundaries: Wicca, Celtic Spirituality and the New Age*, Milton Keynes: Open University/Ashgate, pp. 15–54.

Pearson, J. (2002b), 'Witches and Wicca', in Pearson, J., ed., *Belief Beyond Boundaries: Wicca, Celtic Spirituality and the New Age*, Milton Keynes: Open University/Ashgate, pp. 133–72.

Pettifor A.E., Rees H.V., Kleinschmidt I., Steffenson A.E., MacPhail C. and Hlongwa-Madikizela L. (2005),'Young People's Sexual Health in South Africa', *AIDS*, 19/14: 1525–34.

Pink, S. (2007), *Doing Visual Ethnography: Images, Media and Representation in Research*, London: Sage.

Planet, M. and Planet, M. (1992) *Risk-Takers: Alcohol, Drugs, Sex and Youth*, London: Routledge.

Plaskow, J. (1990), *Standing Again at Sinai: Judaism from a Feminist Perspective*, New York: HarperCollins.

Post, P., Pieper, J. and van Uden, M. (1998), T*he Modern Pilgrim: Multidisciplinary Explorations of Christian Pilgrimage*, Leuven: Peeters.

Prosser, J. (1998), *Image-based Research: A Sourcebook for Qualitative Researchers*, London: Routledge.

Putnam, R.D. (2000), *Bowling Alone: The Collapse and Revival of American Community*, New York: Simon and Schuster.

Qualifications and Curriculum Authority (QCA) (2004), *Religious Education – The Non-statutory National Framework*, London: QCA.

Raby, R. (2007), '"Across a Great Gulf?" Conducting Research With Adolescents', in Best, A.L., ed., *Representing Youth: Methodological Issues in Critical Youth Studies*, New York: New York University Press, pp. 39–59.

Radcliffe, T. (2005), *What is the Point of Being a Christian?*, London: Burns and Oates.

Rankin, P. (2005), *Buried Spirituality*, Salisbury: Sarum College Press.

RavenWolf, S. (1998, 2002), *Teen Witch: Wicca for a New Generation*, St. Paul, MN: Llewellyn.

Regnerus, M.D. (2007), *Forbidden Fruit: Sex and Religion in the Lives of American Teenagers*, New York: Oxford University Press.

Regnerus, M.D. and Smith, C. (2005), 'Selection Effects in Studies of Religious Influence', *Review of Religious Research*, 47: 23–50.

Regnerus, M.D., Smith, C. and Smith, B. (2004), 'Social Context in the Development of Adolescent Religiosity', *Applied Development Science*, 8: 27–38.

Reichel-Dolmatoff, G. (1996), *The Forest Within: The World View of the Tukano Amazonian Indians*, Foxole: Themesis Books.

Reproductive Health Research Unit (2003), *HIV and Sexual Behaviour Among Young South Africans: A National Survey of 15–24 Year-olds*, RHRU, University of the Witwatersrand: Johannesburg.

Reynolds, S. (1997), 'Rave Culture: Living Dream or Living Death?', in Redhead, S., Wynne, D. and O'Conner, J., eds, *The Clubcultures Reader: Readings in Popular Cultural Studies*, Oxford: Blackwell, pp. 102–11.

Ribben, J. and Edwards, R. (1998), *Feminist Dilemmas in Qualitative Research: Public Knowledge and Private Lives*, Thousand Oaks, CA: Sage.

Rich, A. (1986), Blood, Bread, and Poetry: Selected Prose 1979–1985, New York: Norton.

Richter, P. (2006), 'Later Developer, Thomas Merton's Discovery of Photography as a Medium for his Contemplative Vision', *Spiritus*, 6: 195–212.

Riley, S., Morey, Y. and Griffin, C. (2008), 'Ketamine: The Divisive Dissociative – A Discourse Analysis of the Constructions of Ketamine by Participants of a Free Party Scene', *Addiction Research and Theory*, Special Issue on the Social and Cultural Uses of Ketamine, 16: 217–30.

Roach-Higgins M.E. and Eicher J.B. (1992), 'Dress and Identity', *Clothing and Textiles Research Journal*, 10: 1–8.

Roach-Higgins, M.E., Eicher J.B. and Johnson, K.K.P. (1995), *Dress and Identity* New York: Fairchild.

Robbins, J. (2003), 'What is a Christian? Notes Toward an Anthropology of Christianity', *Religion*, 33 (3): 191–9.

Robbins, J. (2007), 'Continuity Thinking and the Problem of Christian Culture', *Current Anthropology*, 48 (1): 5–17.

Robbins, M. (2000), 'Leaving before Adolescence: Profiling the Child no Longer in the Church', in Francis, L.J. and Katz, Y.J., eds, *Joining and Leaving Religion: Research Perspectives*, Leominster: Gracewing, pp. 103–28.

Robbins, M. (2005), 'Attitude to Smoking among Female Adolescents: Is Religion a Significant but Neglected Factor?' in Francis, L.J., Astley, J. and Robbins, M., eds, *Religion, Education and Adolescence: International Empirical Perspectives*, Cardiff: University of Wales Press, pp. 94–106.

Robbins, M. and Francis, L.J. (2009), 'The Spiritual Revolution and Suicidal Ideation: An Empirical Enquiry among 13 to 15 Year-old Adolescents in England and Wales', *International Journal of Children's Spirituality*, 14: 261–72.

Roebben, B. (2004), 'The Mirror Effect: Reflective Theological Education and Religious Consciouness in Young Adult Ministry', in Larsson, R. and Gustavsson, C., eds, *Towards a European Perspective on Religious Education*, Uppsala: Artos and Norma, pp. 332–43.

Roof, W.C. (1993), *A Generation of Seekers: The Spiritual Journeys of the Baby Boom Generations*, New York: HarperCollins.

Roof, W.C. (1999), *Spiritual Marketplace: Baby Boomers and the Remaking of American Religion,* Princeton, NJ: Princeton University Press.

Roy, O. (2004), *Globalised Islam: The Search for a New Ummah*, London: Hurst and Company.

Ruby, J. (1996), 'Visual Anthropology', in Levinson, D. and Ember, M., eds, *Encyclopedia of Cultural Anthropology*, Vol. 4, New York: Henary Holt and Co., pp. 1345–51.

Ruel, M. (1982), 'Christians as Believers', in Davis, J., ed., *Religious Organization and Religious Experience*, ASA Monograph 21, London and New York: Academic Press, pp. 9–32.

Runnymede Trust, Commission on British Muslims and Islamophobia (1997), *Islamophobia: A Challenge for Us All*, London: Runnymede Trust.

Rutenberg, N, Kehus-Alons, C., Brown, L., MacIntyre, K., Dallimore, A. and Kaufman, C. (2001), *Transitions to Adulthood in the Context of AIDS in South Africa: Report of Wave 1*, Horizons Population Council/University of Natal, Washington, DC: Horizons.

Ryan, M.P. (1981), Cradle of the Middle Class: T*he Family in Oneida County, New York, 1790–1865*, New York: Cambridge University Press.

Sacks, J. (1997), *The Home We Build Together: Recreating Society*, London: Continuum.

St John, G. (2003), ed., *Rave Culture and Religion*, London: Routledge.

St John, G. (2006), 'Electronic Dance Music Culture and Religion: An Overview', *Culture and Religion*, 7: 1–25.

St John, G. (2008), 'Trance Tribes and Dance Vibes: Victor Turner and Electronic Dance Culture', in St John, G., ed., *Victor Turner and Contemporary Cultural Performance*, New York: Berghahn, pp. 149–73.

Santelli, J.S., Lindberg, L.D, Abma, J., McNeely, C.S. and Resnick, M. (2000), 'Adolescent Sexual Behaviour: Estimates and Trends from Four Nationally Representative Surveys', *Family Planning Perspectives*, 32 (4): 156–65, 194.

Savage, S., Collins-Mayo, S., Mayo, B. and Cray, G. 2006 *Making Sense of Generation Y: The World View of 15 to 25 Year-olds*, 1st edn, London: Church House Publishing.

Schieber, A. and Olson, A., eds (1999), *What Next? Connecting Your Ministry with the Generation Formerly Known as X,* Minneapolis, MN: Augsburg.

Schmid, Paul (2001), 'Understanding turbans', Seattle Times, September 27th 2001, http://seattletimes.nwsource.com/news/lifestyles/links/turbans_27.html, accessed 22 July 2007.

Scholefield, L. (2004), '"Bagels, Schnitzel and McDonalds" – Fuzzy Frontiers of Jewish Identity in an English Jewish Secondary School', *British Journal of Religious Education*, 16: 237–48.

Schuman, H. and Scott, J. (1989), 'Generations and Collective Memories', *American Sociological Review*, 54: 359–81.

Schweitzer, F. (2000), 'Religious Affiliation and Disaffiliation in Late Adolescence and Early Adulthood: The Impact of a Neglected Period of Life', in Francis L.J. and Katz, Y.J., eds, *Joining and Leaving Religion: Research Perspectives*, Leominister: Gracewing, pp. 87–102.

Schweitzer, F. (2004), T*he Postmodern Life Cycle: Challenges for Church and Theology*, St Louis, MO: Chalice Press.

Schweitzer, F. and Elsenbast, V. (2009), *Konfirmandenarbeit erforchen*, Gütersloh: Gutersloh Verlag.

Schweitzer, F., Ilg, W. and Simojoki, H., eds (forthcoming), *Confirmation Work in Europe: Empirical Results, Experiences and Challenges: A Comparative Study from Seven Countries*, Gütersloh: Gutersloh Verlag

Seeger, A. (1987), *Why Suyá Sing: A Musical Anthropology of an Amazonian People*, Cambridge: Cambridge University Press.

Sennett, R. (1998), *The Corrosion of Character: The Personal Consequences of Work in the New Capitalism*, New York: W.W. Norton.

Sered, S.S. (2000), '"Woman" as Symbol and Women as Agents: Gendered Religious Discourses and Practices', in Ferree, M.M., Lorber, J. and Hess, B.B., eds, *Revisioning Gender*, Lanham, MD: AltaMira Press, pp. 193–217.

Shaffir, W. and Stebbins. R.A. (1991), *Experiencing Fieldwork: An Inside View of Qualitative Research*, Thousand Oaks, CA: Sage.

Sherif B. (2001), 'The Ambiguity of Boundaries in the Fieldwork Experience: Establishing Rapport and Negotiating Insider/Outsider Status', *Qualitative Inquiry*, 7: 436–47.

Sherkat, D.E. (2003), 'Religious Socialization: Sources of Influence and Influences of Agency', in Dillon, M., ed., *Handbook of the Sociology of Religion*, Cambridge: Cambridge University Press, pp. 151–63.

Sidhu, D.S. and Gohil, N.S. (2008), 'The Sikh Turban: Post-9/11 Challenges to this Article of Faith', *Rutgers Journal of Law and Religion*, 9. 10, available at http://ssrn.com/abstract=962779, accessed 29 July 2007.

'Sikh Teen Lied about Hair Attack', *BBC News*, 24 December 2006, http://news.bbc.co.uk/1/hi/scotland/edinburgh_and_east/6207509.stm, accessed 22 July 2007.

Simon, B.E. (1995), 'Body Image and Plastic Surgery'. in Roach-Higgins, M.E., Eicher, J.B. and Johnson, K.K.P., eds, *Dress and Identity*, New York: Fairchild, pp. 44–50.

Sinclair, J. and Milner, D. (2005), 'On Being Jewish: a Qualitative Study of Identity among British Jews in Emerging Adulthood', *Journal of Adolescent Research*, 20: 91–117.

Singh G. (2005), 'British Multiculturalism and Sikhs', *Sikh Formations*, 1: 157–73.

Singh, G. (2000), 'Importance of Hair and Turban', in Singh M., ed., *Sikh Forms and Symbols*, New Delhi: Manohar, pp. 39–44.

Singh, G. and Tatla, D.S. (2006), *Sikhs in Britain: The Making of a Community*, London: Zed Books.

Singh, P. and Barrier, N.G., eds (2001), *Sikh Identity: Continuity and Change*, New Delhi: Manohar.

Singh, S. and Darroch, J. (2000), 'Adolescent Pregnancy and Childbearing: Levels and Trends in Developing Countries', *Family Planning Perspectives*, 32: 14–23.

Singh, S.P. (1997), 'Failing the Turban Test', *New Statesman*, 29 August, p. 31.

Smith, C. with Denton, M. (2005), *Soul Searching: The Religious and Spiritual Lives of American Teenagers*, Oxford: Oxford University Press.

Smith, C. Denton, M.L., Faris, R. and Regnerus, M. (2002), 'Mapping American Adolescent Religious Participation', *Journal for the Scientific Study of Religion*, 41: 597–612.

Smith, C., Faris, R., Denton, M.L. and Regnerus, M. (2003), 'Mapping American Adolescent Subjective Religiosity and Attitudes of Alienation Toward Religion: A Research Report', *Sociology of Religion*, 64: 111–33.

Smith, M.K. (2003), 'From Youth Work to Youth Development: The New Government Framework for English Youth Services', *Youth and Policy* 79, Available in *the informal education archives*: http://www.infed.org/archives/jeffs_and_smith/smith_youth_work_to_youth_development.htm, accessed 1 October 2009.

Smith, W.C. (1967), *Problems of Religious Truth*, New York: Scribner's.

Smith, W.C. (1977), *Belief and History*, Charlottesville, VA: University of Virginia Press.

Smith, W.C. (1978), *The Meaning and End of Religion*, London: SPCK.

Smith, W.C. (1979), *Faith and Belief*, Princeton, NJ: Princeton University Press.

Smith, Z., Measham, F. and Moore, K. (2009), 'MDMA Powder, Pills and Crystal: The Persistence of Ecstasy and the Poverty of Policy', *Drugs and Alcohol Today*, 9(1): 13–19.

Social Compass (2004), *Religion et générations: Le fait religieux à l'épreuve des générations/Religion and Generations*. Proceedings of the 27th International Conference of the Sociology of Religion (21–25 July 2003, Turin), 51 (2).

Sontag, S. (1979), *On Photography*, Harmondsworth: Penguin.

Spalek, B. and Imtoual, A. (2008), *Religion, Spirituality and the Social Sciences: Challenging Marginalisation*, Bristol: Policy Press.

Squires, P., ed. (2008), *ASBO Nation: Anti-social Behaviour – Critical Questions and Key Debates*, Bristol: Policy Press.

Stack, C.B. (1974), *All Our Kin: Strategies for Survival in a Black Community*, New York: Harper and Row.

Stark, R. and Finke, R. (2000), *Acts of Faith: Explaining the Human Side of Religion*. Berkeley, CA: University of California Press.

Starkey, M. (1997), *God, Sex and Generation X*, London: Triangle.

Statistics South Africa Census (2001), Primary Tables South Africa Census '96 and 2001 compared, http://www.statssa.gov.za/census01/html/C2001PrimTables.asp, accessed March 2007.

Steinman, K.L., Wright, V., Cooksey, E.C., Myers, L.J., Price-Spratlen, T. and Ryles, R. (2005), 'Collaborative Research in a Faith-based Setting: Columbus Congregations for Healthy Youth', *Public Health Reports*, 120: 213–16.

Stolz, J. (2009), 'A Silent Battle: Churches and their Secular Competitors', *Review of Religious Research*, forthcoming.

Stratton, J. (2000), *Coming Out Jewish: Constructing Ambivalent Identities*, London and New York: Routledge.

Strauss, W. and Howe, N. (1991), *Generations: The History of America's Future, 1584 to 2069*, New York: William Morrow and Co.

Sugar Special Report (December 2001), 'Wild about Wicca', *Sugar*, London: Hachette.

Surratt, G., Ligon, G. and Bird, W. (2006), *The Multi-Site Church Revolution: Being One Church in Many Locations*, Grand Rapids, MI: Zondervan.

Sweetman, P. (2003), 'Twenty-first Century Dis-ease? Habitual Reflexivity or the Reflexive Habitus', *Sociological Review*, 51: 528–49.

Tacey, D. (2004), *The Spirituality Revolution: The Emergence of Contemporary Spirituality*, London: Routledge.

Tacey, D. (2001), *Jung and the New Age*, London and New York: Routledge.

Tacey, D. (2003), *The Spirituality Revolution: The Emergence of Contemporary Spirituality*, Pymble, NSW: HarperCollins.

Taylor, C. (2002), *Varieties of Religion Today: William James Revisited*, Cambridge, MA: Harvard University Press.

Taylor, C. (2007), *A Secular Age*, Cambridge, MA: Belknap Press of Harvard University Press.

Thornton, S. (1995), *Club Cultures: Music, Media and Subcultural Capital*, Cambridge: Polity.

Thumma, S. (2007), *Beyond Megachurch Myths: What We Can Learn from America's Largest Churches*, San Francisco: Jossey-Bass.

Thurén, B-M. (1998), 'Att erövra barerna. Former och platser för kulturell förhandling kring genus i Spanien' ['Conquering the Bars. Forms and Places for Cultural Negotiation on Gender in Spain'], *Kvinnovetenskaplig tidskrift*, 19(3): 4.

Tilley, J. and Heath, A. (2007), 'The Decline of British National Pride', *The British Journal of Sociology*, 58: 661–78.

Towler, R. (1974), *Homo Religiosus*, London: Constable.

Turner, V. and Turner, E. (1978), *Image and Pilgrimage in Christian Culture*, New York: Columbia University Press.

UNAIDS (2004), 'Focus on HIV and Young People: The Threat for Today's Youth. Report on the Global AIDS Epidemic', http://www.unaids.org/bangkok2004/GAR2004_pdf/Focus_youth_en.pdf, accessed September 2006.

'Understanding Turbans', http://seattletimes.nwsource.com/news/lifestyles/links/turbans_27.html, accessed 5 December 2007.

Valentine, G. (1999), 'Being Seen and Heard? The Ethical Complexities of Working With Children and Young People at Home or at School', *Philosophy and Geography*, 2: 141–55.

Valins, O. (2003), 'Defending Identities or Segregating Communities? Faith-Based Schooling and the UK Jewish Community', *Geoforum*, 34: 235–47.

Van Gennep, A. (1960), *The Rites of Passage*, London: Routledge and Kegan Paul.

Van Leeuwen, T. (2001), 'Semiotics and Iconography', in Van Leeuwen, T. and Jewitt, C., eds, *Handbook of Visual Analysis*, Thousand Oaks, CA: Sage, pp. 92–118.

Vayne, F., Korpal, M. and Laurent, L. (2007), 'The Sign of the Crowds' in *Lourdes Magazine*, October–November: 37–47.

Verter, B. (2003), 'Spiritual Capital: Theorizing Religion with Bourdieu Against Bourdieu', *Sociological Theory*, 21: 150–74.

Virtanen, P.K. (2006), 'The Urban Manchinery Youth and Social Capital in Western Amazonian Contemporary Rituals', *Anthropos*, 101: 159–67.

Virtanen, P.K. (2007), 'Changing Lived Worlds of Amazonian Native Young People: Manchinery Youths in the City and the Reserve, Brazil-Acre', unpublished PhD thesis, University of Helsinki.

Virtanen, P.K. (2009), 'Shamanism and Indigenous Youthhood in the Brazilian Amazonia', *Amazônica. Revista de Antropologia*, 1: 152–77.

Viveiros de Castro, E. (1996), 'Os Prononomes cosmológicos e o perspectivismo Ameríndio', *Mana. Estudos de Antropologia Social*, 2: 115–44.

Voas, D. (2003), 'Intermarriage and the Demography of Secularisation', *British Journal of Sociology*, 54: 83–108.

Voas, D. (2007), 'Surveys of Behaviour, Beliefs and Affiliation', in Beckford, J. and Demerath, N.J., eds, *Handbook of the Sociology of Religion*, London: Sage, pp. 128–50.

Voas, D. and Bruce, S. (2007), 'The Spiritual Revolution: Another False Dawn for the Sacred', in Flanagan, K. and Jupp, P., eds, *A Sociology of Spirituality*, Aldershot: Ashgate, pp. 43–62.

Voas, D. and Crockett, A. (2004), 'Spiritual, Religious or Secular: Evidence from National Surveys', paper presented at the conference of the British Sociological Association Sociology of Religion Study Group, Bristol, March.

Voas, D. and Crockett, A. (2005), 'Religion in Britain: Neither Believing nor Belonging', *Sociology*, 39(1): 11–28.

Voas, D. and Day, A. (2007), 'Secularity in Great Britain', in Kosmin, B.A. and Keysar, A., eds, *Secularism and Secularity: Contemporary International Perspectives*, Hartford, CT: Institute for the Study of Secularism in Society and Culture, pp. 95–110.

Wallis, R. (1984), *The Elementary Forms of the New Religious Life*, London: Routledge and Kegan Paul.

Walton-Roberts, M. (1998), 'Three Readings of the Turban: Sikh Identity in Greater Vancouver', *Urban Geography*, 19: 311–31.

Warner, R.S. (1993), 'Work in Progress toward a New Paradigm for the Sociological Study of Religion in the United States', *American Journal of Sociology*, 98: 1044–93.

Webb, J., Schirato, T. and Danaher, G. (2002), *Understanding Bourdieu*, London: Sage.

Weinstock, H., Berman, S. and Cates, W. Jr (2004), 'Sexually Transmitted Diseases among American Youth: Incidence and Prevalence Estimates, 2000', *Perspectives on Sexual and Reproductive Health*, 36: 6–10.

Westerhoff, J. (2000), *Will Our Children Have Faith?*, revised edn, Harrisburg, PA: Morehouse.

Whitwell, T. (2007), 'Microtrends: Rate My Turban', *The Times*, August 4, http://technology.timesonline.co.uk/tol/news/tech_and_web/the_web/article 2188176.ece, accessed 22 September 2009.

Wilkins, A. (2008), *Wannabes, Goths and Christians: The Boundaries of Sex, Style and Status*, Chicago, IL: University of Chicago Press.

Willis, P.E. (1977), *Learning to Labour: How Working Class Kids get Working Class Jobs*, Aldershot: Ashgate.

Willis, P.E. (1990), *Common Culture: Symbolic Work at Play in the Everyday Cultures of the Young*, Milton Keynes: Open University Press.

Winograd, M. and Hais, M.D. (2008), *Millennial Makeover: MySpace, YouTube, and the Future of American Politics*, New Brunswick, NJ: Rutgers University Press.

Wolf, C. (2008), 'How Secularized is Germany? Cohort and Comparative Perspectives', *Social Compass*, 55: 111–26.

Woodhead, L. (2005), 'Gendering Secularisation Theory', *Køn og Forskning* [Women, Gender and Research], 1–2: 24–35.

Worth, S. and Adair, J. (1972), *Through Navajo Eyes: Explorations in Film Communication and Anthropology*, Bloomington, IN: Indiana University Press.

Wright, A. (2005), 'On the Intrinsic Value of Religious Education', *British Journal of Religious Education*, 27(1): 25–8.

Wuthnow, R. (1994), *I Come Away Stronger: How Small Groups are Changing American Religion*, Grand Rapids, MI: Eerdmans.

Wuthnow, R. (1998), *After Heaven: Spirituality in America Since the 1950s*. Berkeley and Los Angeles: University of California Press.

Wuthnow, R. (2001), *Creative Spirituality: The Way of the Artist*, Berkeley and Los Angeles: University of California Press.

Wuthnow, R. (2007), *After the Baby Boomers: How Twenty- and Thirty-Somethings are Shaping the Future of American Religion*, Princeton, NJ: Princeton University Press.

York, M. (2003), *Pagan Theology: Paganism as a World Religion*, New York: New York University Press.

Young, L. and Barrett, H. (2001), 'Adapting Visual Methods: Action Research with Kampala Street Children', *Area*, 33 (2): 141–52.

Yuri, I. (2005), 'Influential Factors in the Intergenerational Transmission of Religion: The Case of Soka Gakkai in Hokkaido (Report)', *Japanese Journal of Religious Studies*, 2 (2): 371–82.

Zald, M.N. and McCarthy, J.D., eds (1987), *Social Movements in an Organizational Society: Collected Essays*, New Brunswick, NJ: Transaction.

Zisenwine, D. and Schers, D. (1997), *Making a Difference: Jewish Identity and Education*, Tel Aviv: Tel Aviv University Press.

Index